by Wilma J. Brown-Foreman, ED. S

Academic Initiatives
for Biblical Literacy
AIBL

A Literary Study of the Book of Genesis
(A Bible as/in Literature Online Course Curriculum
for Secondary Education)

By

Wilma J. Brown-Foreman, ED. S

Teachers' Edition with Answers to Study

D1501121

TABLE OF CONTENTS

PRE-ASSESSMENT QUESTIONS
(1st Amendment Rights in Public Education)

The purpose of this pre-assessment is to gain insight into what experiences and knowledge the teachers, parents, and students bring to the course and to offer the basis for planning truly meaningful instruction as the course progresses. Throughout the course, students will complete formal and informal assessments that measure their understanding of the academic content of the lessons and allow them to illustrate and expand their ideas connected to different scholarly biblical topics.

Assignment One

(Suggested Resource(s)/Reference(s):

- The First Amendment in Schools Resource Guide (https://ncac.org/resource/the-first-amendment-in-schools-resource-guide-religious-expression-in-the-public-schools)
- STATEMENT ON THE BIBLE IN PUBLIC SCHOOLS: A FIRST AMENDMENT GUIDE (https://www.aclu.org/other/statement-bible-public-schools-first-amendment-guide)

(Note: Use an online dictionary to define and pronounce unfamiliar terms.)

Directions:

- Use online 1st Amendment guides for teaching about the Bible and religion in public schools to answer the following questions.
- E-mail your responses to me at wilmaforeman@yahoo.com.
- Include any questions about the assignment in your e-mail.
- Label the submission: Pre-Assessment-1st Amendment Rights in Public Education.

Answer (A) YES (B) NO.

1. In 1963, did the U.S. Supreme Court rule against all religious activities in public schools? **(B) NO**
2. Are public school teachers legally allowed to require students enrolled in public education to engage in devotional activities, such as daily Bible readings and prayers that do not relate to academics? **(B) NO**
3. Is the Hebrew Bible connected to Western culture? **(A) YES**
4. Do people in Western civilization recognize the Hebrew Bible as an outstanding literary and historical work? **(A) YES**
5. Do writers in Western cultures rely on the Hebrew Bible to answer questions that humans face in life? **(A) YES**
6. Does "literacy" simply mean that one can read and write? **(B) NO**

7. Should literate people be able to engage in cultural conversations in a way that will earn them respect? **(A)**

8. Did any of America's founding fathers hold the Hebrew Bible in high esteem? **(A) YES**

9. In the 1963 U.S. Supreme Court ruling, *Abington v. Schempp*, did the Court state that the Bible is "worthy of studying for its literary and historical qualities"? **(A) YES**

10. Are English teachers expected to know that biblical literature gives more insight about other literary works, including their overall structures, themes, and background history? **(A) YES**

11. Did Gallup mean that Western cultures do not respect the Hebrew Bible when he said, "We revere the Bible, but we don't read it"? **(B) NO**

12. Based on the legal findings, should public schools be "religious-free" zones because of "separation of church and state" laws? **(B) NO**

13. Is the Hebrew Bible filled with figurative language? **(A) YES**

14. If the Hebrew Bible uses figurative language, should one expect to see symbols, similes, and metaphors in the Scriptures? **(A) YES**

15. If the Hebrew Bible uses figurative language, should one expect the complete text to be literal, or strictly word for word? **(B) NO**

Select the correct choice for each set of statements.

16. Which of the following statements is NOT CORRECT?
   A. Educators widely agree that studying about religion, where proper, is an important part of a complete education.
   B. Constitutionally, academic courses such as literature and history classes are permissible as a part of high schools' curricula.
   C. Understanding biblical narratives and concepts adds to our understanding of literature, history, law, art, and modern society in general.
   D. The Supreme Court has held that public schools may instruct students about the Bible in public education if such teaching is without the attempt to persuade students religiously.
   E. All the above are correct.

17. Which of the following statements is NOT CORRECT?
   A. In 1995 and again in 1998, the U.S. Department of Education sent 1st Amendment clarification guidelines to every superintendent of public schools across America?
   B. Questions concerning religion, the history of religion, comparative religion, the Bible (or other religious teachings) as literature are permissible in public education.
   C. In public education, students may study lessons related to the role of religion in the history of the United States and other countries.
   D. Public school students may consider religious influences on philosophy, art, music, literature, and social studies.
   E. All the above are correct.

18. **Which of the following statements is NOT CORRECT?**

    A. *Not only may public schools teach about religious holidays, but they may engage in religious holidays as religious events and promote such observance. (Incorrect)*

    B. In keeping the 1st Amendment's mandate of governmental neutrality toward religion, any study of religion in a public school must be educational, not devotional.

    C. Teaching about the Bible academically in public education may occur in literature, history, or any other required or elective course.

    D. The lower courts have ruled that the constitutionality of Bible elective courses in public schools' classes is highly dependent on how one teaches the class.

    E. All the above are correct.

19. **Which of the following statements is NOT CORRECT?**

    A. A superintendent or school board should select teachers for a class involving Biblical studies in the same way as all other teachers.

    B. *School districts should assign the responsibility of hiring teachers of Bible electives to an outside committee that selects teachers based upon their religious beliefs or perspectives. (Incorrect)*

    C. Hiring of teachers of academic Bible classes in public education should be based upon their academic qualifications, rather than religious beliefs or non-beliefs.

    D. Disqualification of teachers should not rest upon the fact that they have received training in religious institutions such as Bible colleges or seminaries.

    E. All the above are correct.

20. **Which of the following statements is NOT CORRECT?**

    A. *Outside sources cannot fund religious courses on public school campuses. (Incorrect)*

    B. Decisions concerning instructional materials, including which translation of the Bible to use, should remain under the control of the local board of education.

    C. The Hebrew Bible is permissible as a primary text in Bible electives in public school curricula.

    D. Legal guidelines suggest more than one biblical text for public school Bible elective courses.

    E. All the above are correct.

21. **Which of the following statements is NOT CORRECT?**

    A. *Funding for an elective course in religion cannot come from the state. (Incorrect)*

    B. Instructional materials and lessons that are of a devotional nature, such as those used in a Sunday school, are constitutionally inappropriate for Bible elective courses in public education.

    C. In public education, local school boards should adopt policies on the role of studies about religion in the schools' curricula.

    D. A school district's policy for teaching Bible elective courses should reflect constitutional principles and current law.

    E. All the above are correct.

22. Which of the following statements is NOT CORRECT?

    A. The goals of public schools in teaching about religion and the Hebrew Bible should be academic and not devotional.

    B. Academic teaching about the Hebrew Bible should not intend to either undermine or reinforce the beliefs of those who accept the Bible as sacred scripture or of those who do not.

    C. Faith formation in children is the responsibility of parents and religious communities, not the public schools.

    D. In 1998, a coalition of seventeen religious and educational organizations issued clarification guidelines about religion in public schools and avoidance of religious indoctrination.

    E. All the above are correct.

23. Which of the following statements is NOT CORRECT?

    A. Public educators may strive for student awareness of religions but should not press for student acceptance of any religion.

    B. A public school may sponsor studies about religion but may not sponsor the practice of religion.

    C. The public school may expose students to different religious views, but may not impose, discourage, or encourage any view.

    D. The Jewish and Christian Bibles have two major divisions-the Old and New Testaments. (Incorrect)

    E. All the above are correct.

24. Which of the following statements is NOT CORRECT?

    A. A public school may educate students about all religions, but may not promote or denigrate, or criticize any religion.

    B. Students in public education have the 1st Amendment right to disparage (belittle) other religions. (Incorrect)

    C. Teachers of Bible electives must understand the difference between favoring the practice of religion and teaching a Bible class in a way that does not influence personal feelings or opinions.

    D. Selecting a variety of Bibles for use in literature, history, or elective Bible courses is important since more than one Bible exist in Western cultures.

    E. All the above statements are correct.

25. Which of the following statements is NOT CORRECT?

    A. Teacher advocacy (support for), indoctrination (teaching a doctrine without questions), and proselytizing (trying to convert someone to a belief) are not permissible in Bible electives courses in public education.

    B. In Western cultures, there is a Jewish Bible called the Hebrew Scriptures, or *Tanakh*.

    C. Western cultures have only one official biblical text, the King James Version. (Incorrect)

    D. In Western societies, there are various Christian Bibles – such as Catholic, Protestant, and Orthodox.

E. All the above statements are true.

26. **Which of the following statements is NOT CORRECT?**
    A. To be "objective" is to remain "neutral" in instructional procedures.
    B. Public educators should be nonjudgmental, academic, neutral, balanced, and fair in teaching about religion.
    C. Judaism (Jewish faith) does not include the Christian New Testament in its Bible.
    D. The Catholic Old Testament has forty-six books while the Protestant has thirty-nine books.
    E. *All the statements above are correct.*

27. **Which of the following statements is NOT CORRECT?**
    A. *Catholicism and Protestantism have the same meanings. (Incorrect)*
    B. A Protestant is a member or follower of any of the Western Christian churches that are separate from the Roman Catholic church.
    C. Teachers of Bible course electives in public education should use a biblical sourcebook that includes the key texts of each of the major Bibles or an anthology (a collection or compilation) of various translations.
    D. Parents should be involved in planning academic courses about the Hebrew Bible and religion in public education.
    E. All the statements above are correct.

28. **Which of the following statements is NOT CORRECT?**
    A. In elective Bible courses, teachers should remind students about the differences between the various Bibles.
    B. Students should discuss the major views concerning authorship and the compilation of books of the Bible.
    C. Lessons assigned to Bible courses in public education should reflect on the significance of the differences in various cultures and traditions.
    D. In Judaism, various *rabbinic* (Jewish scholars or teachers) commentators give instruction about the Hebrew Bible.
    E. *All the statements above are correct.*

29. **Which of the following statements is NOT CORRECT?**
    A. Christians and Jews use the findings of modern secular (having no religious or spiritual basis) scholarship to interpret the Bible.
    B. *Modern scholarship (learning) of the Hebrew text is not common to every denomination in Western culture. (Incorrect)*
    C. Religious and secular studies of the Hebrew Bible are common in Western culture.
    D. Public-school teachers should expose students to a variety of interpretations of Hebrew scriptures.
    E. All the statements above are correct.

30. **Which of the following statements is NOT CORRECT?**
    A. Teachers should allow students to engage in reading the Hebrew biblical text directly (like any primary source).
    B. Students should draw on the resources of different religious and secular interpretative traditions for understanding the Hebrew Bible.
    C. Academic studies of the Hebrew scriptures require the use of secondary sources that offer a discussion of the various religious and secular approaches to the Bible.
    D. Teaching about the Bible, either in literature and history courses or in Bible electives, requires extensive (considerable, substantial) preparation.
    E. *All the above statements are correct.*

31. **Which of the following statements is NOT CORRECT?**
    A. School districts and universities should offer in-service workshops and summer institutes for teachers who are teaching about the Bible in literature and history courses.
    B. School districts should look for teachers who have training in the academic study of religion.
    C. Teachers selected to teach a course about the Bible should receive substantive in-service training from qualified scholars before teaching such courses.
    D. Schools should offer electives in biblical studies if there are teachers academically competent to teach them.
    E. *All the above statements are correct*.

32. **Which of the following statements is NOT CORRECT?**
    A. Teaching education should ensure that study of religion, including the Bible, is taught constitutionally in public schools.
    B. Literature and history teachers should take at least one course in religious studies that prepares them to teach about religions in their subject.
    C. Teachers who wish to teach a Bible elective should take college-level courses in biblical studies.
    D. In public education, religious studies will become a certifiable field, requiring at least an undergraduate minor.
    E. *All the above statements are correct.*

33. **Which of the following statements is NOT CORRECT?**
    A. One can expect that eventually, state departments of education will adopt proper academic standards for electives in religious studies.
    B. In a Bible as literature class, students will examine the Bible as they would other literature.
    C. In Bible literature classes, students will study the ways in which later writers have used Bible literature, language, and symbols.
    D. In Western culture, literature draws heavily from the Hebrew Bible.
    E. *All the above statements are correct.*

34. Which of the following statements is NOT CORRECT?

A. A literature elective in the Bible would focus on the Bible as a literary and historical text.

B. A primary goal of a Bible as/in Literature course is basic biblical literacy.

C. Within a Bible as/in Literature course, students will learn a grasp of biblical language, major narratives, and literary elements in the Hebrew Scriptures.

D. A Bible literacy course may explore the influence of the Bible on classic and contemporary poems, plays, and novels.

E. All the above statements are true.

35. Which of the following statements is NOT CORRECT?

A. For various religious traditions, the Hebrew Bible is sacred Scripture.

B. A "Bible as/in Literature" course may include discussions on how various religious traditions understand the text.

C. History classes offer opportunities to study about the Hebrew Bible.

D. When studying the origins of Judaism, students may learn different theories of how the Bible came into existence.

E. All the above statements are true.

36. Which of the following statements is NOT CORRECT?

A. Jews and Christians are followers of the teachings of the Hebrew Bible.

B. A study of the Reformation might include a discussion of how Protestants and Catholics differ in their interpretation and use of the Bible.

C. Protestants and Catholics affirm the Hebrew Bible as Scripture

D. The Hebrew Bible has played a significant role in American life and society throughout history.

E. All the above statements are true.

37. Which of the following statements is NOT CORRECT?

A. Both past and present U.S. presidential addresses and congressional debates have held biblical references.

B. Throughout American history, public-policy debates rely on the Hebrew Scriptures.

C. Social movements such as abolition, temperance, and the civil rights movement have relied on the Hebrew Scriptures to resolve situations.

D. A government or civics course may include discussions on the biblical influences in the America's legal system.

E. All the above statements are correct.

38. Which of the following statements is NOT CORRECT?

A. Public school students cannot express their faith in school. (Incorrect)

B. The Supreme Court said in *Abington vs. Schempp* that the Bible is worthy of study for its literary qualities.

C. The Supreme Court ruled that the Bible is worthy of study for its historic qualities.

D. In public education, a study of the Bible or of religion should be taught objectively.

E. All the above statements are correct.

39. Which of the following statements is NOT CORRECT?
   A. The public school's approach to religion should be *academic*, not *devotional*.
   B. The Supreme Court ruled in Abington vs. Schempp that the Hebrew Bible has no place in public education. (Incorrect)
   C. The Supreme Court ruled that the Hebrew Bible contributes to a quality education.
   D. A study of the Bible or of religion must be neutral in public education.
   E. All the above statements are correct.

40. Which of the following statements is NOT CORRECT?
   A. The public school's approach to religion should be in fairness to all students.
   B. The school may sponsor study about religion but may not sponsor the practice of religion.
   C. The Equal Access Act refers to those student groups not related to the curriculum.
   D. Public schools cannot deny students the right to form religious clubs if they allow secular clubs on their campuses.
   E. All the above statements are correct.

ONLINE SURVEY
(PRE-ASSESSMENT OF FIRST AMENDMENT KNOWLEDGE)

Overview of The Pre-Assessment:

Pre-assessments, also known as diagnostic tests, assess students' strengths, weaknesses, prior knowledge, and skills before instruction. A pre-assessment is an effective tool to help find the needs and interests of students. Pre-assessments allow teachers to see if students have mastered a lesson or unit of studies. By comparing formative and summative assessments, teachers can measure true learning. At the end of a unit or course, the teacher can see what students learned from earlier lessons. Such evaluations also give students a preview of what teachers expect of them. From engaging in pre-assessments, they can learn to focus on the key topics throughout the units or the entire course.

Lesson Objectives:

Students will:

- complete an online pre-assessment survey of prior knowledge about the 1st Amendment topics covered in the course.
- review questions/activities on the survey to become familiar with the course content.

Expected Student Learning Objectives:

At the end of the survey, students and teachers will:

- recognize the course content and measure prior knowledge of the course materials.
- assess their growth in learning by comparing pre-assessments and summative assessments.
- realize their strengths and weaknesses in applying 1st Amendment rights in public education.

Duration: 1-2 hours

Procedure:

- Visit https://freeonlinesurveys.com/app#/1413601/build to take the pre-assessment of your knowledge of 1st Amendment rights of teachers and students in public education.
- Check your score, copy, paste and send your results to wilmaforeman@yahoo.com. This score will not affect your final grade average.
- NOTE: Be sure to write Pre-assessment #1 (Survey) as the subject.

Page intentionally left blank

by Wilma J. Brown-Foreman, ED. S

LESSON ONE
TEACHING ABOUT THE BIBLE IN PUBLIC SCHOOLS
(ONLINE 1ST AMENDMENT GUIDES)

Overview: Students will use online 1st Amendment guides for teaching about the Bible and religion in public schools.

Objectives

Students will:

- use primary sources for contextual understanding and for extracting information to make informed judgments.
- interpret the 1st Amendment in the U.S. Constitution in relation to religious expression in public education. (This lesson will help students and teachers understand their 1st Amendment rights guaranteed by the U.S. Constitution and the U.S. Supreme Court's 1963 ruling in *Abington v. Schempp*).
- apply legal mandates related to teaching Bible electives in secondary public education.
- improve reading comprehension and vocabulary skills by referring to various online academic resources/references, such as online Bible dictionaries, thesauruses, concordances, lexicons, audio Bibles, and commentaries.
- participate in class discussions.
- edit writing to correct errors.

Expected Student Learning Outcomes

By the end of the lesson, students will be able to:

- consult primary and secondary sources to understand and to extract information for making informed judgments.
- interpret the 1st Amendment in the U.S. Constitution in relation to religious expression in public education.
- demonstrate knowledge of First Amendment rules for teaching about the Hebrew Bible and religion in public education.

Duration: 2-3 hours

Materials

To complete the lesson students will need the following guides:

- *Religion in the Curriculum:*
  https://www.adl.org/education/resources/tools-and-strategies/religion-in-public-schools/curriculum#:~:text=Public%20schools%20may%20not%20teach%20religion%2

C%20although%20teaching,of%20the%20Bible%20as%20a%20religious%20document. %202

- _The Bible & Public Schools a First Amendment Guide_: http://users.clas.ufl.edu/kenwald/pos4291/spring_00/bible-publicschools.pdf
- _Religious Activity - Virginia Department of Education_: https://www.doe.virginia.gov/doe/guidance/support/religious_activity.pdf
- _Rights of Teachers | The First Amendment Encyclopedia_: https://mtsu.edu/first-amendment/article/973/rights-of-teachers
- _The First Amendment in Public Schools – ADL_ https://www.adl.org/sites/default/files/documents/cc-first-amendment-in-public-schools_0.pdf
- _AAR Religious Literacy Guidelines_ https://www.aarweb.org/AARMBR/Publications-and-News

Additional Materials Needed:

- Internet access/e-mail/computer editing ability
- Notebook/paper/pen

Procedure:

- Read two of the 1st Amendment guides listed above to answer the study questions below.
- Use a dictionary or other online resource to define any unfamiliar vocabulary terms.
- Respond to the study questions that follow.
- Note the key points for future discussions/assessments.
- Study the italicized terms for future vocabulary assessments.
- Review the study questions throughout this course and apply the 1ˢᵗ Amendment guidelines in the documents.
- If you have questions or need further clarification on any assignment, e-mail me at wilmaforeman@yahoo.com or visit my website: AIBL.INFO to sign up for the online course.

Study Questions (Assignment one-1st Amendment Guides)

Directions:

Based on the 1ˢᵗ Amendment guides listed above, are the following statements are (A) TRUE or (B) FALSE?

1. Public schools may teach about religion in a secular context of the lesson. **(A) TRUE**
2. A study of the Hebrew Bible is permissible in a public school for its historical, cultural, or literary value. **(A) TRUE**
3. In public schools, educators cannot teach the Hebrew Bible devotionally, celebratorily, or doctrinally. **(A) TRUE**
4. As a part of a public high school curriculum, a Hebrew Bible course should encourage acceptance of the Bible as a religious document. **(B) FALSE**

5. Teachers may quote the views of others, such as the Founding Fathers, even when they are reverential toward a religious text if the words connect to the lesson. **(A) TRUE**
6. A *secular* educational program may not include religious studies. **(B) FALSE**
7. The term "secular" means the same as "religious." **(B) FALSE**
8. Academic programs that "teach about religion" instruct students on the role of religion in the historical, cultural, literary, and social development of the United States and other nations. **(A) TRUE**
9. In public schools, classes about religion should instill understanding, tolerance, and respect for a pluralistic society. **(A) TRUE**
10. When discussing religion in an objective context, religious instruction is *neutral*, balanced, and shared factually. **(A) TRUE**
11. In public education, religious classes should educate students about the principle of religious liberty as one of the fundamental elements of freedom and democracy in the United States. **(A) TRUE**
12. Religious indoctrination is acceptable in public school settings if the administration supports the practice. **(B) FALSE**
13. Legally, a public-school curriculum may not be *devotional* or *doctrinal*. **(A) TRUE**
14. A teacher in public education must not *promote* nor *denigrate* any religion, or lack of religious belief. **(A) TRUE**
15. In religious discussions, a public-school teacher may interject personal views or advocate the religious beliefs of certain students, while dismissing the beliefs of others. **(B) FALSE**
16. Teachers in public education must be extremely sensitive to respect a student's religious beliefs and practices. **(A) TRUE**
17. Teachers cannot encourage public-school students to conform to specific religious beliefs or practices. **(A) TRUE**
18. In public education, a Bible literature course is the same as teaching religious doctrine to students. **(B) FALSE**
19. The lessons in a public school's Bible literature class must not be secular, or religiously neutral. **(B) FALSE**
20. Public schools may teach secular values, such as honesty, courage, kindness, respect for human dignity, and good citizenship across the curriculum. **(A) TRUE**
21. Public school officials may not instill in students such values as independent thought, tolerance of diverse views, self-respect, maturity, self-reliance, and logical decision-making in biblical literacy classes. **(B) FALSE**
22. In biblical literacy education, no student should feel that his or her personal religious beliefs or practices are questionable, violated, or compromised. **(A) TRUE**
23. In public education, a student should never feel ostracized because of his or her religious beliefs. **(A) TRUE**
24. Class discussions in public education should include minority as well as majority religions. **(A) TRUE**
25. Public-school students should have opportunities to explain their religious or cultural traditions. **(A) TRUE**
26. Public school teachers should be able to discuss religion without personal biases. **(A) TRUE**
27. "Teaching religion" and "teaching about religion" are different in meaning. **(A) TRUE**

28. While it is constitutionally permissible for public educators to teach about religion, it is unconstitutional for public schools and their employees to engage in religious holidays or to promote a certain religious belief over another. **(A) TRUE**
29. Knowledge *about* religions is not only a characteristic of an educated person, but it is also necessary for understanding and living in a global society. **(A) TRUE**
30. High school graduates should have a basic understanding of religion as a part of the human experience. **(A) TRUE**

Vocabulary Practice – (Assignment two-1st Amendment Guides)

Directions:

Use an online dictionary or other proper resources to select the best word for each definition.

1. denoting attitudes, activities, or other things that have no religious or spiritual basis
A. celebratory   **B. secular**   C. pluralistic   D. fundamental   E. balanced

2. the circumstances that form the setting for an event, statement, or idea, in terms of which it is understood and assessed, such as a _____ clue
A. objective   B. democracy   C. advocate   D. tradition   **E. context**

3. of or used in religious worship
A. neutral   **B. devotional**   C. neutral   D. sensitive   E. prohibited

4. a person who starts or helps to start a movement or institution
A. principle   B. minority   C. citizen   D. element   **E. Founding Father**

5. criticize unfairly; disparage
A. **denigrate**   B. indoctrinate   C. interject   D. promote   E. compromise

Directions (Assignment three):

Indicate whether the following statements are (A) CORRECT or (B) INCORRECT following 1st Amendment mandates for teaching about the Bible and religion in public education.

6. In public schools, Christmas holidays are usually celebratory events that involve all teachers and students devotionally. **(B) INCORRECT**
7. Members of a church should promote their doctrine in public classroom settings. **(B) INCORRECT**
8. A pluralistic society will have only one race of people and one religious doctrine. **(B) INCORRECT**
9. When one stays neutral, expect the person to help or support a single side of a conflict, or disagreement. **(B) INCORRECT**
10. Another word for *neutral* is *impartial*. **(A) Correct**
11. An objective individual works by personal feelings or opinions in considering facts. **(B) INCORRECT**
12. When someone is *impartial*, he or she is fair. **(A) Correct**

13. A *principle* is a basic truth or proposition that serves as the foundation for a system of beliefs. **(A) Correct**
14. Expect societies to have basic *principles* passed down from one generation to another. **(A) Correct**
15. A democracy is a system of government run by the entire population or by all the eligible members of a state, usually through elected representatives. **(A) Correct**
16. *A democratic* society does not consider the opinions of citizens in the *minority* populations. **(B) INCORRECT**
17. Public school teachers should engage in *indoctrinating* students assigned to their classes. **(B) INCORRECT**
18. Public school teachers should require students to accept a set of religious beliefs without *critical* thinking opportunities. **(B) INCORRECT**
19. Something *prohibited* is open to the public for use. **(B) INCORRECT**
20. Expect a *disgruntled* person to *promote* his least favorite idea. **(B) INCORRECT**
21. Teachers in public schools should *proselytize* or advance their personal *religious* beliefs. **(B) INCORRECT**
22. Students in public schools should *disparage* the religious beliefs of other students. **(B) INCORRECT**
23. *Devotional* activities are usually a part of a *secular* program of public education. **(B) INCORRECT**
24. When one *infringes* his or her beliefs upon another person, he or she will have an *objective* view while interacting with others. **(B) INCORRECT**
25. Expect a public-school campus to have a *diverse* population. **(A) Correct**

For Reflection:

Directions (Assignment four):

Write a reflection (5-8 sentences) about your learning experience from this lesson about 1st Amendment rights in public education. Edit your writing to correct errors in spelling, grammar, punctuation, clarity, and structure. Post your reflection on the discussion board. Label the post: Lesson One- A Reflection on 1st Amendment Rights in Public Education.

A Closing Thought:

"The book to read is not one which thinks for you, but the one that makes you think. No other book in the world equals the Bible for that."

-James McCosh

by Wilma J. Brown-Foreman, ED. S

by Wilma J. Brown-Foreman, ED. S

LESSON TWO

UNDERSTANDING THE ESTABLISHMENT CLAUSE

Overview:

This lesson presents two opposed situations involving religion in public schools. The goal of the lesson is to strengthen students' understanding of the two clauses of the First Amendment that relate to religion in the public square: *establishment of religion or prohibiting the free exercise thereof.*

Key Concept:

The Establishment Clause found in the First Amendment to the U.S. Constitution ("Congress shall make no law respecting an establishment of religion, or prohibiting the free exercise thereof...")

Lesson Objectives

Students will:

- understand the types of situations that can result in issues addressed by the Establishment Clause.
- understand how the interpretation of the Establishment Clause has developed over time.
- apply the text, history, and interpretation of the Establishment Clause to current issues.
- understand the current questions that surround the rights to religious freedom in public education.
- cite strong and thorough textual evidence to support analysis of what the text says explicitly as well as inferences drawn from the text.
- apply knowledge of word origins, derivations, and figurative language to extend vocabulary development in authentic texts.
- participate in class discussions.
- edit writing to correct errors.

Expected Student Learning Outcomes

At the end of this lesson, students will:

- decide what an assigned text says explicitly and implicitly.
- make logical conclusions/inferences from assigned readings.
- summarize the key supporting details and ideas in assigned readings.
- cite specific textual evidence to support conclusions drawn from the text.
- interpret key words and phrases as used in the assigned texts.
- demonstrate vocabulary knowledge that is important to comprehension or expression of knowledge of the First Amendment.

- use technology, including the Internet, to produce and publish writing and to interact and collaborate with others.
- participate in class discussions.
- edit writing to correct errors.

Duration: 2-3 hours

Materials:

To complete the lesson, students will need:

- Article: "The Establishment Clause" by the Constitution Center (https://constitutioncenter.org/interactive-constitution/interpretation/amendment-i/interps/264)
- A computer with internet access and editing capability
- An online dictionary

Procedure:

- Read the article:
- Respond to the study questions and reflection.
- Note key details for discussions and future assessments.
- If you have questions or need further clarification on any assignment, e-mail me at wilmaforeman@yahoo.com or visit my website: AIBL.INFO to sign up for the online course.

Study Questions:

Directions: Show the statement in each set that is INCORRECT.

1. Which of the following statements is INCORRECT?
   a. ***America was built upon a single religious principle. (Incorrect)***
   b. America's early settlers came from a variety of religious backgrounds.
   c. During the Colonial Period, the Church of England existed by law in all the southern colonies.
   d. Localized Puritan (or "Congregationalist") establishments settled in the New England states during colonial times.
   e. All the statements above are correct.

2. Which of the following statements is INCORRECT?
   a. In the New England colonies, colonial authorities ordained and disciplined people for religious duties.
   b. The colonists in New England paid religious taxes.
   c. ***"Dissenters" were people who conformed to the doctrine, discipline, and worship of the Church of England. (Incorrect)***
   d. In the early settlements in America, religious authorities punished dissenters for preaching without a license or for refusing to pay taxes to a church they opposed.

e. All the statements above are correct.

3. Which of the following statements is INCORRECT?
   a. After the Declaration of Independence, there was widespread agreement that there should be no nationally established church.
   b. The Establishment Clause of the First Amendment, principally authored by James Madison, reflects this consensus.
   c. The language of the Establishment Clause itself applies to the federal government.
   d. The first part of the Establishment Clause reads: "Congress shall pass no law respecting an establishment of religion."
   e. All the statements above are correct.

4. Which of the following statements is INCORRECT?
   a. All states in America disestablished religion by 1833.
   b. In the 1940s, the Supreme Court held that disestablishment applies to state governments based on the Fourteenth Amendment.
   c. The American government has the authority to compel attendance or financial support of a religious institution. (Incorrect)
   d. The federal government cannot interfere with a religious organization's choice of clergy or religious doctrine.
   e. All the statements above are correct.

5. Which of the following statements is INCORRECT?
   a. The government has the right to extend benefits to religious entities and not others without adequate secular justification. (Incorrect)
   b. In 1971, the Supreme Court surveyed its earlier Establishment Clause cases and found three factors that show whether a government practice violates the Establishment Clause.
   c. Using the "*Lemon* test," Supreme the Court often decides Establishment Clause cases without referring to it.
   d. The Supreme Court Justices have not overruled the *Lemon* test, and the lower courts still are obliged to use it.
   e. All the above statements are correct.

6. Which of the following statements is INCORRECT?
   a. Under the Establishment Clause, the government must be neutral between religious and non-religious institutions that supply education or other social services.
   b. Under the Establishment Clause no taxpayer funds should go to religious institutions if they might be used to communicate religious doctrine.
   c. In the case, *Everson v. Board of Education* (1947), students who attend private religious elementary and secondary schools were allowed to receive transportation and textbook subsidies.
   d. In the case, *Board of Education v. Allen* (1968), for about fifteen years, the Supreme Court attempted to draw increasingly sharp lines against the use of tax-funded assistance for the religious aspects of education.

e. **All the above statements are correct.**

7. Which of the following statements is INCORRECT?
   a. In the case *Aguilar v. Felton* (1985), the Supreme Court prohibited public school teaching specialists from going on the premises of religious schools to provide remedial assistance.
   b. In the case, *Zelman v. Simmons-Harris* (2002), the Supreme Court upheld programs that provide aid to educational or social programs on a neutral basis.
   c. The Supreme Court held in *Rosenberger v. University of Virginia* (1995) that it is unconstitutional under free speech or free exercise principles to exclude otherwise eligible recipients from government assistance solely because their religious activity.
   d. The Court's best-known Establishment Clause decisions, *Engel v. Vitale* (1962), *Abington School District v. Schempp* (1963), held it unconstitutional for public schools to lead schoolchildren in prayer or Bible reading for devotional purposes, even is students volunteer to participate in such activities.
   e. **All the above statements are correct.**

8. Which of the following statements is INCORRECT?
   a. The Supreme Court prohibited prayers at graduation ceremonies in <u>*Lee v. Weisman*</u> (1992).
   b. Prayer at football games on public school campuses was prohibited in the Supreme Court case, <u>*Santa Fe Independent School District v. Doe*</u> (2000).
   c. In general, the Supreme Court allows government-sponsored prayer that occur off public school campuses.
   d. In <u>*Marsh v. Chambers*</u> (1983), the Court upheld legislative prayer, specifically because the practice was immersed in history.
   e. **All the above statements are correct.**

9. Which of the following statements is INCORRECT?
   a. In <u>*Town of Greece v. Galloway*</u> (2014), the Supreme Court approved an opening prayer or statement at town council meetings.
   b. Hundreds of federal, state, and local laws exempt or accommodate religious believers or institutions from laws for whom compliance would conflict with religiously motivated conduct.
   c. American courts recognize religious exemptions for military draft orders, for kosher or halal meals for prisoners, and for parents who do not believe in medical treatment for their ill children.
   d. The Supreme Court held that a state sales tax exemption limited to religious publications was unconstitutional in <u>*Texas Monthly, Inc. v. Bullock*</u> (1989).
   e. **All the above statements are correct.**

10. Which of the following statements is INCORRECT?
    a. The Supreme Court unanimously upheld the exemption of religious organizations from prohibitions on employment discrimination for ministers in *Hosanna-Tabor Evangelical Lutheran Church and School v. E.E.O.C.* (2012).

b. The Supreme Court held that a state sales tax exemption limited to religious publications was unconstitutional in *Texas Monthly, Inc. v. Bullock* (1989).

c. In *Lynch v. Donnelly* (1984), the Court allowed display of a nativity scene surrounded by other holiday decorations.

d. In *County of Allegheny v. American Civil Liberties Union* (1989), most Justices held that the display of a nativity scene by itself at the top of the grand stairway in a courthouse violated the Establishment Clause.

e. ***All the above statements are correct.***

For reflection:

What are the two parts of the Establishment Clause? Give an example of a violation of each part. Use internet sources to respond. Document sources. Edit your writing to correct errors in spelling, grammar, punctuation, and sentence structure. Post your reflection to the discussion board. Label the post: Examples of Violations of the Establishment Clause.

A Closing Statement:

"To know what you know and what you do not know, that is true knowledge."

-Confucius

by Wilma J. Brown-Foreman, ED. S

LESSON THREE

EXAMINING "SEPARATION OF CHURCH AND STATE" ISSUES IN PUBLIC EDUCATION

Lesson Overview:

Coined by Thomas Jefferson, the term, "separation of church and state," is derived from the expression, "wall of separation between church and state." Separation of church and state means that the government cannot exercise its authority to set up a national religion. Since public schools constitute a local extension of the government, they cannot make religion mandatory for all students. To strengthen understanding of the two clauses of the First Amendment, this lesson presents two opposite situations related to religion in public secondary schools.

Key Concepts: Establishment Clause, Separation of Church and State laws

Lesson Objectives

Students will:

- understand the main idea of material heard, viewed, or read.
- interpret or summarize ideas in own words.
- apply an abstract idea in a concrete situation to solve a problem or relate it to a prior experience.
- break down a concept or idea into parts and show the relationships among the parts.
- make informed judgements about the value of ideas or materials.
- apply 1st Amendment rights to everyday situations in public education.

Expected Student Learning Objectives:

At the end of the lesson, students will be able to:

- explain the meaning of the term, "Separation of Church and State."
- apply the Establishment Clause to religious practices in public schools.
- clarify misconceptions about teaching about religion and the Hebrew Bible in public education.

Duration: 2-3 hours

Materials:

- Article*: "Public Schools and Religion"*
  (https://mtsu.edu/first-amendment/encyclopedia/case/98/public-schools-and-religion)
  (https://mtsu.edu/first-amendment/page/religion-public-schools)

- *A Teacher's Guide to Religion in the Public Schools*, by Charles C. Haynes (*https://religiousfreedomcenter.org/wp-content/uploads/2014/08/teachersguide.pdf*)
- *STATEMENT ON THE BIBLE IN PUBLIC SCHOOLS: A FIRST AMENDMENT GUIDE* (*https://www.aclu.org/other/statement-bible-public-schools-first-amendment-guide*)
- *Teaching about the Bible in Public School: How to do it Right* (*https://www.au.org/the-latest/church-and-state/articles/teaching-about-the-bible-in-public-schools/*)
- *The First Amendment Lesson Plan: Religion in Public School* (*https://mtsu.edu/first-amendment/page/religion-public-schools*)
- *Religion in Colonial America: Trends, Regulations, and Beliefs*
- *Finding Common Ground: A Guide to Religious Liberty in Public Schools, by Charles C. Haynes and Oliver Thomas. First Amendment Center, 2011.*
- "How Should We Teach the Bible in Public Schools? *by Mark A. Chancey (2014)* (*https://religionandpolitics.org/2014/01/07/how-should-we-teach-the-bible-in-public-schools/*)
- Internet access/e-mail/computer editing ability
- Notebook/paper/pen/dictionary

Procedure:

- Use a reliable internet resource to read the First Amendment Establishment Clause resources listed above.
- Explain the meaning of and purpose for the Establishment Clause.
- Give examples of how religious liberty might be infringed upon by the local, state, and federal governments.
- Read the two hypothetical situations in the First Amendment Lesson Plan: *Religion in Public School (https://mtsu.edu/first-amendment/page/religion-public-schools)*.
- Contrast the actions of the school officials in both situations.
- Explain why, under the First Amendment, the school officials' actions were wrong.
- Respond to study questions.
- Write a reflection on the lesson.
- Edit your writing.
- Post the reflection on the discussion board.
- Label the reflection: A Reflection on "Separation of Church and State" Issues.
- If you have questions or need further clarification on any assignment, e-mail me at wilmaforeman@yahoo.com or visit my website: AIBL.INFO to sign up for the online course.

Study Questions

Are the following statements **(A) CORRECT or (B) INCORRECT** about the First Amendment Establishment Clause: "Congress shall make no law respecting an establishment of religion or prohibiting the free exercise thereof …"?

1. Under the "establishment" clause of the First Amendment, and in line with U.S. Supreme Court rulings, public school educators should lead students in prayer during the school day. **(B) INCORRECT**
2. As agents of the state, public school teachers may not require prayer or other religious practices from students, even if students do not object to taking part in the devotional activities. **(A) CORRECT**
3. The first religion clause says government and its agencies cannot set up religious beliefs in students. **(A) CORRECT**
4. Local, state, and federal governments cannot set up a national religion. **(A) CORRECT**
5. The Establishment Clause prohibits the government from favoring one religion over another. **(A) CORRECT**
6. School administrators cannot broadcast prayers over a school public-address system. **(A) CORRECT**
7. Under the "free exercise" clause of the First Amendment, public schools may not prevent students from expressing or sharing religious beliefs privately or in lessons related to academic religious studies. **(A) CORRECT**
8. Public school students may express their religious beliefs if they do not disrupt the school environment. **(A) CORRECT**
9. The second part of the Establishment clause says that the government and its agencies may not forbid or interfere with individuals' practice of religion. **(A) CORRECT**
10. Students may not bring religious texts to school to read and discuss them. **(B) INCORRECT**

Study Questions

Reference: **"Teaching about the Bible in Public School: How to do it Right"** by Mark A. Chancey

(*https://www.au.org/the-latest/church-and-state/articles/teaching-about-the-bible-in-public-schools/*)

Directions: Based on this article, are the following statements (A) TRUE or (B) FALSE

11. Teaching about the Hebrew Bible is illegal on public school campuses. (B) FALSE
12. Studies about the Hebrew Bible are permissible on public school grounds only if other religions are in the curriculum also. (B) FALSE
13. Mark Chance, professor of religious studies at Southern Methodist University in Dallas, studied the teaching practices of teachers of Bible Literacy courses in public schools. (A) TRUE
14. According to Chancey, successful Bible literacy courses in public school curricula rely primarily on resources by a variety of biblical scholarship. (A) TRUE
15. Successful Bible literacy classes in public education show sensitivity toward issues resulting from religious diversity. (A) TRUE
16. Bible literacy class assignments should be intellectually challenging and require critical thinking. (A) TRUE
17. Students in Bible literacy classes should avoid creativity so as not to offend other students with different religious persuasions. (B) FALSE

18. Bible literacy lessons in public schools should focus on rote memorization of scriptures. (B) FALSE
19. Bible literacy curriculum should inform students about different Bibles of various religious traditions, including Jewish and Christian. (A) TRUE
20. Bible literacy teachers should recognize biblical texts as historical sources. (A) TRUE
21. Teachers of the Hebrew Bible in public education should present the text as a completely historical document. (B) FALSE
22. Bible literacy classes may include lessons on the theological, ethical, and moral claims of the biblical text. (A) TRUE
23. Teachers of Bible literacy in public education should present the biblical text as the only authoritative text for making theological, ethical, and moral decisions. (B) FALSE
24. Bible literacy classes should treat Judaism as a religion with its own culture. (A) TRUE
25. Teachers of biblical literacy courses recognize the Hebrew Bible as a religious text instead of a science book. (A) TRUE

Extended Assignment:

- Reread the article "How Should We Teach the Bible in Public Schools? by Mark A. Chancey (2014) (https://religionandpolitics.org/2014/01/07/how-should-we-teach-the-bible-in-public-schools/).
- Respond in complete sentences to the following:

   a. What are the problems that Chancey found in the teaching practices of biblical literacy classes in Texas?
   b. Summarize the practices of the successful Bible literacy classes. (Give three-five examples.)
- Edit your writing to correct errors.
- Post your examples on the discussion board. Label the post: Examples of Successful Bible Literacy Classes in Public Education.

A Closing Thought:

"The man who asks a question is a fool for a minute, the man who does not ask is a fool for life."

—Confucius

LESSON FOUR
USING ONLINE BIBLE STUDY TOOLS (PART ONE)
(COPYRIGHT & THE PUBLIC DOMAIN RULES)

Lesson Overview:

Copyright law affects the way we gather, share, create and use the intellectual property that is so readily available in our culture. This lesson focuses on copyright and fair use in relation to materials from mass media, popular culture, and digital media. The lesson helps educators and students understand the legal and ethical uses of copyrighted materials protected under the doctrine of fair use.

Key Concepts:

copyright, fair use, copyfraud, public domain

Lesson Objectives:

Students will:

- use online resources to access and interpret information.
- understand terminology and rules related to copyrighted and public domain materials.
- learn about how copyright law protects both the rights of owners and the rights of users to promote creativity for the good of society.
- learn about Section 107 of the Copyright Act and see how fair use applies to teaching and learning.
- understand that ideas about copyright are in transition because of changes in communication technologies.

Expected Learning Outcomes:

At the end of this lesson, students will be able to:

- demonstrate a knowledge of terminology related to the public domain and copyright rules.
- decide when and how to use copyrighted materials as part of their creative works.
- apply the concepts of copyright laws and fair use to the practices of teaching and learning.

Materials:

To complete the lesson, students will need:

- *Copyright and Fair Use Lesson Plans by Renee Hobbs, Sandra Braman and Katie Donnelly (https://mediaeducationlab.com/copyright-and-fair-use-lesson-plans-high-school-college-and-graduate-education*)

- *Copyright and Fair Use (https://fairuse.stanford.edu/overview/public-domain/welcome/)*
- *Creative Commons (https://creativecommons.org/2017/01/16/public-domain-5-things-not-covered-copyright/)*
- *WIPO Intellectual Property (https://www.wipo.int/edocs/pubdocs/en/wipo_pub_450_2020.pdf)*
- Internet access/e-mail/computer editing ability
- Notebook/paper/pen/dictionary

Procedure:

- Read the assigned articles and respond to the study questions.
- Respond to the reflections and post your work on the discussion board. (Edit your writing to correct errors.)
- If you have questions or need further clarification on any assignment, e-mail me at wilmaforeman@yahoo.com or visit my website: AIBL.INFO to sign up for the online course.

(Read *Copyright and Fair Use Lesson Plans by Renee Hobbs, Sandra Braman and Katie Donnelly (https://mediaeducationlab.com/copyright-and-fair-use-lesson-plans-high-school-college-and-graduate-education*).

Are the following statements (A) CORRECT or (B) INCORRECT?
1. The word, "copyright," relates to the rights of owners to control access to their intellectual property. (A) CORRECT
2. The U.S. Constitution says that the purpose of copyright is to promote the spread of knowledge and innovation. (A) CORRECT
3. The intellectual property rights provision of the Constitution exists because the Founders believed that encouraging the development of innovative ideas and information serves society. (A) CORRECT
4. Today's copyright and fair use rules have increased confusion and anxiety among educators. (A) CORRECT
5. The term "intellectual property" refers to creations of the mind, such as inventions; literary and artistic works; designs; and symbols, names and images used in commerce. (A) CORRECT
6. To protect the value of their intellectual property, owners have lobbied for changes in copyright law. (A) CORRECT
7. In general, educators have incomplete knowledge about copyright law and the doctrine of fair use. (A) CORRECT
8. Lack of knowledge about copyright rules has a negative effect on the quality of teaching and learning. (A) CORRECT
9. Copyright guides can limit the spread of innovative instructional practices and perpetuate misunderstandings about copyright. (A) CORRECT
10. *The Agreement on Guidelines for Classroom Copying in Not-for-Profit Educational Institutions*, the *Fair Use Guidelines for Educational Multimedia*, and the *Guidelines for*

the Educational Use of Music resulted from negotiated agreements between lawyers standing for media companies and lawyers standing for educational groups. (A) CORRECT

11. To clarify how fair use applies to the work of educators, these guidelines specify precise examples of fair use, such as the "ten percent rule," and the "forty-five-day rule." (A) CORRECT

12. Legal scholar Kenneth Crews states that the copyright documents created by the negotiated agreements give them "the appearance of positive law." (A) CORRECT

13. Crews asserts that the copyright rules within the documents are illusory and have had a seriously damaging effect. (A) CORRECT

14. Crews believes that the copyright guides interfere with an actual understanding of the law and weaken confidence in the law as created by Congress and the courts. (A) CORRECT

15. *The Code of Best Practices for Fair Use in Media Literacy Education* names five principles about acceptable practices for the fair use of copyrighted materials. (A) CORRECT

16. This code of best practices for copyright use originated from ten meetings with more than 150 members of leading educational associations and other educators across the United States. (A) CORRECT

17. Copyright law enables the owner to control access to the work he or she created and imposes strong penalties for infringement of owners' rights. (A) CORRECT

18. Copyright law includes the doctrine of fair use, which exempts all uses of copyright material from the owners' control. (B) INCORRECT

19. Part of the Copyright Act of 1976 states that people have a right to use copyrighted materials freely without payment or permission, for purposes such as "criticism, comment, news reporting, teaching, scholarship, and research." (A) CORRECT

20. "Fair use" gives people a right to use copyrighted material when the cost to the copyright holder is less than the social benefit of the use of the copyrighted work. (A) CORRECT

21. Individuals should assess the specific context and situation of the use of a copyrighted work to see if "fair use" applies. (A) CORRECT

22. The expression "fixed copyright rules" is inappropriate since "fair use" requires that people use reasoning and judgment. (A) CORRECT

23. Courts recognize that educators and students use copyrighted materials for scholarship, teaching, and learning. (A) CORRECT or (B) INCORRECT

24. In recent years, courts have ruled that when a user of copyrighted materials adds value to or repurposes materials for a use different from the original intent, it will be considered "fair use." (A) CORRECT

25. "Fair use" embraces the modifying of existing media content, placing it in new context.

(A) CORRECT

Study Questions

Directions:

Read *Copyright and Fair Use* by Stanford University

(https://fairuse.stanford.edu/overview/faqs/copyright-protection/#when_can_i_use_a_work_without_the_author8217s_permission) .

Are the following statements (A) CORRECT or (B) INCORRECT?

1. As a rule, it is wise to work under the assumption that copyright or trademark laws protect works unless conclusive information says otherwise. (A) CORRECT
2. A work is in the public domain simply because it appears on the Internet. (B) INCORRECT
3. Usually, a work is in the public domain if it lacks a copyright notice. (B) INCORRECT
4. One can distribute or copy clip art, shareware, freeware, or materials labeled "royalty-free" or "copyright-free" without authorization. (A) CORRECT
5. Read the terms and conditions in any "Click to Accept" agreements or "Read Me" files going with such materials to be certain that your intended use complies to the statements. (A) CORRECT
6. "Click to Accept" agreements and "Click-Wrap" agreements are the same in meaning. (A) CORRECT
7. Removal of infringing material is also an element of the Digital Millennium Copyright Act (DMCA), a 1998 law showing that an Internet Service Provider (ISP) can avoid liability by following certain rules, including speedy removal of infringing material. (A) CORRECT
8. If someone complains about an unauthorized use of copyrighted materials, one should investigate the claim quickly and seek evidence of copyright ownership and validity from the complaining person. (A) CORRECT
9. The webmaster can verify the facts through copyright research. (A) CORRECT
10. The webmaster will investigate the transfer of any infringing material, if any, to and from the site. (A) CORRECT

Study Questions:

Read *Creative Commons (https://creativecommons.org/2017/01/16/public-domain-5-things-not-covered-copyright/)*. Are the following statements (A) CORRECT or (B) INCORRECT?

1. To receive copyright, a work must be "fixed in a tangible medium of expression." (A) CORRECT
2. A "tangible medium of expression" means that that one has reduced a work to a concrete form. (A) CORRECT
3. A "derivative work" is a copyright term for a work of authorship that is based upon another original work of authorship. (A) CORRECT
4. The author of a "derivative work" cannot claim ownership of the whole work, only to the part he or she created. (A) CORRECT

5. Copyright protection for an original work of authorship does not extend to any idea, procedure, process, system, method of operation, concept, principle, or discovery. (A) CORRECT

6. Copyright does not protect works consisting entirely of information that is commonly known and having no original authorship. (A) CORRECT

7. Copyright protection is not available for any work by the United States Government. (A) CORRECT

8. Domain names have a utilitarian (useful) function and are not copyright protected. (A) CORRECT

9. A work in the public domain is not eligible to claim a copyright. (A) CORRECT

10. Domain status means that there are no legal restrictions on copying, publishing, or making derivative works because of human copyright law. (A) CORRECT

11. With a public domain Bible, one may freely copy, publish, distribute, print, adapt, make derivative works of the content. (A) CORRECT

12. One may quote from the Bible in the public domain as much as he or she wants. (A) CORRECT

13. One does not need permission to use works in the public domain because there is no copyright owner with an exclusive legal right to control these uses. (A) CORRECT

14. A person may not claim a copyright on a song or poem. (B) INCORRECT

15. If a person converts a public domain text to another format, he or she may not claim a copyright on the public domain text for himself. (A) CORRECT

16. "Copyfraud" is a form of stealing intellectual property rights from the public. (A) CORRECT

17. A public domain work stays in the public domain even if someone prints and sells it. (A) CORRECT

18. Anyone may claim a copyright on his/her own creative works. (A) CORRECT

19. Twentieth century Bibles are not in the public domain or are available online. (B) INCORRECT

20. Copyrighted materials belong to the owner of the property to help prevent intellectual property theft. (A) CORRECT

Assignment: Complete the two practice quizzes on copyright rules and fair use listed below. Copy and paste your results on the discussion board. (Include your name.)

- Michigan State University (https://mclellan.law.msu.edu/quizzes/copyright-quiz)
- Proprofs.com (https://www.proprofs.com/quiz-school/story.php?title=copyright-fair-use-quiz)

A Closing Thought:

"*Any fool can know. The point is to understand.*"
— Albert Einstein

by Wilma J. Brown-Foreman, ED. S

LESSON FIVE

EXPLORING ONLINE BIBLE STUDY TOOLS

Lesson Overview:

A serious study of the Hebrew Scriptures involves gaining insight from scholarly Bible study tools. Bible study tools are resources that can aid people in reading, understanding, and studying the Bible. There are distinct types of Bible study tools available online, including study Bibles, commentaries, Bible dictionaries, lexicons, Bible encyclopedias, and concordances. In short, Bible study tools can help supply important academic and historical context, find translation differences between versions, find the true meaning of a passage, and aid readers in applying the lessons to their own experiences in life. This lesson gives students the opportunity to engage in using online Bible study tools.

Key Concepts: commentaries: exegetical, expository, expositional, cultural, devotional, archetypal, theologians, Old and New Testaments, exegetical, expositional, devotional, and cultural commentaries, Bible dictionaries, lexicons, Bible encyclopedias, and concordances

Objectives

Students will:

- use online resources to access, examine, research, discuss, assimilate, and critique information.
- distinguish between available Bible resources useful for enhancing biblical literacy.
- use Bible study tools to enhance writing and research skills.
- participate in class discussions.
- edit writing to correct errors.

Expected Learning Outcomes:

At the end of this lesson students will be able to:

- distinguish between various online Bible study tools.
- use proper study tools to enhance learning.

Duration: 2-3 hours

Materials:

- paper/pen/notebook/dictionary
- Website: *For All Things (19 Websites for Reading and Searching the Bible) (https://forallthings.bible/19-websites-for-reading-and-searching-the-bible/*

- Website: *5 of the Best Free Bible Study Tools (https://freedailybiblestudy.com/5-of-the-best-free-bible-study-tools/)*
- Website*: Think about Such Things.com (https://thinkaboutsuchthings.com/bible-study-tools-online/)*
- Video: *Bible Commentaries: What They Are and How to Use Them (https://www.youtube.com/watch?v=6U67Xvf-T9Y)*
- *Blue Letter Bible* (https://www.blueletterbible.org/study.cfm)
- A computer with internet access/editing capability
- Internet access/e-mail/computer editing ability
- Notebook/paper/pen/dictionary

Procedure:

- Complete each assignment below.
- Note key details for future discussions and assessments.
- If you have questions or need further clarification on any assignment, e-mail me at wilmaforeman@yahoo.com or visit my website: AIBL.INFO to sign up for the online course.

Assignment one

Directions:

- Explain at least ten (10) features of online Bible study tools
- Post key findings to the discussion board.
- Label the post: Ten (10) Features of Online Bible Study Tools.

(Note: You may use more credible online resources to respond to the assignment.)

Study Questions

Directions:

Use websites such as *BibleStudyTools.com* and *Blue Letter Bible.org* to answer the study questions below. Write key points in your notebook.

Based on your study of online Bible study tools, are the following statements (A) CORRECT or (B) INCORRECT?

1. With the software at *Bible Study Tools.com*, users can search the Hebrew Bible, track daily reading plans, and share scripture via copy/paste or links. (A) CORRECT
2. The site *Bible Study Tools* has resources from the public domain. (A) CORRECT
3. When a work is in the public domain, it usually has copyright privileges. (B) INCORRECT
4. Bible commentaries have copyrighted materials. (A) CORRECT
5. The website *Bible Study Tools.com (*https://www.biblestudytools.com/) has dictionaries, encyclopedias, and encyclopedias. (A) CORRECT
6. Old and New Testament *lexicons* at https://www.studylight.org/lexicons/eng/greek.html have classic sermons of scholars and preachers from the past. (A) CORRECT

7. A Bible *concordance* is an alphabetical listing of words and phrases found in the Bible and shows where the terms occur throughout all books of Scripture. (A) CORRECT

8. An *interlinear* Bible on the website at https://www.biblestudytools.com/interlinear-bible/ connects to the Greek and Hebrew texts through *Strong's Concordance*. (A) CORRECT

9. *The Strong's Exhaustive Concordance* is the most complete, easy-to-use, and understandable concordance for studying the original languages of the Bible. (A) CORRECT

10. One can find concordances for great writers, such as Shakespeare, Milton, Spenser, Tennyson, Dante, but more concordances relate to the Bible than for all these authors combined. (A) CORRECT

11. *The Berean Interlinear Bible* uses KJV and NASB as the English translation of Greek and Hebrew words. (A) CORRECT

12. The *Bible Study.com* site has no modern reference tools. (B) INCORRECT

13. Students can find the KJV and NASB in the *Berean Interlinear Bible* to study the original Hebrew language. (A) CORRECT

14. *The Interlinear Bibles* have cross references related to the topics in the passage. (A) CORRECT

15. The *Interlinear Hebrew* text comes from the United Bible Societies. (A) CORRECT

16. The *Bible Hub* is an online *parallel* Bible project. (A) CORRECT

17. Across the top of the *Bible Hub* site is a toolbar that helps people navigate to specific passages in any of the supported translations. (A) CORRECT

18. The *Bible Hub* software has only one translation of the Bible. (B) INCORRECT

19. Study tools such as the context of the biblical passage, cross references, and the *Treasury of Scripture Knowledge* are available on the *Bible Hub* website. (B) INCORRECT

20. The site includes a collection of modern public domain translations of the Hebrew Bible. (A) CORRECT

21. The toolbar on the *Bible Hub* site also includes public domain commentaries, cross references, and a context button that shows the single verse within the pericope. (A) CORRECT

22. Bible Hub links to *Facebook, Twitter, and Google*. (A) CORRECT

23. *Biblia* website offers a simplified version of the *Logos 9* app. (A) CORRECT

24. *Bible Hub* software includes pictures, maps, and outlines. (A) CORRECT

25. Commentaries, lexicons, dictionaries, sermons, and various language translations are on Bible study websites such as *Bible Gateway, Bible Hub, and Bible Study Tools.com*. (A) CORRECT

26. *Bible Hub* interface is quite different from *Bible Gateway.com*. (A) CORRECT

27. *Biblia* gives users access to their *Logos* Bible Software library. (A) CORRECT

28. *Biblia* has a mobile version of the site. (A) CORRECT

29. *The Treasury of Scripture Knowledge's* Bible references link to the King James Version of the Bible. (A) CORRECT

30. All resources on *Bible Hub* are in public domain. (B) INCORRECT

31. All Bible study tools on *Bible Gateway* are in public domain. (B) INCORRECT

32. *The Pursuit of God* written by A.W. Tozer (originally published in 1948) is a Christian Classic in public domain. (A) CORRECT

33. *The Pilgrim's Progress from This World, to That Which Is to Come* is a 1678 Christian allegory written by John Bunyan that is in the public domain. (A) CORRECT
34. *The Pilgrim's Progress* is one of the most significant works of religious theological fiction in English literature. (A) CORRECT
35. John Bunyan's *The Pilgrim's Progress* is written in more than two hundred languages and has never been out of print. (A) CORRECT
36. *Blue Letter Bible.org* is a free, searchable online Bible program that supplies access to different Bible translations including: KJV, NKJV, NLT, ESV, NASB20, NASB95. (A) CORRECT
37. *Blue Letter Bible.org* provides in-depth study tools with access to commentaries, encyclopedias, dictionaries, and other theological resources. (A) CORRECT
38. *The Darby Bible* refers to the Hebrew Bible as translated from Hebrew and Greek by John Nelson Darby. (A) CORRECT
39. Noah Webster wrote the *Webster Bible*.
40. The Greek Old Testament, known as the *Septuagint*, is the earliest *extant* Greek translation of books from the Hebrew Bible. (A) CORRECT
41. In academia, the abbreviation for the *Septuagint* is LXX (the Roman numeral for seventy). (A) CORRECT
42. The expression "extant" means "still in existence; surviving." (A) CORRECT
43. The *Vulgate* is a Latin version of the Bible by St Jerome. (A) CORRECT
44. *The Berean Study Bible*, like the *NKJ*, has words such as "unto," and "behold," but sometimes it reads like the *NIV*. (A) CORRECT
45. In the New Testament times, the Bereans were residents of the city of Berea in Macedonia. (A) CORRECT
46. Paul and Silas preached to the Bereans during Paul's second missionary journey (Acts 17:11). (A) CORRECT
47. Bible lexicons have definitions and meaning of Biblical expressions found in the original New Testament Greek and Old Testament Hebrew languages of the Bible. (A) CORRECT
48. Bible encyclopedias have articles and definitions to thousands of words and terms used in Scripture. (A) CORRECT
49. A concordance has an alphabetical index of the principal words in a book or the works of an author with their immediate contexts. (A) CORRECT
50. Exhaustive concordances, such a *Strong's Exhaustive Concordance of the Bible*, list every word found in the Bible, including articles and conjunctions like "the," "and," "but." (A) CORRECT

Study Questions

Reference: *Bible Commentaries: What They Are and How to Use Them*

(https://www.youtube.com/watch?v=6U67Xvf-T9Y))

Are the following statements (A) CORRECT of (B) INCORRECT?

1. In studying the Bible, scholars should limit their resources to one interpretation only. (B) INCORRECT

2. *Commentaries* are books written about the books of the Bible to help supply background information that will help someone understand biblical text better. (A) CORRECT

3. In general, there are four distinct kinds of commentaries. (A) CORRECT

4. The first type of Bible commentary is an *expository* commentary, written by pastors for pastors. (A) CORRECT

5. An *expository* commentary gives ministers ideas for sermon outlines. (A) CORRECT

6. *Expository* commentaries are useful for scholars in a high school English classroom. (A) CORRECT

7. *The Moody Bible* is an *exegetical* commentary. (A) CORRECT

8. *Theologians* and professors write *exegetical* commentaries. (A) CORRECT

9. *Exegetical* Bible commentaries provide readers with insight and understanding through the "*exegesis*" of the biblical text. (A) CORRECT

10. The English word "*exegesis*" comes from a Greek word that literally means "to draw out." (A) CORRECT

11. *Exegetical* commentaries aim to "draw out" the original meaning of Scripture. (A) CORRECT

12. The statement, "The quintessential commentary is an exegetical commentary" means that the exegetical commentary is a perfect example of the type of writing that draws out understanding. (A) CORRECT

13. A *devotional* commentary gives thoughts for reflection and life application. (A) CORRECT

14. The Bible commentary by Jay Vernon McGee is devotional. (A) CORRECT

15. *Cultural* commentaries, such as the *IVP Bible*, provide the background on the culture to help with relating the biblical text to one's own life experiences. (A) CORRECT

16. A commentary may focus on a single book in the Hebrew Bible. (A) CORRECT

17. A commentary can have sub-sections. (A) CORRECT

18. A commentary can be a study on the Old and New Testaments in Christian Bibles. (A) CORRECT

19. A one-volume commentary covers the entire Bible in one collection. (A) CORRECT

20. In scholarly Bible study, readers should spend more time on reading biblical text than on Bible commentaries. (A) CORRECT

Extended Learning Study Questions

Directions:

- Read the following passage from *Ellicott's Commentary for English Readers (THE CREATIVE DAYS)*.
- Write unfamiliar vocabulary terms in your notebook.
- Use an online resource to define each term based on the context of the passage.
- Respond to the study questions that follow the excerpt.
- Note key points in your notebook for future discussions and assessments.
- Post questions for added clarification on the discussion board.

THE CREATIVE DAYS. (from Ellicott's Commentary for English Readers)

(3) And God said. --Voice and sound there could be none, nor was there any person to whom God addressed this word of power. The phrase, then, is metaphorical, and means that God enacted for the universe a law; and ten times we find the command similarly given. The beauty and sublimity of the language here used has often been noticed: God makes no preparation, He employs no means, needs no secondary agency. He speaks, and it is done. His word alone contains all things necessary for the fulfilment of His will...God, then, by speaking, gives to nature a universal and enduring law. His commands are not temporary, but eternal; and whatever secondary causes were called into existence when the Elohim, by a word, created light, those same causes produce it now, and will produce it until God recalls His word. We have, then, here nature's first universal law. What is it?

Light is not itself a substance but is a condition or state of matter; and this primaeval light was electric, arising from the condensation and friction of the elements as they began to arrange themselves in order. And this, again, was due to what is commonly called the law of gravitation, or of the attraction of matter. If, on the first day, electricity and magnetism were generated, and the laws given which create and control them, we have in them the two most powerful and active energies of the present and of all time--or two forms of one and the same busy and restless force. And the law thus given was that of gravitation, of which light was the immediate result.

Study Questions

1. Based upon this passage, which of the following statements is NOT CORRECT?
   A. God uses His voice during creative acts.
   B. He speaks to no other being.
   C. God's speech is authoritative.
   D. The opening verse to the Book of Genesis is both literal and metaphorical.
   E. All statements are CORRECT.

2. Which of the following statements is NOT CORRECT?
   A. God enacted for the universe a law...means that God erased all universal laws. (Incorrect)
   B. *"And God said..."* occurs at least ten times in the opening chapter of the Book of Genesis.
   C. If a statement is metaphorical, then it is symbolic, standing for something else.
   D. A metaphor is a figure of speech that compares one thing to another without using the words "like" or "as."
   E. All statements are CORRECT.

3. Which of the following statements is NOT CORRECT?
   A. To *designate* is to appoint or assign someone or something to a specified position.
   B. Based on this passage, light follows a pattern of gravitational pull.
   C. Light consists of busy and unstable waves.
   D. Light waves are a mixture of electricity and magnetism.
   E. All statements are correct.

For Reflection

Explain the significance of the statement: "Our civilization is built upon words." How does this statement relate to the passage above? Mention the power of the words in the Hebrew Scriptures. Tell how the Hebrew Bible has played an invaluable role in building Western civilization through the power of words. (5-8sentences) Use reliable sources to respond. Document sources. Edit your writing to correct errors. Post your reflection on the discussion board, Label the post: A Reflection on How Biblical Words Have Help Build Western Civilization."

Closing Thought:

"The Bible is endorsed by the ages. Our civilization is built upon its words. In no other book is there such a collection of inspired wisdom, reality, and hope."

–Dwight D. Eisenhower, 34th President

LESSON SIX

INTRODUCTION TO THE TORAH

(OLD TESTAMENT)

Lesson Overview:

This lesson is an overview of the literary unity found in the Torah in Jewish tradition and the Old Testament in Christian communities. Students will examine the structure and literary design of the writings and discuss the artistry and purposes of the biblical text. This lesson will focus on the unity of the Torah (Old Testament) by studying the characters, plot, structure, themes, and historical settings of the Hebrew Bible.

Key Concepts:

> etiology, Torah, Tanakh, Old Testament, the Hebrew Bible, prologue, epilogue, macro frame, Bible structure, Pentateuch, the Law, Suzerain, covenants, the prophets, Tanakh, literary genre

Objectives:

Students will:

- examine the structure of the Torah in Jewish tradition.
- understand basic biblical terminology used in the Jewish and Christian traditions.
- distinguish between the structures of the Jewish Torah and the Old Testament in Christian Bibles.
- examine the unity of the Torah (Old Testament) by an introduction to the characters, plot, structure, themes, and historical settings of the Hebrew Bible.

Expected Learning Outcomes:

At the end of this lesson, students will be able to:

- use biblical terms, such as Torah, Old Testament, Pentateuch, and Tanakh.
- state differences in the structural content of Jewish and Christian Hebrew Bibles.
- explain the literary unity in biblical text by connecting the characters, plot, structure, themes, and historical settings of the Hebrew Bible
- cite evidence from an informational text about the Torah to support responses in a collaborative discussion.
- develop vocabulary skills relevant to the understanding of biblical text.
- write a reflection on the key concepts in the lesson.
- correct writing errors.
- participate in discussion board collaboration.

Duration: 2-3 hours

Materials:

To complete the lesson, students will need:

- Internet access/e-mail/computer editing ability
- Notebook/paper/pen/dictionary
- Video: *The Torah: A Quick Overview (https://www.youtube.com/watch?v=7e-z1R62FtI)*
- Video: *"Who Wrote the Bible: A History of the Torah"* (*https://www.youtube.com/watch?v=k8vYLSBCAF8&t=19s*
- Article: "The Torah/the Pentateuch" by Shalom Haverim (*http://www.shalomhaverim.org/English/torah/bereshit_english_1.htm*)
- Article: "The Torah" by Jeffrey Kranz | Aug 16, 2019 |Bible Books (https://overviewbible.com/torah)

Procedure:

- View the videos: *The Torah: A Quick Overview* (*https://www.youtube.com/watch?v=7e-z1R62FtI*) and *"Who Wrote the Bible: A History of the Torah"* (*https://www.youtube.com/watch?v=k8vYLSBCAF8&t=19s*
- Respond to the study questions.
- Write at least five (5) of the video presentation's key points/terminology in your notebook.
- Explain the purpose(s) of the video presentation(s).
- Use a Bible dictionary, Bible encyclopedia, or other resources to define unfamiliar terms.
- Study the terms for future assessments (quizzes/tests).
- Respond to the study questions that follow.

- If you have questions or need further clarification on any assignment, e-mail me at wilmaforeman@yahoo.com or visit my website: AIBL.INFO to sign up for the online course.

(Note: You may use added credible online resources to respond to the questions. Use a pronunciation dictionary to learn to pronounce unfamiliar words.)

Study Questions (Assignment one)

Directions:

- View the video: *The Torah: A Quick Overview-https://www.youtube.com/watch?v=7e-z1R62FtI*.
- Respond appropriately to the following study questions/activities.
- Write the answers in your notebook.

1. How does the speaker define the *Torah*? (*Answer: the five Books of Moses*)
2. Why is the Torah called "the Law of Moses"? (*Answer: Moses is credited as the "mediator" who transmitted information about God's 10 Commandments and other statutes, principles, and instructions to the nation of Israel.*)
3. What is the *etiology* of the word *Torah*? (*Answer: from Hebrew "torah," is literally "instruction, law" -verbal noun from horah "he taught, showed"*)
4. Which individual books lay the foundation for the *Torah*? (*Answer: five-Genesis, Exodus, Leviticus, Numbers, and Deuteronomy*)
5. What do the Torah and the Old Testament in Christian Bibles have in common? (*Answer: The Torah is the first five Books of the Hebrew Bible. In the Jewish faith, the Torah is one part of the "bible." It contains information about Jewish history and laws for worship and daily living.*)

Study Questions (Assignment two)

View the video: *"Who Wrote the Bible: A History of the Torah"* (*https://www.youtube.com/watch?v=k8vYLSBCAF8&t=19s*).

Fill in the blanks to the statements below.

6. The *Torah* is the compilation of the first____ books of the Hebrew Bible, namely the books of Genesis, Exodus, Leviticus, Numbers and____. (*Answers: five; Deuteronomy*)
7. In the Book of Genesis, Chapter 12, God chooses a man called Abram, who later becomes the "father" of the nation____. (*Answer:* Israel)
8. God promises Abram that He will ___him and give him a special land on the eastern coast of the Sea. (*Answer: bless*)
9. The land called "The Promised Land" is ___, a place that the Canaanites occupied. (*Answer: Canaan*)
10. God promises Abram that he will have descendants and that he will become a blessing to other ___of the world. (*Answer: nations*)
11. As the story continues, Abram and his family travel to _____escape a famine. (*Answer: Egypt*)
12. In the Book of ___, the descendants of Abraham become enslaved to the Egyptians. (*Answer*: *Exodus*)
13. In the second Book of the Hebrew Bible, called____, God rescues the children of Israel from their Egyptian captors. (*Answer: Exodus*)
14. God says to the Israelite leader named_____: "Let them (the Israelites) make for Me a sanctuary so that I may dwell among them." (Ex 25:8) (*Answer*: *Moses*)
15. A *sanctuary* is a place of refuge or_____. (*Answer: safety*)
16. God frees Israel from both their _____. (*Answer: oppressors*)
17. God goes to war and executes judgment on the Egyptian_____. (*Answer: pharaoh*)
18. In the wilderness, God makes a special pact, or _____, with the Israelites. (*Answer: covenant*)
19. A wilderness is a place that has not been ____ by human activity. (*Answer: inhabited*)
20. God gives the children of Israel the Ten____ (the Law) while they are wandering in the wilderness. (*Answer: Commandments*)

21. *The Law* is a series of solemn _____. (*Answer: commandments; mandates*)

22. *The Law* is a binding agreement between two _____. (*Answer: parties*)

23. This kind of agreement common to the people of Ancient Near East is a_____. (*Answer: covenant*)

24. In ancient times, mighty kings had *suzerainty* (rulership) over smaller kingdoms and could exert _____ over them. *Answer: power*)

25. During biblical times, landholders, held the smaller kingdoms on conditions of homage and _____. (*Answer: allegiance.*)

26. To show *homage* is to give public_____. (*Answer: respect; reverence*)

27. The *suzerain* would give_____ to loyal vassals, but there would also be curses if vassals were to break the rules of loyalty. (*Answer: protection*)

28. The people engaged in rituals so that they would not _____the agreements. (*Answer: break; forget*)

29. A *ritual* is a religious or solemn _____consisting of actions performed according to a prescribed order. (*Answer: ceremony*)

30. During ancient rituals, people would usually *invoke* their own national_____ to bear witness to the covenant, or agreement. (*Answer: deity; god*)

31. In the case of the Israelites in the Book of Exodus, the God of the *cosmos* replaces _____kings. (*Answer: earthly; human*)

32. For the ancient Israelites, the God of the cosmos had a special_____ with them. (*Answer: relationship*)

33. Throughout the Hebrew Scriptures, God reminds the children of Israel that He rescued them from the Egyptians to take them into the land that He promised _____. (*Answer: Abraham*)

34. God expects the children of Israel to keep the sacred _____. (*Answer: covenant*)

35. If something is sacred, expect it to be _____ to a religious purpose. (*Answer: set apart*)

36. The Books of Exodus, Leviticus, Numbers, and Deuteronomy focus of God's_____ with the Israelites. (*Answer: relationship*)

37. In summary, God wants love and _____from the nation of Israel. (*Answer: obedience or loyalty*)

38. Israel is not to worship other _____beings. (*Answer: divine; supernatural*)

39. God also wants a relationship with other_____. (*Answer: humans*)

40. The Ten Commandments forbid the people to murder, steal, covet, or _____their parents. (*Answer: disrespect*)

41. As He dwells among the people, God manifests (reveals) His presence as a fiery_____. (*Answer: cloud*)

42. God moves alongside this *nomadic* nation of mortals in a *portable* _____or place of worship. (*Answer: tabernacle; tent*)

43. The Book of Leviticus explores the different rules and rituals that the ancient Israelites believe would make it possible for them to coexist with_____. (*Answer: God*)

44. The Book of Numbers records the famous forty-year journey from the Mount _____outside Egypt to the edge of the Promised Land. (*Answer: Sinai*)

45. During the journey, the children of Israel _____against God. (*Answer: grumble; complain*)

46. Because of their recalcitrant (stubborn) disposition, the children of Israel must wait forty years for a new _____ to remain loyal to God. *(Answer: generation)*

47. God disciplines the disobedient Israelites, but He also preserves them and _____them from their enemies along the way. *(Answer: protects)*

48. In the Book of Deuteronomy, Moses acts as a _____between God and the people. *(Answer: mediator)*

49. If the people break the_____, they will not remain in the Promised Land. *(Answer: Commandments)*

50. Throughout the Hebrew Bible, prophets remind the Israelites of the _____between them and God. (Answer: covenant)

Study Questions

Directions:

- Read the article: *"THE OLD TESTAMENT: A Christian Name for the Jewish Bible (My Jewish Learning "(https://www.myjewishlearning.com/article/the-old-testament* .
- Use the article to respond to the study questions below.
- Review the answers for discussions and assessments.

(Note: You may use added credible online resources to respond to the questions. Use a pronunciation dictionary to learn to pronounce unfamiliar words.)

Are the following statements (A) TRUE or (B) FALSE?

1. In Jewish tradition, the Hebrew Scriptures consist of *the Torah*, the *Books of the Prophets* and *the Books of the Writings*. (A) TRUE
2. Within Judaism, this trio is known simply as the Hebrew Bible, or *the Tanakh*. (A) TRUE
3. *Tanakh* is an acronym derived from *Torah* (Teaching), *Nevi'im* (Prophets), and *Ketuvim* (Writings). (A) TRUE
4. In Christian tradition, the term *Old Testament* differs from the *New Testament*. (A) TRUE
5. The *Old Testament* is the first division of the Christian biblical *canon.* (A)
6. The term *canon* refers to a general rule for categorizing, which is based primarily upon the twenty-four (24) books of the *Hebrew Bible* or *Tanakh*. (A) TRUE
7. *The Hebrew Bible* or *Tanakh* is a collection of ancient religious Hebrew writings. (A) TRUE
8. The second division of *Christian Bibles* is the *New Testament*, originally written in the Greek language. (A) TRUE
9. The order and categorization of the books in the Christian Bibles are different from the traditional arrangement in the Jewish Bible. (A)
10. According to Jewish tradition, the *Tanakh* comprises of twenty-four (24) books including narratives, law codes, short stories, etiological tales, prophecies, exhortations, poetry, and wisdom writing. (A) TRUE
11. An *etiological* tale is a short story, with a simple structure- the story answers the "why" question in the beginning. (A) TRUE
12. A *prophecy* is a message inspired by God, or a divine revelation. (A) TRUE

13. An *exhortation* is an address or communication emphatically urging someone to do something. (A) TRUE
14. *Exhortations* are meant to encourage someone. (A) TRUE
15. Wisdom literature is a literary *genre* that consists of statements from *sages* or wise men that teach about life, *virtue,* and the nature of God. (A) TRUE

For Reflection:

View the video: *Who Wrote the Bible: A History of the Torah (https://www.youtube.com/watch?v=k8vYLSBCAF8&t=19s)*. Briefly explain the "Documentary Hypothesis." (Write 3-5 paragraphs. Employ terminology from this lesson in your response. Document sources. Edit your work to remove writing errors. Post your reflection on the discussion board. Label the post: The Torah and the "Documentary Hypothesis.")

A Closing Thought:

"The book to read is not one which thinks for you, but the one that makes you think. No other book in the world equals the BIBLE for that."

- James McCosh

by Wilma J. Brown-Foreman, ED. S

LESSON SEVEN

AN OVERVIEW OF THE GENESIS STORY

Lesson Overview:

In this lesson, students will understand the Book of Genesis as the foundational work for the entire Hebrew Bible. They will learn basic biblical terms that will help them understand the text and to be able to engage in logical exchanges about the Bible's account of the history of humanity and the shaping of Israel as a nation.

Key Concepts: *Bereshit* (in the beginning), epic, Torah, Pentateuch, Yahweh (God), Abraham, Mesopotamian, Canaan, covenant, prologue, blessing, curse, repentance, genealogy, motif, inheritance

Objectives:

Students will:

- understand the Book of Genesis as a foundational work for the entire Hebrew Bible.
- become familiar with the most basic biblical terms that are useful in interpreting textual meaning.
- follow the literary patterns of storytelling in the Hebrew Bible.
- write a reflection on key details of the lesson.
- edit writing to correct composition errors.
- engage in discussions of the lesson via a discussion board.

Expected Learning Outcomes:

At the end of this lesson, students will be able to:

- explain how the Book of Genesis is a foundational work for the entire Hebrew Bible.
- use basic biblical terms to interpret textual meaning and purpose.
- demonstrate knowledge of the literary patterns of storytelling found in the Hebrew Bible.
- understand how the Book of Genesis gives an account of the early history of humankind and how Israel became a nation.
- write a reflection on key details of the lesson.
- edit writing to correct composition errors.
- engage in discussions of the lesson via a discussion board.

Duration: 2-3 hours

Materials:

- Internet access/e-mail/computer editing ability
- Notebook/paper/pen/dictionary
- Article: "Genesis: the Bible's story begins" by Jeffrey Kranz (https://overviewbible.com/genesis/_)

Procedure:

- Read the assigned article.
- Respond to the study questions and reflection.
- Post the reflection on the discussion board.
- If you have questions or need further clarification on any assignment, e-mail me at wilmaforeman@yahoo.com or visit my website: AIBL.INFO to sign up for the online course.

Study Questions

Directions:

Read "Genesis: the Bible's story begins" by Jeffrey Kranz (https://overviewbible.com/genesis/_). Are the following statements (A) TRUE or (B) FALSE about the article? (Note: You may use additional online resources to answer the study questions. Use a pronunciation dictionary to learn to pronounce unfamiliar words.)

1. The Book of Genesis is the first book of the Hebrew Scriptures and in the Christian Old Testament. **(A) TRUE**
2. The word "Genesis" in Hebrew means "beginning," the same as the first words in the biblical text (*Bereshit*). **(A) TRUE**
3. Genesis is a record of the creation of the world, the early history of humanity, and of Israel's ancestry and the origins of the Jewish nation. **(A) TRUE**
4. The Book of Genesis opens with one of the most famous first sentences of any literary work: "*In the beginning, God created the heavens and the earth.*" **(A) TRUE**
5. The Book of Genesis has the famous stories of Adam and Eve, Cain and Abel, Noah and the ark, Abraham and Isaac, and the life of Joseph. **(A) TRUE**
6. Narratives in the book of Genesis read like a string of *epic* stories. **(A) TRUE**
7. Genesis a "stand-alone" book. **(B) FALSE**
8. The Book of Genesis is the first book the five-part *Torah* (or *Pentateuch*). **(A) TRUE**
9. The Torah is the foundational work of the Hebrew Bible (Old Testament). **(A) TRUE**
10. The Torah is Israel's *origin* story. **(A) TRUE**
11. The Torah records the history of how the nation of Israel got its population, its land, and its religion. **(A) TRUE**
12. After the Book of Jeremiah, Genesis is the second-longest book of the Bible. **(A) TRUE**
13. Another name for God is *Yahweh*—the creator of heaven and earth, including the humans Adam and Eve. **(A) TRUE**

14. Based on the narrative, God describes all Creation as "very good." (A) TRUE

15. When both humans and divine creations rebel against God, the world slips back into chaos. (A) TRUE

16. According to Genesis, only the people rebel against God. (B) FALSE

17. The sinful nature of humans brings a curse on the world. (B) FALSE

18. Humankind becomes so violent that God destroys everyone except Noah and his family. (B) FALSE

19. God chooses Abraham to begin the work of restoring the world. (A) TRUE

20. Abraham, a Mesopotamian, is formerly known as "Abram." (A) TRUE

21. Abraham becomes the first patriarch of a special nation later called Israel. (A) TRUE

22. Abraham journeys through the land of Canaan, which God promises to give to his descendants. (A) TRUE

23. God makes a covenant (a special binding agreement) with Abraham. (A) TRUE

24. The covenant that God makes with Abraham is the beginning of Israel's story as a nation. (A) TRUE

25. Jacob is Abraham's grandson who tricks his father and brother into receiving a special blessing. (A) TRUE

26. Jacob has twelve sons from whom the twelve tribes of Israel trace their lineage. (A) TRUE

27. Joseph, who has prophetic dreams of greatness, is Jacob's favorite son. (A) TRUE

28. Joseph's brothers sell him into slavery, but through his God-given wisdom, he ascends to the position of second-in-command over all Egypt. (A) TRUE

29. The story of Genesis sets the stage for the rest of the Pentateuch. (A) TRUE

30. The Book of Genesis is a long *prologue* to Israel's beginnings as a nation. (A) TRUE

31. A "prologue" is an introduction. (A) TRUE

32. The Book of Genesis is a story of the promises God makes to humans that He begins to fulfill through the rest of the Bible. (A) TRUE

33. The focus of Genesis is on the words that God says to Abraham: "And I will establish my covenant between me and thee and thy seed after thee in their generations for an everlasting covenant, to be a God unto thee, and to thy seed after thee." *(Gen.17:7 KJV)* (A) TRUE

34. A covenant is a solemn, binding agreement between two or more parties. (A) TRUE

35. Covenants usually involve promises, conditions, and blessings for keeping the covenant, and curses for breaking it. (A) TRUE

36. The Book of Genesis records God's agreement with the post-flood world (Genesis 9:1–17) and his covenants with Abraham (Genesis 15, 17). (A) TRUE

37. The theme of covenants moves the story forward in Genesis. (A) TRUE

38. God promises the childless Abraham that he will be the father of nations, that his descendants will have land, and that they will be a blessing to the world. (A) TRUE

39. Thirty-eight of Genesis' fifty chapters follow Abraham's family as God begins fulfilling the first part of His promise. (A) TRUE

40. In the Book of Genesis, the word, "swear" relates to making covenants. (A) TRUE

41. After Genesis, the next four books in the Pentateuch tell the story of how Abraham's descendants become a nation and begin to claim their promised land. (A) TRUE

42. In the twelfth chapter of Genesis, God promises to bless Abraham and his allies, and to curse his enemies. (A) TRUE

43. Through Abraham, God promises to bless only Israel. **(B) FALSE**
44. The Book of Genesis records the promises of God as they unfold in time. **(A) TRUE**
45. Jacob "inherits" the blessing that God gives to Abraham and Isaac. **(A) TRUE**
46. The narrator proposes that Jacob escapes to a distant land to start a new life before another "Cain and Abel situation" takes place. **(A) TRUE**
47. Jacob wrestles with God, and God blesses him. **(A) TRUE**
48. Another theme in the Book of Genesis centers on owning the land of Canaan. **(A) TRUE**
49. Abraham wanders through Canaan, Isaac settles there, and Jacob eventually lives there also. **(A) TRUE**
50. At the end of the Book of Genesis, the patriarchs of the nation of Israel in its early stage of development dwell in Egypt. **(A) TRUE**

For Reflection:

The word "beginning" (Heb. *Bereshit*) occurs throughout Hebrew Scriptures. Find at least five (5) examples of the use of the Hebrew word *Bereshit* and explain the meanings based on the context of the Scriptures. Use reliable internet Bible study tools to respond effectively. Document sources. Post your findings on the discussion board. Label the post: A Reflection on the Use of the Expression "*Bereshit*" in Hebrew Scriptures.

A Closing Thought:

"There was no such thing as new truth. Error might be old or new; but truth was as old as the universe."

-Frederick Douglass

LESSON EIGHT

THE LITERARY PLOT OF GENESIS

Lesson Overview:

The first eleven chapters of the Hebrew Bible, also known as "primeval history," have definitive literary plots. In literature, the plot of a story is the sequence of events where each affects the next one through the principle of cause-and-effect. The Book of Genesis opens with an account of how the universe came into existence. Beginning with the Creation narratives, the early chapters of Genesis focus on humanity's proliferation of rebellion against their Creator. After gaining the knowledge of good and evil, humans live in disharmony with God and among themselves. The proclivity to turn to evil leads humankind to continual trouble and a need for redemption. This lesson gives students more insight into the underlying messages and events conveyed within the stories.

Key Concepts: historical narratives, primeval history, plots, theme, rebellion, disharmony, judgment, grace, repentance, redemption

Lesson Objectives:

Students will:

- use online Bible study tools to access, read, interpret, and explain information.
- summarize the common themes (main ideas) in the biblical text (Genesis, Chapters 1- 11).
- use information in biblical resources to support analysis, reflection(s), and research.
- make inferences and draw conclusions based on explicit and implied information using evidence from the text as support.
- state the writer's intended purpose for writing the text.
- synthesize information from various sources.
- draw conclusions and make inferences from primary and secondary sources.
- discuss the literary and historical aspects of narratives in Genesis, Chapters 1-11.

Expected Learning Objectives

At the end of this lesson, students will:

- recognize and understand common plots and themes in biblical literature.
- discuss literary and historical elements found in biblical text, including common unifying themes.
- participate in class discussions.
- edit writing to correct errors.

Duration: 3-4 hours

Materials:

- Video: *Genesis: the Bible's story begins* by Jeffrey Kranz (https://overviewbible.com/genesis/)
- Video: *The Book of Genesis by Bill Barrick* (*https://www.learnoutloud.com/Free-Audio-Video/Religion-and-Spirituality/The-Bible/The-Book-of-Genesis/116730*)
- A computer with internet access and editing capability
- Paper, pen, pencil/dictionary

Procedure:

- View the video: *Genesis: the Bible's story begins* by Jeffrey Kranz (https://overviewbible.com/genesis/)
- Respond to the study questions.
- Use an online dictionary to define and pronounce unfamiliar terms.
- View the video: *The Book of Genesis by Bill Barrick* (*https://www.learnoutloud.com/Free-Audio-Video/Religion-and-Spirituality/The-Bible/The-Book-of-Genesis/116730*)
- Respond to the study questions.
- Respond to the reflection. (Post the reflection on the discussion board.)
- If you have questions or need further clarification on any assignment, e-mail me at wilmaforeman@yahoo.com or visit my website: AIBL.INFO to sign up for the online course.

Study Questions:

Reference: Video: *Genesis: the Bible's story begins* by Jeffrey Kranz

https://overviewbible.com/genesis/)

Based on the video, are the following statements (A) CORRECT or (B) INCORRECT?

1. The book of Genesis is the first book of the Hebrew Bible. (A) CORRECT
2. It is the second longest book of the entire Bible. (A) CORRECT
3. The interesting and well-loved stories in Genesis are thousands of years old. (A) CORRECT
4. The stories in Genesis began as an oral tradition. (A) CORRECT
5. They passed down from one Hebrew generation to another until they became a part of the law of Moses in the Torah. (A) CORRECT
6. The law of Moses began as a list of conditions that an ancient prophet gave to the Israelites about how they should interact with their God. (A) CORRECT
7. The stories in the book of Genesis are foundational to how the people of Israel came to be associated with the law of Moses. (A) CORRECT
8. Over centuries, scribes worked on the books of Moses to construct the Tanakh. (A) CORRECT

9. The Book of Genesis sets the stage for divinity to interact in human affairs throughout the rest of the Bible. (A) CORRECT

10. The Hebrew Bible records God's relationship to humans through the nation Israel and through His son, Jesus, in the New Testament in Christian Bibles. (A) CORRECT

11. Genesis recounts a default relationship between humans and God. (A) CORRECT

12. The Hebrew Bible explores humans' purpose in life, as well as human nature. (A) CORRECT

13. Throughout the Book of Genesis, one sees elements of humanity that are not commendable. (A) CORRECT

14. Genesis tells of Israel's origin as a nation and gives a message of hope for non-Jews. (A) CORRECT

15. The Book of Genesis has fifty chapters that fall into two sections. (A) CORRECT

16. The first section of Genesis, Chapters 1-11, focuses on the relationship between God and all humanity. (A) CORRECT

17. Genesis, Chapters 12-50 reveal God's relationship with the nation of Israel's ancestors. (A) CORRECT

18. In section 1, God brings order out of chaos and creates humans to help govern the earth. (A) CORRECT

19. Based on the presentation, humans were created to reflect God's character. (A) CORRECT

20. The narrator refers to the Garden of Eden as a "Garden Temple." (A) CORRECT

21. The setting of the Book of Genesis is in the Ancient Near or Near East. (A) CORRECT

22. Garden temples were important to the ancient Hebrews. (A) CORRECT

23. The Hebrew temple in Jerusalem takes center stage for a large part of the Old Testament. (A) CORRECT

24. In the first major section of Genesis, a sense of the supernatural surrounds the narrative about an evil serpent that comes into the garden and tricks the woman into rebelling against God. (A) CORRECT

25. After the first major section, the Genesis narratives continue with an account of the sons of God having relationships with humans. (A) CORRECT

26. In ancient Jewish tradition, the Nephilim were fully human. (B) INCORRECT

27. People believed that the Nephilim were regular humans that eventually became so powerful that they were worshipped as gods. (A) CORRECT

28. In Genesis, supernatural evils, along with the human disobedience, corrupt the world. (A) CORRECT

29. As the stories progress in the Book of Genesis, the world becomes increasingly corrupt. (A) CORRECT

30. In Genesis, Chapter 3, a glimmer of hope for humanity appears when God foretells that a human will defeat the serpent that is a representative of evil. (A) CORRECT

31. The Flood narrative is one of divine judgment upon humankind from which God spares only one family. (A) CORRECT

32. In the Genesis stories, God values human life, and He wants humanity to continue to grow and flourish. (A) CORRECT

33. In the last sub-section, people repopulate the earth and decide to build their own structure that will reach into heaven. (A) CORRECT

34. In the Tower of Babel narrative, God disburses humanity into various nations so that each group speaks a distinct language. (A) CORRECT

35. In the Torah, ancient Israelites believed that God also distributed the nations to different gods. (A) CORRECT
36. The second section of Genesis begins with a man named Abram. (A) CORRECT
37. God promises to make Abraham a very great person in history. (A) CORRECT
38. God says that Abram will have innumerable descendants. (A) CORRECT
39. Abram, later named Abraham, obeys God's order to leave his home. (A)
40. God promises Abraham a place called Canaan, also known as the Promised Land. (A) CORRECT
41. God's promises pass from Abraham to his son Isaac, to Isaac's son Jacob, and on to the nation of Israel. (A) CORRECT
42. God instructs Abraham to leave his relatives and travel to Canaan, but Abraham never settles in the land. (A) CORRECT
43. Chapters thirty-seven to fifty focus on the sons of Jacob, Abraham's grandson. (A) CORRECT
44. Jacob has twelve sons that later became the tribes of Israel. (A) CORRECT
45. The story about Joseph, one of Jacob's sons, tells of a coat with assorted colors. (A) CORRECT
46. The story centers on sibling rivalry and divine intervention. (A) CORRECT
47. God tests Joseph's loyalty and integrity of character. (A) CORRECT
48. Joseph has *vicissitudes* in his life. (A) CORRECT
49. He stays upright in character. (A) CORRECT
50. Joseph becomes an Egyptian leader and saves his family from starvation. (A) CORRECT

Study Questions

Directions:

- View the video: *The Book of Genesis by Bill Barrick*

(https://www.learnoutloud.com/Free-Audio-Video/Religion-and-Spirituality/The-Bible/The-Book-of-Genesis/116730)

- Respond to the study questions. (If necessary, use credible online sources to answer study questions.)

Based on the video, are the following statements (A) TRUE or (B) FALSE?

1. The Hebrew Bible in Jewish tradition begins with Genesis and ends with II Chronicles. (A) TRUE
2. The New Testament in Christian Bibles discusses the Creation from the Book of Genesis, Chapters 1 and 2. (A) TRUE
3. At least one hundred references to Genesis, Chapters 1-11 are in the New Testament. (A) TRUE
4. Nine references in the New Testament are direct quotations from the Book of Genesis. (A) TRUE
5. Jesus in the New Testament of Christian Bibles refers to events in Genesis, Chapters 1-7 fifteen times. (A) TRUE

6. A "canonical approach" to studying the Bible means that one offers an alternative to the traditional and modern hermeneutical methods. (A) TRUE
7. The term "hermeneutical" means biblical or literary interpretation. (A) TRUE
8. The Book of Genesis can be studied geographically. (A) TRUE
9. In Genesis, Chapters 1-3, the setting is in Eden. (A) TRUE
10. In Genesis, Chapters 4-6, is East of Eden. (A) TRUE
11. The setting for Genesis, Chapters 7-9 is in the mountains of Ararat. (A) TRUE
12. In Genesis, Chapters 10-11, the setting is in Babel or Babylon. (A) TRUE
13. The settings in Genesis, Chapters 12-36 are in Ur and Canaan. (A) TRUE
14. In Genesis, Chapters 37-50, the setting is in Egypt. (A) TRUE
15. The geography of the Book of Genesis points to a book of world history. (A) TRUE
16. Penned by Moses, the Book of Genesis is written solely for Israel. (A) TRUE
17. The Book of Genesis has a global or universal focus. (A) TRUE
18. As a nation, the name "Israel" does not exist in the Book of Genesis. (A) TRUE
19. The lecturer mentions a study of the Book of Genesis by generations. (A) TRUE
20. The Tablet Theory is a Jewish approach to interpreting Genesis. (A) TRUE

For Reflection:

The stories in Genesis, Chapter 1-11 contain profound insights about the relationship between God and humankind. The themes of human rebellion against a faithful God, consequential judgment, human remorse, and God's grace unify the narratives in Genesis, Chapters 1-11. Discuss one lesson learned from the stories? Give specific details and Scripture references. (Write at least five-eight sentences.) Edit writing to correct errors. Label the post: An Overview of Genesis, Chapters 1-11. Post the response to the discussion board.

A Closing Thought:

"Life is a culmination of the past, an awareness of the present, an indication of a future beyond knowledge, the quality that gives a touch of divinity to matter."- Charles Lindbergh

by Wilma J. Brown-Foreman, ED. S

by Wilma J. Brown-Foreman, ED. S

LESSON NINE
HEBREW CREATION NARRATIVES IN JEWISH AND CHRISTIAN TRADITIONS

Lesson Overview:

The early chapters of Genesis present two accounts of cosmic and human origins in the language and ideas of the ancient Hebrews. This lesson explores the differences between the two historical accounts of creation according to the Jewish and Christian traditions and the literary style of the ancient Hebrew biblical narratives.

Key Concepts: cosmic and human origins, foundational Abrahamic religions, biblical allusions, idioms

Lesson Objectives:

Students will:

- read and summarize the main ideas of the first two chapters of the Book of Genesis.
- explain terminology associated with the literary elements of biblical text.
- distinguish between the figurative and literal textual expressions.
- write an effective reflection paragraph on Genesis, Chapters 1-2.
- edit writing to correct errors standard English usage.
- participate in class discussions.

Learning Outcomes

At the end on this lesson, students will be able to:

- demonstrate a general knowledge of the creation narratives in the Book of Genesis.
- use terminology associated with the literary elements of biblical text.
- distinguish between the figurative and literal textual expressions.
- recognize biblical allusions in idiomatic expressions.
- write an effective reflection paragraph on a given topic.
- edit writing to correct errors standard English usage.
- participate in class discussions.

Duration: 3-4 hours

Materials:

- a Hebrew Bible
- video: *Creation (Genesis1-2)* (737) Creation (Genesis 1-2) - YouTube

- a computer with internet access, email, and editing capability
- chart (below): An Overview of Genesis, Chapters 1-2
- notebook/paper/pen/dictionary
- internet access/e-mail/computer editing ability

Procedure (Assignment one):

- View the video: *Creation (Genesis1-2)* (737) Creation (Genesis 1-2) - YouTube
- Read Genesis, Chapters 1-2 (any translation).
- Review the chart of Genesis, Chapters 1-2.
- Note details from assigned readings not mentioned on the chart.
- Use a dictionary or other credible online sources to define unfamiliar vocabulary terms.
- Respond in full sentences to the study questions on the overview chart.
- Post questions about the assignment on the discussion board to receive help in completing the assignment(s).
- View the video: *Understanding the Creation Story in Genesis* (*https://www.youtube.com/watch?v=Iv2mePpin6A*).
- Respond to the study questions.
- Respond to the reflection questions in complete sentences.
- Edit writing to correct errors.
- Post the reflection(s) and extended assignment(s) on the discussion board.
- If you have questions or need further clarification on any assignment, e-mail me at wilmaforeman@yahoo.com or visit my website: AIBL.INFO to sign up for the online course.

Genesis, Chapter 1

Title of the Narrative	Literary Themes	Plot Summary	Study Questions
"The First Creation Account" (Gen. 1:1-25)	<ul><li>The Origin of the Universe</li><li>Order in Creation</li><li>Goodness in Creation</li><li>God's Sovereignty</li><li>The Self Existence of God</li><li>Boundaries</li></ul>	*Genesis* means "origins." The first account of the origin of creation begins with its famous declaration of God creating the heavens and the earth. During the six days of creation, everything that is now a part of the world has its existence from a sovereign God. In a series of affirmations, Genesis declares the *goodness* of God's creation. With the creation of humanity as the climax, the work of creation ends. The theme of goodness of creation is central to the Book.	1. What is the state of the earth before the Creation narrative begins? 2. How does God show His sovereignty in this narrative? 3. What is "good" about God's the Creation of the world? 4. How does God set boundaries in His Creation?

		The high point of this creation narrative is God's creation of humanity. It is at this point that the Bible introduces the only creature to bear the image of God. The Hebrew word cited in this passage for "man" is humanity in general, rather than as a male human being. Genesis depicts humanity, male and female, as created in the likeness of God (1:26-27).	1. In what ways is the creation of humans the apex of God's Creation?
"Humanity Created" (Gen. 1:26-31)	• Man Created in the Image of God • Equality between Male and Female		2. Define the use of the expression "man" in the second Creation narrative. 3. Explain the concept of humans created in the "image" of God.

Genesis, Chapter 2

Title of the Narrative	Literary Themes	Plot Summary	Study Questions
"The Second Account of Creation" (Genesis 2)	• God's Sovereignty • God's Love for Humanity • Man-Created in the Image of God • Goodness of Creation • Orderliness in the World • Boundaries • The Sabbath	The second account of creation (Genesis 2:4b–25) describes how God creates man, and the Garden of Eden. Then, He makes Adam a female companion. In Genesis 2:4b–25, "the LORD God formed man from the dust of the earth. He blew into his nostrils the breath of life, and man became a living being." (Genesis 2:7) This *anthropocentric* account differs from the *cosmos centric* account in the first narrative.	1. How does the second Creation narrative differ from the first? 2. What is God's plan for humans after the Creation? 3. How does Adam respond to his companion? 4. What is God's plan for all creation? 5. What does this narrative reveal about God's character?

Study Questions

Directions: Respond to the study questions.

(Video*: Understanding the Creation Story in Genesis)*

(*https://www.youtube.com/watch?v=Iv2mePpin6A*).

Are the following statements (A) CORRECT or (B) INCORRECT based on the video?

1. The lecturer states that Genesis 1:1 and 2:4 serve as echoes of the beginning of Creation. (A) CORRECT
2. These two verses serve as opening and closing summary statements, enclosing the "creating" days. (A) CORRECT
3. The term "create" relates to the expression "to make." (A) CORRECT
4. The speaker refers to the first three days of creation as "forming" days. (A) CORRECT
5. Based on the presentation, the separation of light from darkness, heavens from the seas, and land from the seas are "forming" days. (A) CORRECT
6. Days four, five, and six are called "filling" days. (A) CORRECT
7. On the "filling" days, the heavens are filled with lights, the seas are filled with fish and flying creatures, and the land is filled with vegetation, animals, and humans. (A) CORRECT
8. "To create" means to separate and to fill with light and life. (A) CORRECT
9. In the Creation narratives, "to separate" refers to a physical function. (A) CORRECT
10. Based on the presentation, "light and life" are *metaphorical* concepts. (A) CORRECT
11. The speaker proposes that Creation is a separation unto life while sin is a separation unto death. (A) CORRECT
12. Based on the speaker, rebellion produces death. (A) CORRECT
13. According to the lecturer, sin is an anti-creational action. (A) CORRECT
14. The speaker asserts that sin creates a contradiction in the hearts of fallen humans made in the image of God. (A) CORRECT
15. Contradiction in the human heart resulting from sin is a central part of the Genesis story. (A) CORRECT

For Reflection:

Compare the two accounts of Creation in Genesis, Chapters 1 and 2. Find at least three similarities and three differences in the details. Proofread your writing before posting your reflection on the discussion board. Label the reflection: Three Similarities and Differences in the Creation Narrative in the Hebrew Bible.

A Closing Thought:

"In the beginning God created man in His own image, and man has been trying to repay the favor ever since."

— Voltaire

LESSON TEN

THE LITERARY DESIGN OF GENESIS,

(CHAPTER ONE)

Lesson Overview

   This lesson focuses on the intentional literary design of the first chapter of Genesis and how the chapter sets the stage for the entire Hebrew Bible. The prologue (1:1-2) and the epilogue (1:31-2:3) of Genesis, Chapter One serve as a macro frame around the internal sequence of six days. Students will examine the precise structure of the chapter and the linguistic artistry that brings to life the rest of the Hebrew text.

Key Concepts: literary design, epilogue, prologue, exposition, macro frame, forward symmetry, eschatology, triads, structure, themes, literary framework, triad literary framework view, framework theory, framework hypothesis

Lesson Objectives

Students will:

- understand the literary structure of Genesis, Chapter One.
- explain terminology associated with the literary structure of biblical text.
- distinguish between the literary expressions *prologue* and the *epilogue*.
- write an effective reflection paragraph on literary design.
- edit writing to correct errors.
- participate in class discussions.

Learning Outcomes

At the end on this lesson, students will be able to:

- explain the meaning of the literary design of the first chapter of Genesis.
- distinguish between different terms related to the literary design of the biblical text.
- respond to reading comprehension questions logically and accurately.
- write a reflection on the literary design of Genesis, Chapter One.
- edit writing to correct errors.
- participate in class discussions.

Duration: 2-3 hours

Materials:

- Video: *The Literary Design of Genesis: (737) The Literary Design of Genesis 1 - YouTube*

- Article: "COMPARISONS BETWEEN GENESIS 1 AND 2" by William H. Shea at: Geoscience Research Institute | Literary Structural Parallels Between Genesis 1 and 2 (grisda.org)
- A computer with editing capability
- Internet access
- A notebook/pen/pencil/dictionary

Procedure:

- View the video: *The Literary Design of Genesis: (737) The Literary Design of Genesis 1 - YouTube.*
- Respond to the video study questions.
- Read the article by William H. Shea.
- Answer the study questions.
- Respond to the reflection question(s).
- Use an online dictionary to define and pronounce unfamiliar terms.
- If you have questions or need further clarification on any assignment, e-mail me at wilmaforeman@yahoo.com or visit my website: AIBL.INFO to sign up for the online course.

Study Questions

(The Literary Design of Genesis: (737) The Literary Design of Genesis 1 - YouTube.)

Based on the video, are the statements below (A) CORRECT or (B) INCORRECT?

1. The first book in the Bible focuses on *beginnings*. (A) CORRECT
2. Genesis, Chapter 1 is organized into a linear sequence with seven days. (A) CORRECT
3. The literary structure of the first chapter of Genesis is precise. (A)
4. In the presentation, the lecturer compares the sets of days in the Creation narrative to a three-tiered house. (A) CORRECT
5. The sun and the moon are compared to humans in that they have rulership over God's Creation. (A) CORRECT
6. The speaker asserts that God has an organizational pattern to His Creation. (A) CORRECT
7. The pattern of Creation has social organizational space with hierarchy and assigned duties. (A) CORRECT
8. Moral obligations are included in the Creation pattern in Genesis 1. (A)
9. The literary structure of the first chapter of Genesis reveals the character of the Creator-God. (A) CORRECT
10. Details of the Creation narrative are subtle and require deeper thinking to uncover the plot and character development.
(A) CORRECT

Study Questions:

Directions: Read the passages below from Genesis 2:8-9 and 2:15-17. Tell if the statements that follow are (A) TRUE or (B) FALSE.

Passage 1	Passage 2
Genesis 2:8-9 (King James Version)	Genesis 2:15-17 (Young's Literal Translation)
[8] And the LORD God planted a garden eastward in Eden; and there he put the man whom he had formed. [9] And out of the ground made the LORD God to grow every tree that is pleasant to the sight, and good for food, the tree of life also in the midst of the garden, and the tree of knowledge of good and evil.	[15] And Jehovah God taketh the man, and causeth him to rest in the garden of Eden, to serve it, and to keep it. [16] And Jehovah God layeth a charge on the man, saying, `Of every tree of the garden eating thou dost eat; [17] and of the tree of knowledge of good and evil, thou dost not eat of it, for in the day of thine eating of it -- dying thou dost die.'

TRUE (A) or FALSE (B)?

1. Each passage uses the divine name of God to introduce them. (A)
2. Both passages mention the Garden of Eden and the humans that God places in it. (B)
3. The two passages speak of the human's duty to till the garden and keep it in order.
4. The second passage mentions the trees in the garden. (A)
5. The first passage refers to all the trees of the garden, including the Tree of Life. (A)
6. The second passage makes a statement about death. (A)
7. The mention of death is a warning against violating God's instructions. (A)
8. In subject matter, the two passages are evenly balanced. (A)
9. Another word for "dost" is "do." (A)
10. Both passages mention that the human rests in the garden. (B)

Directions: Read "COMPARISONS BETWEEN GENESIS 1 AND 2" by William H. Shea at: Geoscience Research Institute | Literary Structural Parallels Between Genesis 1 and 2 (grisda.org), Respond to the study questions. Use a dictionary to pronounce and define italicized words.

Based on the article are the following statements (A) CORRECT or (B) INCORRECT?

1. The narratives in Genesis, Chapters 1 and 2 have clear similarities in their literary structure. (A) CORRECT
2. Both Genesis, Chapters 1 and 2 have a *chiastic* construction. (A) CORRECT
3. The details in the two chapters are *parallel*. (A) CORRECT
4. Days 1-3 in Genesis 1 are paralleled by those described for Days 4-6. (A) CORRECT
5. The seventh day is an *epilogue* to both Genesis 1 and 2. (A) CORRECT
6. In Chapter 1, the epilogue balances the epilogue in Chapter 2. (A) CORRECT
7. The introduction to each chapter is the same in content and structure. (B) INCORRECT
8. In the first chapter, the whole earth is empty, shapeless, and void. (A) CORRECT
9. The earth is uninhabited in Chapter 1, while in Chapter 2, the agricultural fields are empty because humans are not there to till them. (A) CORRECT
10. The second Creation narrative emphasizes the double use of words, such as "heaven and earth." (A) CORRECT
11. In the second passage, the use of doubles is reversed to make it a *chiastic* marker. (A) CORRECT
12. An account of four rivers is found in Genesis, Chapter 2. (A) CORRECT
13. The second chapter of Genesis contains the first geographic descriptive of the world of humankind. (A) CORRECT
14. The location and description of the four rivers are outlined in a *decrescendo* form with each successive descriptions becoming shorter and shorter.
15. "Yahweh God" is an example of doubling the use of names in both passages. (A) CORRECT
16. In the first creative action, the creation of humans is described in one *triplet* of statements. (A) CORRECT
17. The woman is described in a pair of *couplets* in the second act of creation. (A) CORRECT
18. The double use of "heaven and earth" is emphasized in the second creation narrative. (A) CORRECT
19. The expression "heaven and earth" is only used once at the beginning of the first creation narrative. (A) CORRECT
20. The rivers and the garden are interrelated in Genesis 1 and 2 and cannot be completely separated. (B) INCORRECT

For Reflection (1):

Summarize the literary design of Genesis, Chapter 1 (five-eight sentences). Mention the organizational structure of the prologue, the use of triads, and the design of the epilogue. If necessary, use other reliable internet Bible study tools to respond effectively. Document sources. Post your findings on the discussion board. Label the post: A Reflection on the Literary Design of Genesis, Chapter One."

For Reflection (2):

How is literary design important to the depth of meaning in biblical text? Write-5-8 sentences. Edit your writing to correct errors. Post your response on the discussion board. Label the post: The Significance of the Literary Design in Biblical Text.

A Closing Thought:

"Suppose a nation in some distant Region should take the BIBLE for their only law Book, and every member should regulate his conduct by the precepts there exhibited! Every member would be obliged in conscience, to temperance, frugality, and industry; to justice, kindness, and charity towards his fellow men; and to piety, love, and reverence toward Almighty G-D ... What a Utopia, what a Paradise would this region be"

- John Adam

by Wilma J. Brown-Foreman, ED. S

LESSON ELEVEN
"THE CREATION AND THE FALL OF HUMANITY"
(GENESIS, CHAPTERS ONE-THREE)

Lesson Overview:

Central to Judaism, Christianity, and Islam is the concept of the divine word of God. The narratives in Genesis, Chapters 1-3 rely deeply on the use of God's language as He calls the world into being, blesses it, and gives commands to order and balance what He has created. This lesson focuses on the Bible's account of God's Creation and the "Fall of Humanity" narratives in the first three chapters of Genesis. Students will demonstrate a general knowledge of the Genesis record of Creation in Chapters 1 and 2 and the "Fall of Humanity" in Chapter 3.

Key Concepts*:* theological foundation, monotheism versus polytheism, theistic versus naturalistic viewpoints. human fallibility, "inherited curse," God's mercy, innocence, and experience

Lesson Objectives:

Students will:

- read and summarize the main ideas of the first three chapters of the Book of Genesis.
- explain terminology associated with the literary elements of biblical text.
- distinguish between the figurative and literal textual expressions.
- write an effective reflection paragraph on Genesis, Chapters 1-3.
- edit writing to correct errors standard English usage.
- participate in class discussions.

Expected Learning Outcomes

At the end on this lesson, students will be able to:

- demonstrate a general knowledge of chapters 1-3 of the Book of Genesis.
- use terminology associated with the literary elements of biblical text.
- distinguish between the figurative and literal textual expressions.
- write an effective reflection paragraph on Genesis, Chapters 1-3.
- edit writing to correct errors standard English usage.
- participate in class discussions.

Duration: 3-4 hours

Material(s):

- Article: "What We Can Learn from Genesis 1 and 2" by Phillip Eichman, Ph. D
- . (Does God Exist? - What We Can Learn from Genesis 1 and 2 - Month/Month YEAR
- Essay: "The Hebrew Creation Narrative (Genesis 1-3)"
  (https://www2.nau.edu/~gaud/bio301/content/hebnar.htm)
- Lecture: *The Genesis Story: Reading Biblical Narratives* from Hillsdale College
  (https://online.hillsdale.edu/courses/genesis
- Internet access/e-mail/computer editing ability
- Notebook/paper/pen/dictionary

Procedure:

- Read Genesis, Chapters 1-3 in any translation.
- Follow directions to respond to the study questions.
- Respond to assigned reflection(s) for each lesson.
- Edit your writing to correct errors.
- Post the reflection(s) on the discussion board.
- Use an online dictionary to define and pronounce unfamiliar terms.
- If you have questions or need further clarification on any assignment, e-mail me at wilmaforeman@yahoo.com or visit my website: AIBL.INFO to sign up for the online course.

Study Questions

Directions:

Read "The Creation and the Fall "at https://www2.nau.edu/~gaud/bio301/content/hebnar.htm. Indicate if the following statements are (A) CORRECT or (B) INCORRECT.

1. The naming of the Tigris and Euphrates as rivers flowing from the Garden of Eden places the location of the original "Paradise" in Mesopotamia. (A) CORRECT
2. The Hebrews trace their ancestry to Mesopotamia. (A) CORRECT
3. The biblical text reflects the notion that the ancient Jewish culture shunned nudity. (A) CORRECT
4. In Hebrew, the term *Satan i*s usually translated as "opponent" or "adversary," and he is often understood to represent the sinful impulse or the forces that prevent human beings from submitting to divine will. (A) CORRECT
5. Adam refers to Eve in the statement: "This at last is bone of my bones and flesh of my flesh." (A) CORRECT
6. The expression relates to the way that God uses Adam's rib to form Eve. (A) CORRECT
7. Adam is asleep when God makes the woman. (A) CORRECT
8. In their first state of innocence, the people are naked, but they are not ashamed. (A) CORRECT

9. The serpent speaks to the woman in half-truths. (A) CORRECT
10. Ironically, both Adam and Eve have divine attributes before they disobey God. (A) CORRECT
11. After they eat from the forbidden Tree, their eyes open, and they realize that they are naked. (A) CORRECT
12. The humans hide from God after they discover their nakedness. (A) CORRECT
13. God punishes the humans and the subtle serpent for being disobedient. (A) CORRECT
14. The humans are banned from the Garden of Eden. (A) CORRECT
15. Guilt and shame are the result of human disobedience. (A) CORRECT
16. Mainstream Judaism does not support the doctrine of an inherited curse called the "original sin." (A) CORRECT
17. Genesis does not specify the fruit from the Tree of the Knowledge of Good and Evil. (A) CORRECT
18. In the early Middle Ages, the forbidden fruit was a fig. (A) CORRECT
19. The expression *malum* in Latin means both "apple" and "evil." (A) CORRECT
20. According to legend, snakes originally had legs like other animals, but lost them because of the curse. (A) CORRECT

Study Questions:

Directions: Read "The Hebrew Creation Narrative (Genesis 1-3)" at

https://www2.nau.edu/~gaud/bio301/content/hebnar.htm and answer the following study questions.

Based on the assigned reading, are the following statements (A) CORRECT or (B) INCORRECT.

According to the writer, the opening to the Creation narratives in Genesis 1-3 is grand, but simple. (A) CORRECT

The first creation narrative answers the question "Where did we come from?" (A) CORRECT

The second Creation story shows the significance of working. (A) CORRECT

God creates a woman who is subordinate to her husband from the start.

In the first Creation narrative, God rules the universe alone.

The first two narratives in the Hebrew Bible supply a foundation for the Jewish concept of the Sabbath.

The Hebrew Creation narratives in Jewish and Christian traditions reject the idea of ancient Mesopotamian polytheism.

Like other ancient Mesopotamian creation narratives, the Hebrew biblical version shares features such as land emerging from a watery chaos and waters above and beneath the earth.

Over time, the "divine word of God" became a central concept in Judaism, Islam, and Christianity.

The term "dome" in the first Creation narrative refers to the sky.

The expression "lights in the dome of the sky" in Genesis 1:14 refers to the sun and the moon.

In Jewish and Christian Bibles, humans resemble God.

Both Jewish and Christian Bibles, record humans as having authority over the animals.

The expression, "…and it was good…" flows throughout the Genesis Creation narratives.

On the seventh day, or the sabbath, God rests.

Genesis, Chapter 3

Title of Narrative	Literary Themes	Plot Summary	Study Questions
"The Fall" (Gen. 3:1-24)	• Deceit • Good against Evil • Rebellion • Human Gullibility • Origin of Sin • Paradise Lost • Man's inadequacies • Disobedience and punishment • God's Mercy	Having given two accounts of how the world came into being, Genesis moves on to deal with the origin of sin. The third chapter of Genesis gives a vivid account of the rebellion of humanity against his creator. Adam and Eve, representatives of humanity, choose to break free from God's authority. The fellowship that they had with God in the Garden does not last. The figure of the deceptive serpent appears (3:1) as a subtle creature who manages to lure Eve into disobeying God by eating the forbidden fruit from the Tree of Knowledge of Good and Evil. She convinces her husband to do the same. When God confronts their disobedience, they try to place the blame on someone else. God, however, punishes them and expels them from the Garden.	1. What is the origin of sin? 2. How does sin affect the harmony between God and humanity? 3. How is the serpent depicted in this chapter? 4. What methods does the serpent use to trick Eve. 5. What is the meaning of "the power of suggestion? 6. How does the woman affect her husband's future? 7. How do the humans blame others for their misbehavior? 8. How does God punish the serpent and the humans?

Study Questions

Directions: Read the article "What We Can Learn from Genesis 1 and 2" by Phillip Eichman, Ph.D. (Does God Exist? - What We Can Learn from Genesis 1 and 2 - Month/Month YEAR. Answer the study questions.

1. Which statement is NOT CORRECT?

   a. The Book of Genesis is thousands of years old.
   b. To interpret the Book accurately, one needs to consider the cultural background, language, and literary style of the writing.
   c. Genesis was originally written for a Hebrew audience.
   d. The Book of Genesis gave the Hebrew people a *theological foundation* for their faith.
   e. *All the above statements are CORRECT.*

2. Which statement is NOT CORRECT?

   a. Genesis explains God's role in the universe.
   b. The Book of Genesis explains the relationship between God and human beings.
   c. Genesis explains the place of humans in God's world.
   d. The main purpose of the Book of Genesis is theological.
   e. *All the above statements are CORRECT.*

3. Which statement is NOT CORRECT?

   a. Chapters 1 and 2 of Genesis outline God's creative activities in simplicity.
   b. This article is written in a Christian's scientific point of view.
   c. The writer proposes that the universe had a beginning.
   d. Science cannot explain the existence of matter.
   e. *All the above statements are CORRECT.*

4. Which statement is NOT CORRECT?

   a. God's words, "Let there be" are the shaping and forming of basic created matter.
   b. The word "kind" was used in Hebrew to describe a small or a large group of living things.
   c. The writer proposes that the term "kinds" refers to groups of organisms that God created.
   d. Both accounts of Creation in Genesis show that human beings were created separately from the other animals.
   e. *All the above statements are CORRECT.*

5. Which statement is NOT CORRECT?

   a. The writer asserts that in the Creation process, humans possessed all the characteristics that we associate with human beings.
   b. According to Genesis, humans were made from dirt.
   c. The writer states that the physical bodies of people are made of the same *elements* as other living things, as well as nonliving things.

d.   The term "breath of life" is used to refer to both humans and animals.

All the above statements are CORRECT.

6.   Which statement is NOT CORRECT?

a.   Like the animals, humans have a "biological life" that ends in death and a physical body that returns to the earth.
b.   Based on the phrase "It was good," the writer believes that the original creation was in a state of well-being.
c.   The article says that there were natural laws in place that maintained and sustained God's universe.
d.   In the article, the expression "breath of life" relates to both animals and humans.
e.   **All the above statements are CORRECT.**

7.   Which statement is NOT CORRECT?

a. The chemical processes that take place within the cells of the bodies of humans are like those found in other living things.
b. Only humans are made in the image of God.
c. The "Godlikeness" that only humans possess makes them unique from all other parts of Creation.
d. Humans have a distinct status in God's Creation.
e. **All the above statements are CORRECT.**

8.   Which statement is NOT CORRECT?

a. The writer asserts that human personalities reflect God's makeup.
b. Based on this article, human have a moral capacity.
c. Modern science assumed that the universe and the laws governing it were created by God.
d. Modern science assumed that the universe and the laws governing it were created by God.
e. **All the above are CORRECT.**

For Reflection (Article: ""What We Can Learn from Genesis 1 and 2"by Dr. Phillip Eichman)

Explain these statements that Dr. Eichman makes in his article: *"Modern science began with the assumption that the universe and the laws governing it were created by God and most of the early scientists were Christians, or at least held a theistic worldview with God as the Creator in the center. For many today, the theistic worldview has been replaced with a naturalistic worldview in which man is the center and natural processes the dominant force in the universe.* (Write five-eight sentences. Edit your writing to correct errors. Post the reflection on the discussion board. Label the post: A Reflection on Humanity and the Forbidden Tree of the Knowledge of Good and Evil.)

A Closing Thought:

"The observant Jew has his own sense of values. Torah Judaism is his blueprint for this life, his target for existence."

–Meir Kahan

LESSON TWELVE

FORESHADOWING IN GENESIS 3:15
(THE PROTOEVANGELIUM)

Lesson Overview:

Genesis 3:15 reads, "I will put enmity between you and the woman, and between your offspring and hers; he will crush your head, and you will strike his heel." This passage of Hebrew Scriptures introduces the two elements basic to the Christian faith- the curse on humanity because of Adam's sin in the Garden of Eden and God's provision for man's redemption through His son, Jesus. In Christian tradition, Jesus takes the curse upon Himself to redeem humanity. Genesis 3:15 is known as the *Protoevangelium,* or the first Gospel. In the Christian faith, Jesus crushes the head of the serpent through His sacrificial death by crucifixion. The ultimate victory is God's by removing the serpent's power over humanity. This lesson examines the literary device of foreshadowing in Genesis 3:15 in which the OT writer gives an advance hint of what develops later in the Christian biblical plot development.

Key Concepts:

gospel, adjudication, protoevangelium, foreshadowing, curse, symbol, pronouncement, seed, enmity

Lesson Objectives:

Students will:

- summarize the main ideas in Genesis 3:15.
- explain terminology associated with the literary elements of biblical text, including foreshadowing.
- understand the Christian concept of protoevangelium.
- distinguish between the figurative and literal textual expressions.
- edit writing to correct errors standard English usage.
- participate in class discussions.

Learning Outcomes:

At the end on this lesson, students will be able to:

- demonstrate a general knowledge of the Book of Genesis, Chapter 3.
- use terminology associated with the literary elements of biblical text, such as protoevangelium, foreshadowing, and prophecy.
- distinguish between the figurative and literal textual expressions.
- edit writing to correct errors standard English usage.

- participate in class discussions.

Duration: 2-3 hours

Materials:

- Article: Genesis 3:15 The Protoevangelium or "First Gospel" *(https://biblescripture.net/First.html)*

- Article: What is Protoevangelium? by Mark Slick (https://carm.org/about-theology/what-is-the-protoevangelium/)

- Video: *How Is Jesus Shown in the Book of Genesis? By Josh Moody* *(ttps://www.christianity.com/jesus/is-jesus-god/old-testament-prophecies/how-is-jesus-shown-in-the-book*-of-genesis.html)

- Internet access/a computer with editing ability
- Paper/pencil/ pen/dictionary

Procedure:

- Read the articles.
- Respond to the study questions.
- Watch the video.
- Respond to the study questions.
- Write a reflection on the assigned topic.
- Edit writing to correct errors.
- Post the reflection on the discussion board.
- Use an online dictionary to define and pronounce unfamiliar terms.
- If you have questions or need further clarification on any assignment, e-mail me at wilmaforeman@yahoo.com or visit my website: AIBL.INFO to sign up for the online course.

Study Questions:

Article: Genesis 3:15 The Protoevangelium or "First Gospel"

Directions: Show whether the statements are (A) CORRECT or (B) INCORRECT**.**

1. Genesis, Chapter 3 begins with the serpent that tempts the woman to eat from the Tree of the Knowledge of Good and Evil. (A) CORRECT
2. In the conversation with Eve, the serpent calls God *Elohim* instead of *Yahweh Elohim.*
3. *Yahweh Elohim* means *Lord God.* (A) CORRECT
4. After the humans succumb to the temptation of eating the forbidden fruit, God questions them, but He does not question the serpent. (A) CORRECT
5. The *adjudication* for the serpent's role in the rebellion is in Genesis, Chapter 3, verses 14-19. (A) CORRECT

6. To "*adjudicate*" a matter is to make an official decision about who is right in a dispute. (A) CORRECT

7. The serpent is the initiator of the sin of disobedience. (A) CORRECT

8. Adam is the last punished. (B) INCORRECT

9. According to the writer, the serpent is the only one that receives a curse. (A) CORRECT

10. A *curse* is the same as a punishment. (B) INCORRECT

11. To curse someone or something is to invoke harm or injury to come upon one. (A) CORRECT

12. Another word for a curse in an *imprecation*. (A) CORRECT

13. Genesis 3:15 is prophetic in that it foretells a future event. (A) CORRECT

14. The passage (Genesis 3:15) is the *Protoevangelium*, or the first *proclamation* of the Good News. (A) CORRECT

15. A *proclamation* is a public or official announcement, especially one dealing with a matter of foremost importance. (A) CORRECT

16. God refers to the future when He says that there will be one "who will crush the head of the serpent." (A) CORRECT

17. The proclamation in Genesis 3:15 has hope for humanity. (A) CORRECT

18. God's *mitigation* for the punishment pronounced on the humans is found within Genesis 3:15. (A) CORRECT

19. According to the article, the structure of the punishment for the serpent is in the form of two pronouncements that are independent of each other. (A) CORRECT

20. The serpent is the only animal that can speak in the narrative. (A) CORRECT

21. According to the article, the serpent *demotes* or lowers God's status by calling him *Elohim* instead of *Yahweh Elohim*. (A) CORRECT

22. The narrator in the beginning of the Book of Genesis refers to God as *Elohim*. (A) CORRECT

23. The serpent refutes God's integrity in the conversation with Eve. (A)

24. The Hebrew scholar, Cassuto, notes that the serpent is a *symbol* of evil in the tradition of the ancient Hebrews. (A) CORRECT

25. In Jewish tradition, the Old Testament Book of Wisdom reads that God made man to be *imperishable*. (A) CORRECT

26. The same Book says the God's wisdom is inside humankind. (A) CORRECT

27. In Jewish tradition, the devil was jealous of humankind. (A) CORRECT

28. The Devil's jealousy of humanity resulted in death. (A) CORRECT

29. Based on the Book of Wisdom, those whom the Devil owns will experience death. (A) CORRECT

30. St. Augustine commented on Genesis, Chapter 3 in *The Literal Meaning of Genesis* that the serpent was wise because of the devil dwelling in it. (A)

Study Questions:

Article: "What is Protoevangelium"? by Mark Slick

(https://carm.org/about-theology/what-is-the-protoevangelium/)

Directions: Show whether the following statements are (A) CORRECT or (B) INCORRECT.

1. In Genesis 3:15, God is speaking to the serpent when He says, *"I will put enmity between you and the woman, and between your offspring and hers; he will crush your head, and you will strike his heel."* (A) CORRECT

2. In Christian tradition, Genesis 3:15 is known as the *protoevangelium*—the first gospel. (A) CORRECT

3. To Christians, Genesis 3:15 introduces two elements—the curse on humanity because of Adam's sin and God's provision for a Savior to fulfill the consequences of sin. (A) CORRECT

4. In Christian tradition, Jesus takes upon Himself the curse of human sin. (A) CORRECT

5. Biblical interpreters use Genesis 3:15 to predict the defeat of evil by the victory of Jesus Christ during the crucifixion episode as recounted in the New Testament gospel narratives. (A) CORRECT

6. The term "gospel" refers to the *episodic* narrative of the words and deeds of Jesus. (A) CORRECT

7. The gospels culminate in the trial and death of Jesus of Nazareth and concludes with various reports of His post-resurrection appearances. (A) CORRECT

8. The prefix *"proto"* means *first.* (A) CORRECT

9. *"Evangelium"* means the *evangelistic message of salvation.* (A) CORRECT

10. In Genesis 3:15, the phrase, "I will put enmity between you and the woman…," means that the offspring of Eve and the serpent will become enemies. (A) CORRECT

11. Eve's posterity (offspring) includes Jesus. (A) CORRECT

12. In Christian tradition, the serpent *symbolizes* (represents) Satan. (A) CORRECT

13. Genesis 3:15 *foreshadows* hostility between the "seed" of the woman and the "seed" of the serpent. (A) CORRECT

14. The writer of this article proposes that Jesus was a distant descendant of Eve. (A) CORRECT

15. Based on the writer of this article, Jesus, the Messiah, was "bruised" via (by) the crucifixion. (A) CORRECT

16. The writer of the article asserts that the serpent (devil) will lose the battle between good and evil. (A) CORRECT

Study Questions:

Video: *How Is Jesus Shown in the Book of Genesis? By Josh Moody*

(ttps://www.christianity.com/jesus/is-jesus-god/old-testament-prophecies/how-is-jesus-shown-in-the-book-of-genesis.html)

Directions:

Based on the video, show whether the following statements are (A) CORRECT or (B) INCORRECT.

1. The speaker suggests that Chapter 3 in the Book of Genesis *foreshadows* Jesus in the New Testament of Christian Bibles. (A) CORRECT.
2. In Christian tradition, the New Testament (NT) is the second division of the Hebrew Bible. (A) CORRECT
3. The New Testament in Christian Bibles discusses the teachings and person of Jesus. (A) CORRECT
4. The *protoevangelium* is the term used to describe the first mention of the *gospel* in reference to Genesis 3:15. (A) CORRECT
5. In Christian tradition, Genesis 3:15, *"I will put enmity between you and the woman, and between your offspring and hers; he will crush your head, and you will strike his heel"* is known as the protoevangelium—the first gospel. (A) CORRECT

For Reflection (1):

How does the description of the serpent in the Book of Revelation 20:2-3 compared to the depiction in Genesis 3:15? Mention the term "protoevangelium." (Write 5-8 sentences. Edit writing to correct errors. Post your work on the discussion board. Label the post: A Reflection on Genesis 3:15 as a Protoevangelium.)

"And the great dragon was thrown down that ancient serpent, who is called the Devil and Satan the deceiver of the whole world. -he was thrown down to the earth, and his angels were thrown down with him."

-Revelation 12:9

For Reflection (2):

Directions:

Explain the literal and symbolic meanings of God's pronouncement of enmity between the serpent and the woman in Genesis 3:15. Discuss the meaning of the term "seed" in the context of this biblical text. (Write 5-8 sentences. Edit writing to correct errors. Post your work on the discussion board. Label the post: A Reflection on Genesis 3:15 as a protoevangelium.)

A Closing Thought:

"Knowledge is power. Information is liberating. Education is the premise of progress, in every society, in every family."

-Kofi Annan

by Wilma J. Brown-Foreman, ED. S

LESSON THIRTEEN
THE CAIN AND ABEL NARRATIVE

Lesson Overview:

The historical Hebrew narrative in Genesis, Chapter 4 records the first murder when Cain kills his brother Abel in a fit of angry jealousy. The hostility erupts when God refuses Cain's grain sacrifice but accepts his brother's blood offering. The murder of Abel is evil in God's eyes and results in Cain becoming a vagabond, or homeless wanderer. Showing mercy toward Cain, however, God places a mark on his forehead so that no one can exact vengeance on him. The mark is often alluded to as "the curse of Cain" or "the mark of Cain." Students will read and analyze the Cain and Abel narrative with a focus on the moral issue of honoring human life.

Key Concepts: sacrifices/offerings, human jealousy/anger, sibling rivalry, consequences of behavior, "mark of Cain," "curse of Cain," dynamic or static character, personification, sarcasm, synecdoche, motivation, hyperbole

Lesson Objectives:

Students will:

- summarize the main ideas in Genesis, Chapter 4.
- explain terminology associated with the literary elements of biblical text.
- distinguish between the figurative and literal textual expressions.
- author an effective full-length essay on Genesis, Chapters 4.
- edit writing to correct errors standard English usage.
- participate in class discussions.

Learning Outcomes:

At the end on this lesson, students will be able to:

- demonstrate a general knowledge of chapters 4 of the Book of Genesis.
- use terminology associated with the literary elements of biblical text.
- distinguish between the figurative and literal textual expressions.
- author an effective full-length essay on Genesis, Chapters 4.
- edit writing to correct errors standard English usage.
- participate in class discussions.

Duration: 3-4 hours

Materials:

- Article: "Cain" by Pamela Barmash)

(*https://www.bibleodyssey.org/people/main-articles/cain*)

- Article: "The Cry of Abel's Blood" by David Carri.
  (*https://www.bibleodyssey.org/en/people/related-articles/cry-of-abels-blood*)
- Essay: "Cain and Abel in the Bible" by Elie Wiesel
  (*http://home.nwi.net/~clark/library/Cain%20and%20Abel%20in%20the%20Bible.pdf*)
- Internet access/e-mail/computer editing ability
- Notebook/paper/pen/dictionary

Procedure:

- Read Genesis, Chapter 4 from any Bible translation.
- Study the review chart of Genesis, Chapter 4 and respond to the study questions.
- Respond to the reflection(s). (Edit your writing to correct errors.)
- Post the reflection(s) on the discussion board.
- Use an online dictionary to define and pronounce unfamiliar terms.
- If you have questions or need further clarification on any assignment, e-mail me at wilmaforeman@yahoo.com or visit my website: AIBL.INFO to sign up for the online course.

Genesis, Chapter 4

Title of Narrative	Literary Themes	Plot Summary	Study Questions
"Cain Murders Abel" Gen. 4:1-16	<ul><li>Sacrifices/Offerings to God</li><li>Human Jealousy</li><li>Sibling Rivalry</li><li>Hatred</li><li>Anger</li><li>Rebellion</li><li>Consequences of Behavior</li><li>Death</li><li>God's Sovereignty</li><li>God's Mercy</li><li>God's Interaction with His Creation</li><li>God's Judgment</li></ul>	Cain and Abel are the children of Adam and Eve. Both bring offerings to God, but God does not favor the sacrifice of Cain. As a result, Cain becomes so jealous of his younger brother Abel that he kills him. God punishes Cain by making him a vagabond and a fugitive. He spares his life, however, and places a mark on him as a sign that no one can harm him.	True (A) or False (B)? 1. Sibling rivalry is a vital part of the narrative. 2. In Shakespeare's, *Hamlet*, Act 3, Scene 3), Hamlet's uncle Claudius murders his own brother to become king. He confesses, "*Oh, my offence is rank. It smells to heaven. It hath the primal eldest curse upon't, A brother's murder.*" The "primal eldest curse" is an *allusion* to the biblical curse of Adam and Eve's Cain, who slew his brother Abel. 3. Cain and Abel become vagabonds *(*wanderers). 4. God's preference of Abel's offering over Cain's is a *motif* (literary

			pattern or *theme*) in the Bible, where the younger child rises above his or her siblings.
			5. If the eldest siblings were supposed to protect the younger brothers and sisters, Cain's response to God's question is not only *sarcastic* but *ironic* when he retorts, "Am I my brother's keeper?" (Gen. 4:8).
			6. Abel's blood calling out to God and implicating his brother as the murderer is an example of personification.
			7. " The ground" opening its mouth to receive Abel's blood is an example of *personificatio*n. (Gen 4:11)
			8. God sentences Cain to wander over the earth where there is no law or morality.
			9. When Cain fears for his life, God shows compassion by giving him a mark on his forehead so that no one will kill him.
			10. Cain's lawlessness costs him his family, his livelihood, and his property.

Study Questions

(Article: "Cain" by Pamela Barmash) (*https://www.bibleodyssey.org/people/main-articles/cain*)

Directions: Based on the article, write down whether the following statements are (A) CORRECT or (B) INCORRECT.

1. In the fourth chapter of Genesis, the first son of Adam and Eve kills his only sibling, Abel. (A) CORRECT
2. The placement of the misdeed early in the Genesis narrative depicts the horrendous nature of the act. (A) CORRECT
3. The narrative explores Cain's inner life and the nature of the human impulse to sin. (A) CORRECT
4. The biblical text is explicit in revealing why Cain murders Abel. (B) INCORRECT
5. Jealousy motivates Cain to become angry when God prefers Abel's sacrifice over his. (A) CORRECT
6. Abel is more gregarious than Cain. (B) INCORRECT
7. Cain and Abel have different temperaments. (A) CORRECT
8. In telling the story, the writer of the biblical text moves directly from Cain's disappointment to Abel's murder. (A) CORRECT
9. God responds to Cain's dismay by warning him about his anger. (A) CORRECT
10. God tells Cain that he cannot overcome the impulse to sin. (B) INCORRECT
11. God says that Cain can withstand the proclivity to sin. (A) CORRECT
12. God states that Cain's jealousy needs not spiral downward into murder. (A) CORRECT
13. Based on the article, God is responding to Cain's change in physical appearance and altered personality in the question: "*Why are you angry, and why has your countenance fallen?*" (A) CORRECT
14. "*Sin is lurking at the door; its desire is for you, but you must master it*" (Gen 4:6-7) is a poetic expression that *personifies* the sinful action. (A) CORRECT
15. The expression means that Cain's character has not become so fallen that killing his brother is inevitable. (A) CORRECT
16. Cain dismisses God's warning and kills his brother in a field. (A) CORRECT
17. In biblical times, the field was a dangerous place because of the unlikelihood of discovering and punishing the murderers. (A) CORRECT
18. The fact that Cain asks his brother to go with him to the field reveals his cunning nature. (A) CORRECT
19. Cain's emotional and psychological complexities surface when he responds to God's question, "Where is thy brother?" (Genesis 4:9). (A) CORRECT
20. To avoid punishment for his actions, Cain lies to God. (A) CORRECT
21. Cain is defiant and sarcastic when he asks God, "Am I my brother's keeper?" (Genesis 4:9). (A) CORRECT
22. This article focuses on a character's motivation for his decisions and actions. (A) CORRECT
23. Cain is a *dynamic* character. (B) INCORRECT

24. Abel is a *static* character. (A) CORRECT
25. Anger and jealousy *motivate* Cain's murderous behavior. (A) CORRECT

Extended Learning Study Questions

Article: "The Cry of Abel's Blood" by David Carr

(https://www.bibleodyssey.org/en/people/related-articles/cry-of-abels-blood)

Based on the article, are the following statements (A) CORRECT or (B) INCORRECT?

1. According to the writer, Cain is "cursed from the ground." (A) CORRECT
2. The expression "*cursed from the ground*" means that the earth will become an enemy to him. (A) CORRECT
3. David Carr proposes that Cain is the first human being on whom God inflicts a curse. (A) CORRECT
4. The writer suggests that the curse on Cain will arise from the part of the earth previously won and subdued by man. (A) CORRECT
5. The soil will resist Cain as an enemy by refusing "to yield unto him her strength." (A) CORRECT
6. Ironically, the blood of Abel exerts power over Cain after his death in that it prevents Cain from ever settling again to farm the ground. (A) CORRECT
7. The literal interpretation of Genesis 4:10-16 is: "Your brother's bloods are crying out." (A) CORRECT
8. The expression stands for violently shed blood that demands payment or restitution. (A) CORRECT
9. The expression, "your brother's bloods' and "rivers of blood" are both *hyperbolic*. (A) CORRECT
10. Both expressions are literal and understood as historical facts. (B) INCORRECT
11. A *hyperbole* is an extreme exaggeration for the sake of emphasis. (A) CORRECT
12. The word for *cry* (Hebrew *tsa'aq*) is used for human expressions of the most desperate and extreme need. (A) CORRECT
13. A paraphrased statement of Genesis 4:10 is: "The rivers of your brother's blood desperately cry to me from the ground for revenge." (A) CORRECT
14. The writer asserts that Cain is "cursed from the ground" which has "opened its mouth" to receive his murdered brother's blood (Gen 4:11). (A) CORRECT
15. In this Genesis narrative, the first human death is a foreshadowing of the widening violence in the future of humanity. (A) CORRECT
16. Jewish and Christian interpreters across the centuries have seen the Cain and Abel narrative as a *precursor* to future murders of innocent people. (A) CORRECT
17. A *precursor* is a person or thing that comes before another, or a forerunner. (A) CORRECT
18. In the biblical narrative, Abel is a *precursor* to Cain. (B) INCORRECT
19. According to the article, *bloods* in Gen 4:10-11 and the present tense of the verb, *is crying out*, in Gen 4:10 point to the blood of later generations crying out to God in a desperate plea for a reckoning. (A) CORRECT

20. A *reckoning* is a settlement of an account or a payment for something. (A) CORRECT

For Reflection (1):

In five-eight (5-8) sentences, discuss what Genesis, Chapter 4 reveals about the value of human life, and how God feels about murder? Edit your writing to correct errors. Post your reflection on the discussion board. Label the post: A Reflection on "The Cry of Abel's Blood."

For Reflection (2):

A static character does not change or develop throughout a narrative. Their personalities, beliefs, and worldview remain the same. They do not expand or adapt to external situations. On the other hand, a dynamic character changes or grows over the course of a story. An event might alter his or her personality, attitude, or overall view of life. Sometimes, the character may have a personal revelation that changes his or her whole perspective. Write a reflection (5-8 sentences) on the characterization of Cain in Genesis, Chapter 4. Overall, is he a *static* or *dynamic* character? Explain your response. Give Scripture references to support your position. You may also use other reliable online resources to make your points. Document your sources. Edit your writing to correct errors. Post your reflection to the discussion board. Label the post: The Biblical Characterization of Cain.

For Reflection (3):

How did the biblical Cain become a precursor or forerunner to other literary, historical, as well as contemporary figures in our world? Give examples. (Write 5-8 sentences.) You may use reliable online resources to make your points. Document your sources. Edit your writing to correct errors. Post your reflection to the discussion board. Label the post: Cain as a Precursor to Murderers.

For Reflection (4):

- Read the Essay: "Cain and Abel in the Bible" by Elie Wiesel
(*http://home.nwi.net/~clark/library/Cain%20and%20Abel%20in%20the%20Bible.pdf*)

- Explain Wiesel's statement in your own three-five paragraph essay: "He who kills, kills his brother."
- Include an introduction, body, and conclusion.
- Use the MLA or APA styles for formatting the essay.
- Use the computer's editing capability to correct errors in writing.
- Submit your work to the instructor by email or the discussion board.

A Closing Thought:

"The Bible is still loved by millions, read by millions, and studied by millions."

- Bernard Ram

LESSON FOURTEEN

THE GREAT FLOOD

(A BIBLICAL HISTORICAL NARRATIVE)

Lesson Overview:

The Genesis Flood narrative is among the best-known historical narratives in the Hebrew Scriptures. There are almost two hundred different accounts around the world of a great flood. This narrative is an account of the continual worsening of evil among humans resulting in the withdrawal of God's Spirit from them (Genesis 6:3). God makes an exception for the "blameless" Noah (Genesis 6:5-8) and his family. God instructs Noah to build an ark (Genesis 6:13-17) and a universal deluge destroys all the people on earth except Noah and his family. After the deluge, God establishes a covenant with Noah that impacts the future of all humanity (Genesis 6:18-22). Students will examine the historical and literary aspects of the Flood narrative.

Key Concepts:

deluge, patriarchs, moral state, judgment, repentance, redemption, covenants, anthropomorphism, literal versus figurative language, ark, cubit, grace, deluge, metonymy, synecdoche, idiom, symbolic, personifies, altar, antithesis, sacrifices, chiasm, reverse order, prologue, epilogue, genealogical account, chronological account, ring structure, literary design, epic, monotheism, polytheism, Mesopotamia

Lesson Objectives:

Students will:

- cite strong and thorough textual evidence to support analysis of what the text says explicitly as well as inferences drawn from the text.
- find a theme or central idea of a text and analyze in detail its development over the course of the text.
- find the meaning of words and phrases as used in the text, including figurative and connotative meanings.
- analyze how an author's choices concerning how to structure a text, order events within it.
- analyze multiple interpretations of a story.

Expected Student Learning Outcomes:

By the end of this lesson, students will be able to:

- use online Bible study tools to access, read, interpret, and explain information.
- summarize the main ideas in the biblical text (Genesis, Chapters 6-9).
- recognize and define literary terms common in writing.

- use information in biblical commentaries to support analysis, reflection, and research.
- make inferences and draw conclusions based on explicit and implied information using evidence from the text as support.
- state the writer's intended purpose for writing the text.
- synthesize information from various sources.
- draw conclusions and make inferences from primary and secondary sources.
- discuss the literary aspects of Creation narratives in Genesis, Chapters 6-9.
- share information about assigned biblical passages logically and accurately.
- edit writing for correct spelling, punctuation, grammar, sentence structure.

Duration: 3-4 hours

Materials:

- Article:" Noah and Human Etymology" by Bengt Sage
- A computer with editing capability
- Internet access
- Paper, pen, pencil/dictionary

Procedure:

- Read/Review Genesis, Chapters 6-9 from any Bible translation.
- Study the review chart of Genesis, Chapters 6-9 and respond to the study questions.
- Read the article: "Noah and Human Etymology" by Bengt Sage
- Respond to the study questions.
- Note key points/vocabulary terms to study for future discussions and assessments.
- Use an online dictionary to define and pronounce unfamiliar terms.
- If you have questions or need further clarification on any assignment, e-mail me at wilmaforeman@yahoo.com or visit my website: AIBL.INFO to sign up for the online course.

Genesis, Chapters 6-9

Title of the Narrative	Literary Themes	Plot Summary	Study Questions
"The Great Flood" Gen. 6-9	<ul><li>God's Mercy</li><li>Man's Obedience</li><li>Man's Disobedience</li><li>God's Sovereignty</li><li>Man's Rebellion</li><li>God's Judgment</li></ul>	Genesis records the account of "The Great Flood" as God's means of purging the earth of evil. Noah, identified as "righteous," receives instructions from God to build an ark as a means of	**True (A) or False (B)?** 1. In contrast to members of his generation, Noah is both "righteous" and "blameless." 2. Noah's conduct contrasts with the sinful nature of humanity in general.

	• Covenants • Consequences for behavior • Redemption	saving humanity and various kinds of creatures from impending destruction. Noah obeys God, and he and his family survive the deluge. God sets up a covenant with Noah in the form of a rainbow. He promises that never again will a flood destroy the earth. Noah's blessing of Shem and Japheth entails their brother Canaan becoming their servant (9:25-26).	3. Throughout the narrative, Noah is amoral and completely unregenerate. 4. The Hebrew Bible depicts Noah as a moral, God-fearing man. 5. From the beginning to the end, Noah is sinless, perfect man. 6. The expression, "blameless" in Hebrew pertains to someone who is exceptionally obedient to God. 7. By character, reputation, and practice, Noah is blameless, or perfect. 8. Noah, like Enoch in Genesis 5, literally "walked with God" (physically). 9. The expression "walked with God" means that one has a close relationship with God. 10. Gen. 6:9-22 records the *genealogy* of Noah. 11. A *genealogy* is the study of a family history and the tracing of its lineages. 12. This historical Hebrew narrative records the violence and sinfulness of early humans. 13. In the narrative, God chooses to declare to Noah His plan to end all land-dwelling life. 14. God plans to save Noah and his family from the global flood, along with every living animal. 15. Noah obeys God's command to build an ark (an enormous boat) that will preserve humanity from destruction during the flood.

			16. In Genesis, 6:19, God tells Noah to take a pair of every animal, male and female, into the Ark.
			17. In Genesis 7:2-3, God supplements His original instruction by telling Noah to take more of the clean animals into the ark.
			18. In the narrative, rain falls onto the earth for forty days and forty nights.
			19. Genesis 6-8 is one of the greatest stories of *redemption* in the Old Testament.
			20. In Christian tradition, the story of Noah is a foreshadow of the ministry of Jesus and the *redemption* of sinful humans.

Study Questions:

(Article:" Noah and Human Etymology" by Bengt Sage at: Noah and Human Etymology | The Institute for Creation Research (icr.org)

Are the following statements (A) CORRECT or (B) INCORRECT?

1. The name "Noah" is as universal as the story of the Great Flood. (A) CORRECT
2. The "post-Ararat" migrations pertain to the mountains of Ararat in Turkey. (A) CORRECT
3. The ancient Sanskrit language is an Old Indo-Aryan language. (A) CORRECT
4. "*Manu*" was the name of the flood hero in India. (A) CORRECT
5. Like Noah in the Hebrew Bible, Manu is believed to have built an ark. (A) CORRECT
6. In the tradition of the narrative about Manu, eight people were saved from drowning in the flood waters. (A) CORRECT
7. "Ma" is an old term for "water." (A) CORRECT
8. The English word "marine" is associated with the term "*ma*." (A) CORRECT
9. In the Sanskrit language, the word *Manu* eventually became to mean "man" or "mankind." (A) CORRECT
10. "Manu" is connected to Noah as the father of all post-flood humans. (A) CORRECT
11. The German word *Mannus* is known as the founder of the West Germanic people. (A) CORRECT
12. The Roman historian Tacitus mentioned *Mannus* in his book *Germania*. (A) CORRECT
13. Lithuanian, and Eastern Baltic language belonging to the Baltic branch of the Indo-European language family used the name *Mannus* for Noah. (A) CORRECT
14. "*Manusa*" and "*manniska*" mean "human being." (A) CORRECT

15. The Egyptian name *Menes* (founder of the first dynasty of Egypt) and *Minos* (founder and first king of Crete) reflect the name *Manu*. (A) CORRECT
16. "Manu" became "maru," a word which is included in the name of most Japanese ships. (A) CORRECT
17. In ancient Chinese mythology, *Maru* came down from heaven to teach people how to make ships. (A) CORRECT
18. In Hawaii, *mano* is the word for "shark," and the word for "mountain" is *mauna*.
19. *Ararat* is the same as *Armenia* in the Bible. (A) CORRECT
20. The prefix "*Ar*" means "Mountain." (A) CORRECT

Study Questions

Directions: Read any Bible version of the Great Flood narrative in Genesis 6:5-9:17. 5 and respond to the questions that follow. Use additional credible internet sources if necessary. Document sources in your notebook.

Are the following questions (A) CORRECT or (B) INCORRECT?

1. This narrative opens with an account of the wickedness that increases among the humans as they begin to multiply in population. (A) CORRECT
2. God's dismay results from the people's evildoings. (A) CORRECT
3. Based on the narrative, humans are relentless in their immoral behavior. (A) CORRECT
4. As a result, God decides to destroy humankind. (A) CORRECT
5. The expression "*it repented me*" shows God's displeasure. (A) CORRECT
6. The expression "*Noah found grace*" implies that only one man among millions obtained approval from God. (A) CORRECT
7. "Grace" is divine help given to humans for their restoration. (A) CORRECT
8. The term "*grace*" implies that one has earned the right or entitlement to God's favor. (B) INCORRECT
9. The phrase "*eyes of the Lord*" is an *anthropomorphic* expression in that it attributes humanlike qualities to God. (A) CORRECT
10. The statement, "*Noah is a just man who is perfect among his generations*," implies that Noah is completely sinless. (B) INCORRECT
11. The expression "*Noah walked with God*" means that Noah followed godly principles. (A) CORRECT
12. The statement, "Noah *begat* three sons Shem, Ham, and Japheth," means that Noah fathered three boys. (A) CORRECT
13. When God tells Noah that "*the end of all flesh has come, for the earth is filled with violence through them,*" this means that humans have become brutal, and God will destroy them. (A) CORRECT
14. God gives Noah specific instructions for building the *ark*. (A) CORRECT
15. The *unrestrained*, careless nature of humans *grieves* God. (A) CORRECT
16. A "*cubit*" is an ancient measure of length, equal to the length of a forearm. (A) CORRECT
17. God instructs Noah to build a three-story boat. (A) CORRECT
18. God's judgment affects every living thing during Noah's time. (A) CORRECT

19. God makes a *covenant* with Noah before the flood begins. (A) CORRECT
20. By God's *grace*, Noah and his family escape the devastation. (A) CORRECT
21. God instructs Noah to take only two of every clean and unclean animal inside the ark. (B) INCORRECT
22. Rain, a familiar occurrence of nature during Noah's times, falls forty days and nights. (B) INCORRECT
23. Only eight humans survive the *deluge*. (A) CORRECT
24. As used in this narrative, the term "*flesh*" is an example of the literary technique *metonymy* or *synecdoche*. (A) CORRECT
25. "Flesh" is the human body. (A) CORRECT
26. At the end of the narrative, God remembers Noah and every living thing inside the ark. (A) CORRECT
27. God causes a wind to pass over the earth to make the waters subside. (A) CORRECT
28. "*The fountains of the deep*" is a literary expression that can refer to the earth's volcanic activity. (A) CORRECT
29. "*The windows of heaven*" is a poetic expression that refers to the torrent (surging water) standing for God's judgment. (A) CORRECT
30. According to the Flood story, God restrains the rain from the heavens, and the waters roll away from the earth continually. (A) CORRECT
31. At the end of the narrative, after one hundred and fifty days, the waters *abate* and become still. (A) CORRECT
32. Historians believe that the ark settles on top of Mount Ararat, a place in Turkey. (A) CORRECT
33. Based on the unfolding of the narrative, the flood waters decrease within a brief time. (B) INCORRECT
34. At the end of forty days, Noah opens the window of the ark and sends forth a raven to fly in search of dry land. (A) CORRECT
35. Based on the narrative details, a raven is a "clean" bird. (B) INCORRECT
36. Noah also sends forth a dove to search for dry land. (A) CORRECT
37. A dove is the *antithesis* of the raven. (A) CORRECT
38. The expression, "*the face of the ground*," is an *idiom* that means *everywhere in the world*. (A) CORRECT
39. The expression "*no rest for the sole of her foot*" means that the dove cannot find a dry place to land. (A) CORRECT
40. In Genesis 8:9, the statement, "*But the dove found no place to rest her foot, and she returned to him in the ark, because the waters were still covering the surface of all the earth,*" the writer personifies the bird. (A) CORRECT
41. Noah's gentle nature surfaces when he pulls the dove back inside the ark and waits another seven days before he sends her out again. (A) CORRECT
42. After Noah releases the dove into the world again, the bird returns with an olive leaf. (A) CORRECT
43. The dove and the olive branch are *symbolic* of peace. (A) CORRECT
44. After the flood, God commands the living creatures to multiply. (A) CORRECT

45. Noah honors God by building an altar and by offering a sacrifice of clean animals and birds. (A) CORRECT
46. God accepts Noah's offerings and promises never to curse the ground again because of the sins of humans. (A) CORRECT
47. God declares that the human imagination is continually evil. (A) CORRECT
48. God promises never to destroy other living creatures because of the wickedness of humankind. (A) CORRECT
49. God sets a rainbow in the sky to serve as a sign of the covenant that He will never again destroy all life with flood waters. (A) CORRECT
50. The narrative portrays Noah both as a "tiller of the soil" and as a drinker of wine. (A) CORRECT
51. The first thing Noah does when he enters the new earth is to build an *altar* for the LORD and to *proffer* (offer) Him *sacrifices*. (A) CORRECT
52. In doing so, he acknowledges that God has every right to the new earth. (A) CORRECT
53. In biblical times, making a *sacrifice* was an act of slaughtering an animal or surrendering a possession as an offering to God. (A) CORRECT
54. In ancient cultures, humans offered sacrifices to divine or supernatural figures. (A) CORRECT
55. During biblical times, sacrifices usually required *altars*. (A) CORRECT

Extended Learning Study Questions

Directions:

- Read the document: "Literary Analysis of the Flood."
(http://helpmewithbiblestudy.org/5system_moses/print/dh11LiteraryAnalysisOfTheFlood.pdf)

- Use online dictionaries and other resources to define unfamiliar terms.
- Respond to the study questions that follow.
- Write the answers in your notebook.
- Note key points to study for future discussions and assessments.
- Post clarification questions on the discussion board.

Based on the document, "Literary Analysis of the Flood," are the statements below (A) CORRECT or (B) INCORRECT? (Items 1-40)

1. The literary structure of the Flood Narrative is a detailed and organized *chiasm*. (A) CORRECT
2. A *chiasm* is a literary device in which the writer presents a sequence of ideas and then, repeats the ideas *in reverse order*. (A) CORRECT
3. A *chiasm* has a "mirror" effect as the writer reflects ideas in a passage. (A) CORRECT
4. In using a chiasm, the writer connects an idea to its "reflection" by a repeated word, often in a related form. (A) CORRECT

5. The term *chiasm* comes from the Greek letter *chi*, which looks like the letter *X*. (A) CORRECT

6. Another term for a *chiastic* pattern is the "*ring structure*." (A) CORRECT

7. The Flood narrative has a *prologue* and an *epilogue*. (A) CORRECT

8. The *prologue* introduces the sinful and wicked state of humankind before the Flood and shows that the immoral state of humans is the cause of God's judgment (Gen 6:1-8). (A) CORRECT

9. A second *genealogical account* mentions Noah's sons, Shem, Ham, and Japheth (Gen 6:9-10). (A) CORRECT

10. In Genesis 6:11-20, God *decrees* that He will destroy human life. (A)

11. God's second *decree* to Noah in Genesis 6: 21-22 concerns the preservation of animal life. (A) CORRECT

12. Genesis 7:11-16, a part of the *prologue*, shows Noah and his family entering the ark. (A) CORRECT

13. In Genesis 7, the Flood rises and lasts for forty days and forty nights. (A) CORRECT

14. The *epilogue* concludes the Flood narrative with a comment about the state of humanity's moral character. (A) CORRECT

15. At the end of the story, Noah becomes intoxicated, and God *curses* his son, Ham, because he disrespects his father's nakedness (Gen 9:20-27). (B) INCORRECT

16. The Hebrew verb for "*saw*" in Gen 9:22 shows that Ham looked upon his father with more than a harmless glance. (A) CORRECT

17. Archeologists have found that Canaan, descendants of Ham, were well known for their deviant sexual practices. (A) CORRECT

18. The Bible does not tell Noah's age when God first speaks to him about building an ark. (A) CORRECT

19. By Noah's 600th birthday, the ark is ready to board. (A) CORRECT

20. God's second divine address to Noah (Gen 7:1- 10) occurs years after the first divine address. (A) CORRECT

21. The Flood narrative is a *chronological account* of a global deluge. (A) CORRECT

22. In the first divine decree (Gen 6:19-22), God informs Noah of the impending Flood and instructs him to admit pairs of animals so that they will not drown. (A) CORRECT

23. In the second divine address, God gives Noah specific details about boarding the animals and birds: clean animals by seven pairs, birds by seven pairs, and unclean animals by one pair (Gen 7:2-3). (A) CORRECT

24. Within the entire Flood narrative, there are only two places that tell the day, month, and year of an event. (B) INCORRECT

25. The *chronological* dates in the narrative have a *literary design*. (A) CORRECT

26. In the biblical narrative, the writer gives the complete date when Noah enters the Ark. (A) CORRECT

27. The writer gives the month and day when God remembers Noah (Gen 8:4). (A) CORRECT

28. The Bible records the complete date when Noah leaves the ark (Gen 8:13). (A) CORRECT

29. The biblical account of the Flood connects to other ancient Mesopotamian flood accounts. (A) CORRECT

30. Two of the earliest writings about a global Flood are the *Atra-hasis Epic* (1646-1626 BC) and the *Gilgamesh Epic* (650-700 BC). (A) CORRECT
31. An earlier Sumerian version (2000 BC) of the Great Flood exists, but only one-third of the fragments are in possession. (A) CORRECT
32. The biblical account of the Flood is exactly like the other ancient accounts. (B) INCORRECT
33. The biblical account of the Great Flood and other ancient accounts differ significantly in the portrayal of God. (A) CORRECT
34. In the biblical account, God is a *monotheistic* Creator. (A) CORRECT
35. Based on the Hebrew Bible, one can conclude that God is *omniscient* and *omnipotent*. (A) CORRECT
36. Other accounts of the Flood feature *polytheism*. (A) CORRECT
37. In the Hebrew Flood narrative, God has a supreme concern for humanity. (A) CORRECT
38. God has compassion on all living creatures in the Hebrew Flood account. (A) CORRECT
39. In the Hebrew Flood narrative, God lives and judges by an impeccable moral standard. (A) CORRECT
40. In ancient Sumerian flood accounts, the gods break their own vows. (A) CORRECT

Reading Comprehension/Biblical Characterization/Vocabulary Development

41. Which of the words best describe Noah according to the lines extracted from the Bible commentaries?

> *Noah was a just man and perfect in his generations.* — *"Just" is righteous, one whose actions were sufficiently upright to exempt him from the punishment inflicted upon the rest of humanity. "Perfect" means sound, healthy, and conveys no idea of sinlessness. It answers to the Latin integer, whence our word integrity, and not to perfectus....*
>
> (*Elliott's Commentary for English Readers*, Genesis 6:8)

    a. wicked/sinful
    b. ***virtuous/upright***
    c. guilty/amiss
    d. reprehensible/dishonorable
    e. none of the above

42. Which of the words best describe God according to the lines below?

> *But Noah found grace in the eyes of the Lord. This man and his family were the only exception to the general apostasy; God always reserves some, in the worst of times, for himself; there is a remnant, according to the election of grace; it was but a small one, and that now appeared; and this was owing to the grace of God, and His choice upon that, and not to the merits of the creature. This grace, which Noah found and shared in, was the favour and good will of God...*
>
> (*Gill's Exposition of the Entire Bible*, Genesis, Chapter 6)

a. unceremonious/unchanging
b. undemanding/wanting
c. unpatriotic/unpredictable
d. *benevolent/kind*
e. none of the above

43. Which of the words best describe God in Genesis 6:5-7 (KJV) according to the lines below?

   ⁵ *And Jehovah seeth that abundant [is] the wickedness of man in the earth, and every imagination of the thoughts of his heart only evil all day.*

   ⁶ *and Jehovah repenteth that He hath made man in the earth, and He grieveth Himself -- unto His heart.*

   ⁷ *And Jehovah saith, `I wipe away man whom I have prepared from off the face of the ground, from man unto beast, unto creeping thing, and unto fowl of the heavens, for I have repented that I have made them.'*

   a. *downhearted/disheartened*
   b. unsympathetic/callous
   c. wroth/irascible
   d. loquacious/garrulous
   e. *none of the above*

44. Which of the words best describe Noah in Genesis 6:8-9 (KJV) according to the lines below?

   ⁸ *And Noah found grace in the eyes of Jehovah.*

   ⁹ *These [are] births of Noah: Noah [is] a righteous man; perfect he hath been among his generations; with God hath Noah walked habitually.*

   a. iniquitous/corrupt
   b. fallen/irreverent
   c. nefarious/ungodly
   d. *principled/decent*
   e. none of the above

Extended Learning Study Questions:

Video: *Noah's Ark Discovered Documentary! Evidence for Its Location, Genesis Flood! Proof Bible Is True!* (*https://www.youtube.com/watch?v=9f4uF4Va9gI*)

Directions: Respond to the following questions based on the video presentation.

1. What is the difference between a historical narrative and a myth? (*Narrative history tells when, where, and why a certain event occurred, its larger significance or context, and who the important participants were. A myth is a widespread belief or tradition that has grown up around something or someone*)

2. What is the meaning of *geology*? (*Geology is the field of study concerned with the solid earth.*)
3. Where is the *Durupınar site* found? (*Turkey*)
4. How does this site relate to the biblical account of the Great Flood? (*The size and shape of the structure led to its promotion by believers as the petrified ruins of the original Noah's ark.*)
5. Why is Mount Ararat significant to the Flood story? (*In the Book of Genesis, the mountains of Ararat in what is now eastern Turkey is the region in which Noah's Ark comes to rest after the Great Flood.*)

For Reflection:

Write a reflection (essay) on the biblical character *Noah* in Genesis, Chapters 6-9 (three-five paragraphs). Use vocabulary terms from this lesson to elaborate on Noah's dominant character traits. Give at least one example to support your reflection. Include an introduction, supporting details, and a conclusion to your essay. Follow writing guidelines at: *Learn to Write a First Class Essay (https://www.researchprospect.com/essay-writing-guidelines/).* Edit writing to correct errors in grammar, spelling, punctuation, sentence structure, and clarity. Post the reflection on the discussion board. Label the post: A Reflection on the Biblical Character Noah (Genesis, Chapters 6-9).

A Closing Thought:

"*The more this BIBLE enters into our national life, the grander and purer and better will that life become.*"

-David Josiah Brewer

LESSON FIFTEEN
THE TOWER OF BABEL NARRATIVE
(GENESIS, CHAPTER ELEVEN)

Lesson Overview:

"The Tower of Babel" historical narrative in Genesis, Chapter 11 is an origin narrative meant to explain why people of the world speak different languages. This biblical account of the building of the tower in ancient Babel and God's scattering of the people continues the overarching storyline about the relationship between God and humans. Students will examine the narrative from a literary and historical perspective.

Key Concepts:

overarching storyline, origin narrative, hubris, themes

Lesson Objectives:

Students will:

- cite strong and thorough textual evidence to support analysis of what the text says explicitly as well as inferences drawn from the text.
- find a theme or central idea of a text and analyze in detail its development over the course of the text.
- recognize and define literary terms common in writing.
- find the meaning of words and phrases as used in the text, including figurative and connotative meanings.
- analyze the cumulative impact of specific word choices on meaning and tone (e.g., how the language evokes a sense of time and place; how it sets a formal or informal tone).
- analyze how an author's choices concerning how to structure a text, order events within it.
- analyze the representation of a subject or a key scene in two different artistic mediums.
- analyze multiple interpretations of a story.

Expected Learning Outcomes:

By the end of this lesson, students will be able to:

- use online Bible study tools to access, read, interpret, and explain information.
- summarize the main ideas in the biblical text (Genesis, Chapter 11).
- recognize and define literary terms common in writing.
- use information in biblical commentaries to support analysis, reflection, and research.
- make inferences and draw conclusions based on explicit and implied information by using evidence from the text.

- state the writer's intended purpose for writing the text.
- synthesize information from various sources.
- draw conclusions and make inferences from primary and secondary sources.
- discuss the literary aspects of Creation narratives in Genesis, Chapters 6-9.
- share information about assigned biblical passages logically and accurately.
- edit writing for correct spelling, punctuation, grammar, sentence structure.

Duration: 3-4 hours

. **Materials:**

- Video: The Tower of Babel: Biblical Archaeology (https://www.youtube.com/watch?v=ZNc-hyIRrCs)

- A computer with editing capability
- Internet access
- Notebook/paper/pen/dictionary

Procedure:

- Read Genesis, Chapter 11. (Compare various translations.)
- Add details to the chart below as you read the narrative.
- Respond to the study questions.
- Edit your writing to correct errors.
- Post the reflection on the discussion board.
- Label the reflection: A Reflection on Babel (1)
- Watch the video: *The Tower of Babel: Biblical Archaeology (https://www.youtube.com/watch?v=ZNc-hyIRrCs .*
- Answer the study question(s).
- Respond to the reflection question(s).
- Post the reflection on the discussion board.
- Label the reflection: A Reflection on the "Tower of Babel."
- Use an online dictionary to define and pronounce unfamiliar terms.
- If you have questions or need further clarification on any assignment, e-mail me at wilmaforeman@yahoo.com or visit my website: AIBL.INFO to sign up for the online course.

Genesis, Chapter 11

Title of the Narrative	Literary Themes	Summary	Study Questions
"The Tower of Babel" (Gen. 11:1-9)	• Strength in Unity • Origin of Different Languages • The Sovereignty of God • Vaunting Ambition/Human Pride • Crossing Boundaries • Divine Intervention	This Pentateuch narrative begins with the whole earth having one language. As men migrate from the East, they find a plain in the land of Shinar and settle there. They say to one another, "Come, let us make bricks, and burn them thoroughly." They use brick for stone, and bitumen for mortar. Then they say, "Come, let us build ourselves a city, and a tower with its top in the heavens, and let us make a name for ourselves, lest we be scattered abroad upon the face of the whole earth." Then, God comes down to see the city and the tower which the sons of men have decided to build. So, God scatters them abroad from over the face of all the earth, and they cease from building the city. The name of the place became known as Babel because God confused the language of all the earth. (Genesis 11:1-9). This story explains the origin of different languages.	True (A) or False (B)? 1. According to Genesis 10:9-10, Shinar is one of the Babylonian cities founded by King Nimrod. 2. Historians believe that the location of the Tower of Babel was in ancient Mesopotamia on the eastern bank of the Euphrates River. 3. The Tower was a type of stepped pyramid called a *ziggurat* that was common throughout ancient Babylonia. 4. The Tower of Babel (2242 BC) was a post-Flood rebellion against God by Noah's descendants. 5. From their own egotism, pride, and rebellion, the people in the story plan to build a great tower. 6. The tower is offensive to God because it is a monument to the people themselves for their own achievements rather than to honor God. 7. When God sees the intentions of people and the purpose of their efforts, His judgment against humankind comes forth. 8. At the center of the story is humanity's transition from speaking one language and living in one place to speaking different

			languages and living across the world.
			9. In the narrative, the words of God suggest that people pose a threat to the order in the divine realm.
			10. A recurring literary theme in the narrative centers on God requiring humans to respect boundaries.

Study Questions

Directions: Read story about the Tower of Babel (in Genesis 11:1–9) in any Bible translation. If necessary, refer to additional credible online sources. Document your sources for future reference. Write down whether the following statements are (A) CORRECT or (B) INCORRECT about the narrative.

1. In the Tower of Babel narrative, humans unify in their efforts to build a tower without God's approval. (A) CORRECT
2. In this story, humans remain scattered and unproductive. (B) INCORRECT
3. The Babel idea to exercise human autonomy without God's consent is a duplicate of the Eden narrative in Genesis, Chapter 3. (A) CORRECT
4. Based on the Tower of Babel story, humans can become dangerous when using a single unifying principle. (A) CORRECT
5. The story depicts humans as becoming unimaginative and nonproductive in their rebellion against God's boundaries. (B) INCORRECT
6. The Babel narrative shows that when humanity seeks unity apart from God, the result is usually wickedness. (A) CORRECT
7. In this narrative, since humans are created in the image of God, they adhere to what is good instead of evil. (B) INCORRECT
8. Based on the story, when humans create their own definition of good and evil, they become a source of conflicts in their relations with God and with one another. (A) CORRECT
9. The narrative supports the premise that all humans bear the image of God, even when they speak in different languages. (A) CORRECT
10. According to the narrators of this podcast, Nimrod, the son of Cush is the father of the city of Babel. (A) CORRECT
11. *Shinar* is another name for Babylonia. (A) CORRECT
12. The Babel narrative accounts for separate languages that originated in Babylon. (A) CORRECT
13. The narrative relates a misguided attempt at human unity that fails without God's permission. (A) CORRECT
14. Babylon stands for humanity's attempt to *deify* its own cultural heritage and *homogenize* humanity. (A) CORRECT
15. To *deify* something is to make a god of it. (A) CORRECT

16. The people's attempt to *deify* their own culture in the "Tower of Babel" story means that they worshipped their knowledge, beliefs, and constructions. (A) CORRECT
17. A *homogenized* group is uniform in structure and purpose. (A) CORRECT
18. The phrase "Tower of Babel" appears in the Genesis 11 narrative in biblical text. (B) INCORRECT
19. The city Babel received its name from the Hebrew verb that means "to jumble" or "to confuse." (A) CORRECT
20. The event involves the building of a city with a tower made of baked bricks. (A) CORRECT
21. The narrative of the Tower of Babel is an *etiology* or *explanation* of why the world's people speak different languages. (A) CORRECT
22. *Etiologies* are narratives that explain the origin of a custom, ritual, geographical feature, name, or other phenomenon. (A) CORRECT
23. The story of the Tower of Babel explains the origins of the multiplicity of cultures. (A) CORRECT
24. One of the dominant themes in the story is about the tension between God and humanity when humans decide for themselves what is good and bad. (A) CORRECT
25. The theme about man's independence of God appears in the story of Adam and Eve in the Garden of Eden. (A) CORRECT
26. The Tower of Babel narrative centers on the consequences of mankind's excessive pride. (A) CORRECT
27. In this narrative, humans make poor judgment when given autonomy. (A) CORRECT
28. The Tower of Babel story shows how overconfidence can drive people to overstep limits in a way that leads. to their downfall. (A) CORRECT
29. Various Bible scholars believe the tower of Babel episode marks the point in history when God divided the earth into separate continents. (A) CORRECT
30. The Tower of Babel is a metaphor for any project that aggrandizes its builders while doing so also suggests an inevitable fall. (A) CORRECT

Extended Learning Study Questions

(The Tower of Babel: Biblical Archaeology) (https://www.youtube.com/watch?v=ZNc-hyIRrCs)

(Note: Use an online dictionary to define and pronounce unfamiliar terms.)

Based on the video, are the following statements (A) CORRECT of (B) INCORRECT?

1. A *ziggurat* is a massive structure built in ancient Mesopotamia. (A) CORRECT
2. A ziggurat has a *terraced* compound of successively receding stories or levels. (A) CORRECT
3. The Sumerians believed that the gods lived in the temple at the top of the ziggurats. (A) CORRECT
4. Only priests and other highly revered individuals could enter the ziggurats. (A) CORRECT
5. Bible scholars believe that the Tower of Babel was a ziggurat. (A) CORRECT or
6. In ancient Mesopotamia, fired brick technology existed around the end of the fifth millennium BC. (A) CORRECT

7. The Canaanites used fired bricks to structure their buildings. (A) CORRECT
8. The ancient Hebrew Scriptures were correct in relaying how the Mesopotamians built large structures. (A) CORRECT
9. The eleventh chapter of Genesis records the tower as having its tops "in the heavens." (A) CORRECT
10. The writings of ancient Mesopotamia describe a temple with its "head in the heavens." (A) CORRECT

For Reflection:

The 1st-century Jewish writer Flavius Josephus explained the construction of the Tower of Babel as a *hubristic act* against God that was ordered by the arrogant tyrant Nimrod. In literature, a hubristic act is one in which a powerful figure shows conceit or excessive pride and self-confidence. The character usually treats others with insolence and contempt. The individual derives pleasure from using his power to treat others dishonorably. How does the Tower of Babel narrative connect to the definition of "*hubris*"? Mention the consequences of excessive pride. Find credible sources to support your response (5-8 sentences). Edit your writing to correct errors. Post your reflection of the discussion board. Label the post: A Reflection on Hubris in the Tower of Babel Narrative.

A Closing Thought:

"Ignorance and power and pride are a deadly mixture, you know."

— Robert Fulghum

LESSON SIXTEEN
COMMON THEMES AND PATTERNS
IN THE BOOK OF GENESIS

Lesson Overview:

Literature, including biblical literature, share common themes (motifs). A motif is a recurring image or detail that highlights the central ideas in a story through repetition. A literary theme is a universal idea, lesson, or message explored throughout a work. Writers convey themes by using characters, setting, dialogue, plot, or a combination of these elements. In simple narratives, the theme may be a moral or message. In more complex stories, the central theme is usually a more open-ended exploration of a fundamental aspect of society or humanity. This lesson explores the biblical themes of *Good versus Evil, The Power of Love, Loss/Redemption, Courage and Perseverance, and Choices and Consequences* through the actions, thoughts, and speech of different biblical figures.

Key Concepts:

themes, motifs, a universal idea, repetition, internal/external conflict, a moral, open-ended exploration, dialogue, rabbinical tradition, avenge redemption, "kinsman" redemption, monetary redemption, spiritual redemption

Learning Objectives:

- Find a theme or central idea of a text and analyze in detail its development over the course of the text.
- Apply knowledge of language to understand how language functions in different contexts, to make effective choices for meaning or style, and to understand more fully when reading or listening.

Expected Outcomes:

After this lesson, students will be able to:

- define the theme/motif of a literary work.
- find the theme or main idea in biblical text.
- find text evidence that supports theme.
- connect biblical literary themes to Western literature.

Duration: 3-4 hours

Materials:

- Article: "6 Common Themes in Literature"
  (https://youronlinepublicist.com/themes-of-literature/)
- Blog: "Biblical Storytelling Techniques: Repetition& Themes" by Tim Macki
  (https://bibleproject.com/blog/biblical-storytelling-repetition-themes /)
- Article: "The Tree of Knowledge of Good and Evil-The Meaning"
  (https://theexplanation.com/the-tree-of-knowledge-of-good-and-evil-the-meaning/)
- Internet access/e-mail/computer editing ability
- Notebook/paper/pen/dictionary

Procedure:

- Read the assigned articles and blog.
- Respond to the study questions,
- Note key points in the lesson to study for class discussions and future assessments,
- Respond to the reflection in complete sentences.
- Edit your writing to correct errors.
- Post the reflection on the discussion board.
- Use an online dictionary to define and pronounce unfamiliar terms.
- If you have questions or need further clarification on any assignment, e-mail me at wilmaforeman@yahoo.com or visit my website: AIBL.INFO to sign up for the online course.

Study Questions

Directions:

Read the Article: "6 Common Themes in Literature" (https://youronlinepublicist.com/themes-of-literature/). Use online resources to define and pronounce unfamiliar terms.

Based on the assigned reading, indicate if the following statements are (A) TRUE or (B) FALSE.

1. Literary themes can center on controversial ideas that result in conflicts for human beings. (A) TRUE
2. The best literary themes explore all aspects of human nature. (A) TRUE
3. Opposing characters create more opportunities for actions, choices, and dialogue. (A) TRUE
4. Conflicts within narratives enable the characters and readers to deal with themes that affect humans universally. (A) TRUE
5. *Motifs*, recurring images, or ideas, reinforce literary themes. (A) TRUE
6. Expect *repetition* of central ideas in biblical literature. (A) TRUE
7. The *external actions* of characters reveal their inner thoughts. (A) TRUE
8. Writers can use *dialogue* to build upon a dominant theme. (A) TRUE
9. A dialogue is a conversation between two or more characters as a feature of a book, play, or movie. (A) TRUE
10. Literary writers use *symbols* to stand for themes within their works. (A) TRUE

11. In literary works, light and darkness often symbolize good and evil. (A) TRUE
12. The battle between good versus evil is a *universal* idea. (A) TRUE
13. In literature, a story about good triumphing over evil may present two characters directly fighting against each other. (A) TRUE
14. The external actions, along with the dialogue of characters, can reflect the theme of a work. (A) TRUE
15. In literature, love can be a force for good that inspires people to sacrifice themselves for others. (A) TRUE
16. The theme of love may show characters controlled by a toxic force that drives them to mental instability or violence. (A) TRUE
17. In Genesis, Chapter 3, Adam faces the dilemma of obeying God or yielding to the temptation of eating the fruit that his wife offers him. (A) TRUE
18. Jewish tradition has four distinct kinds of redemption: *monetary, avenge, "kinsman,"* and *spiritual.* (A) TRUE
19. Monetary redemption relates to money or currency. (A) TRUE
20. The *Goel*, in *rabbinical tradition*, is a person who charged with the duty of restoring the person's rights and avenging his or her wrongs. (A) TRUE
21. In Jewish and Christian, *spiritual redemption* involves the Holy Spirit mentioned in Genesis 1:2. (A) TRUE
22. Biblical literature sometimes depicts a character's *internal struggle* to do the right thing when faced with temptation. (A) TRUE
23. An internal conflict is *man vs self*, as the character opposes him or herself. (A)
24. Internal conflict occurs when a character's external actions do not match his or her inner desires, and the character struggles to come to terms with the conflict. (A) TRUE
25. Love is one of the most universal themes in literature. (A) TRUE
26. In forbidden love stories, lovers often find themselves moving toward a tragic fate. (A) TRUE
27. The theme of family love can occur in stories about the love between parents and children, or between siblings. (A) TRUE
28. In literature, *unrequited love stories* reflect the pain of loving someone who does not return the affection. (A) TRUE
29. *Redemption narratives* often show the main character restored at the end of the story. (A) TRUE
30. The stories in the Book of Genesis portray God as trying to redeem humanity. (A) TRUE

Study Questions

Directions:

Read the article written by Sam Kneller titled "The Tree of Knowledge of Good and Evil- The Meaning," (https://theexplanation.com/the-tree-of-knowledge-of-good-and-evil-the-meaning/).

Based on the assigned article, indicate the INCORRECT statement in each set.

1. Which of the following statements is INCORRECT?
   a. In Genesis, Chapter 3, humans suffer a severe penalty for their misconduct.
   b. The fruit on the Tree is tempting, or "pleasing to the eye."
   c. The writer suggests that the Tree of the Knowledge of Good and Evil signifies four elements: Knowledge, Good, Evil, and Death.
   d. The main idea of the narrative centers around the consequence of man acting apart from God.
   e. *All the above statements are CORRECT.*

2. Which of the following statements is INCORRECT?
   a. *The Genesis 3 narrative depicts man pursuing goodness according to his self-will. (INCORRECT)*
   b. The "goodness" that Eve perceives is based on her own desires.
   c. The conversation with the Serpent causes her to become utterly rapt with delight in her imagination.
   d. The Serpent's words cause Eve to act hastily and impatiently in her seeking after the knowledge that God has not granted.
   e. All the above statements are CORRECT.

3. Which of the following statements is INCORRECT?
   a. The article suggests that man finds trouble when he pursues progress by his own means rather than by trusting God.
   b. According to the writer, "knowledge" is anything that humans acquire independently as a result of the *"nehama"* and *"spirit" in man*.
   c. The writer asserts that the human mind, *neshama*, and mind power, *ruach,* are the fundamental components of each human being.
   d. The human consciousness is composed of the mind and spirit.
   e. *All the above statements are CORRECT.*

4. Which of the following statements is INCORRECT?
   a. The term *knowledge* encompasses all subjects, fields, and branches of information.
   b. *The ability to discover, reach, and accumulate knowledge is available to all Creation. (INCORRECT)*
   c. *Physical* knowledge relates to knowledge about objects in the world, gained through perceptual properties.
   d. Only humanity has been able to obtain volumes of comprehensive knowledge about themselves and their surroundings.
   e. All the above statements are CORRECT.

5. Which of the following statements is INCORRECT?
   a. The modern period that we live in is *the Information-Age.*

b. Words related to the biblical definition of *knowledge* include *discovery, instruction, sensing, understanding, cunningness, awareness, seeing, wit, acquaintance, and observation.*

c. ***Humans are self-contained and limited in their quest of knowledge. (INCORRECT)***

d. Knowledge is at the core of all thoughts, activities, and decision-making.

e. All the above statements are CORRECT.

6. Which of the following statements is INCORRECT?

a. The expression "good" in Genesis, Chapter 3 is *paradoxical* when related to humans.

b. The term *paradoxical* means that something can be contradictory or conflicting.

c. In Genesis, Chapter 3, the expression *good* appears nine times in the account of the Creation story before the same term shows the Tree of the Knowledge in Genesis, Chapter 3.

d. Ironically, the term *good* is associated with a Tree that leads to death.

e. ***All the above statements are CORRECT.***

7. Which of the following statements is INCORRECT?

a. Words associated with *good* include beautiful, best, better, and bountiful.

b. The writer obviously agrees with the *Strong's Concordance* and the KJV's translations of the word *good*.

c. This article explores the question: "How can *good* lead to death?"

d. The writer proposes that both "believers" and "non-believers" know how to perform charitable deeds for their spiritual deliverance.

e. ***All the above statements are CORRECT.***

8. Which of the following statements is INCORRECT?

a. Doing virtuous (good) deeds causes people to have a peaceful conscience.

b. The writer is not supportive of simply performing "good" deeds.

c. According to the writer, Jesus said that no one is "good."

d. ***Kneller asserts that doing honorable deeds suffices for God to attribute eternal life to humans. (INCORRECT)***

e. All the above statements are CORRECT.

9. Which of the following statements is INCORRECT?

a. ***The writer suggests that supplementary necessities, such as "supplementary charitable deeds," will lead to eternal life. (INCORRECT)***

b. Kneller asserts that knowledge without wisdom is destructive.

c. Independent of God's input, man loses the capability to find good.

d. Man has a natural wisdom or goodness sometimes based on shrewdness and other negative motivators.

e. All the above statements are CORRECT.

10. Which of the following statements is INCORRECT?

a. Sometimes, ulterior motives motivate human "goodness."

b. Selfish ambition can be a reason for someone's "good" deeds.

c. True wisdom is the "goodness" that follows a godly path.

d. One can conclude that the writer believes that wisdom from God always leads one along a path that is not harmful to others.

e. ***All the above statements are CORRECT.***

11. Which of the following statements is INCORRECT?

    a. From reading this passage, one can infer that the humans do not have God's permission to access the knowledge of good and evil before they partake of the fruit from the Tree in Genesis, Chapter 3.

    b. ***From reading this passage, one can infer that to access the knowledge of good and evil is God's plans for humanity. (INCORRECT)***

    c. Genesis 3:22 does not say humans came to know only evil, but they gain knowledge of both "good and evil."

    d. Based on the passage, God assigns such knowledge to the spiritual realm.

    e. All the above statements are CORRECT.

12. Which of the following statements is INCORRECT?

    a. In Genesis, Chapter 3, the serpent is subtle in the way that it manipulates Eve's mind.

    b. *Acts of subtility* necessitate skills in thinking.

    c. A subtle person or being is willing to trick or deceive someone.

    d. The word "subtle" carries a negative connotation.

    e. ***All the above statements are CORRECT.***

13. Which of the following statements is INCORRECT?

    a. ***Based on the definition of "knowledge" in a cognitive sense, God originally created human beings as amoral beings. (INCORRECT)***

    b. In the beginning, humans have knowledge of moral concepts or moral categories.

    c. The writer supposes that man has a knowledge of moral concepts because He bears the image of God.

    d. Possessing moral reasoning is part of the *imago Dei* (image of God).

    e. All the above statements are CORRECT.

14. Which of the following statements is INCORRECT?

    a. The Hebrew word for "know" is *yada*.

    b. The word "knowledge" can refer to both *cognitive knowledge*, as well as *experiential knowledge.*

    c. *Cognitive knowledge* refers to the mental action or process of getting knowledge and understanding through thought, experience, and the senses.

    d. *Experiential knowledge* results from experience, as opposed to *a priori* (before experience) knowledge.

    e. ***All the above statements are CORRECT.***

15. Which of the following statements is INCORRECT?
    a. The writer proposes that Adam and Eve had cognitive knowledge of good and evil before the Fall.
    b. They come to know evil in a new way after the Fall.
    c. ***Before their disobedience, the couple has already experienced the knowledge of evil personally.***
    d. The man and his wife gained experiential knowledge after eating the forbidden fruit.
    e. All the above statements are CORRECT.

16. Which of the following statements is INCORRECT?
    a. Eve's choice to eat from the Tree suggests that she places value upon having knowledge.
    b. The knowledge of good and evil embodies four concepts: Knowledge, Good, Evil, and Death (Genesis 2:15-17 15).
    c. Love is one of the most universal themes in literature.
    d. Adam's love for his wife, Eve, propels him to eat the fruit and disobey God's rule.
    e. ***All the above statements are CORRECT.***

For Reflection:

Directions:

Write a three-five paragraph essay about one of the biblical themes below. Refer to the main points presented in this lesson's assigned readings. Follow writing guidelines at: *Learn to Write a First Class Essay (https://www.researchprospect.com/essay-writing-guidelines/)*. Check your writing to correct errors. Post the essay on the discussion board. Label the post: Literary Themes in the Book of Genesis.

- Good Vs Evil in the Universe
- God's Love for Humanity
- Humankind's Rebellion against God
- God's Judgment and Redemption
- Covenants and Promises
- Order in Creation
- Human Character Flaws
- The Paradox of Good and Evil in Humanity

Note: In completing the writing assignment, refer to the website "Tips for Writing an Effective Essay" at https://www.examples.com/education/tips-for-writing-effective-essay.html. Use your computer's editing capability to correct writing errors. Post your essay on the discussion board. Label the essay: Common Biblical Themes.

A Closing Thought:

"An investment in knowledge pays the best interest."

– Benjamin Franklin

LESSON SEVENTEEN
THE BIBLICAL THEME OF GOOD AND EVIL
IN MILTON'S PARADISE LOST

Lesson Overview:

In Christian tradition, Genesis, Chapter 3 is the biblical account of the Fall of humanity from divine favor, resulting in the general sinful or "fallen" condition of humankind. English poet and intellectual John Milton began his epic poem, *Paradise Lost*, with the purpose of explaining the ways of God to man. The author intended to justify God's response to mankind's disobedience and show how, in the fullness of time, God's actions turn evil to good. Students will examine the biblical themes and other literary elements in Milton's classic epic, *Paradise Lost,* as a poetic rewriting of the Book of Genesis.

Key Concepts:

themes, motifs, a universal idea, allusion, epic poem, preface, ethos, logos, justification, blank verse, elevated language, iambic pentameter, and iambic hexameter, muse, Holy Spirit, heroic brokenness

Learning Objectives:

Students will:

- find a theme or central idea of a text and analyze in detail its development over the course of the text.
- find biblical allusions in Western Literature.
- apply knowledge of language to understand how language functions in different contexts, to make effective choices for meaning or style, and to understand more fully when reading or listening.

Expected Outcomes:

After this lesson, students will be able to:

- define literary terms related to the assigned readings (e.g., theme, motif, epic, myth, muse, apostrophe, allusion, preface, ethos, elevated language, pathos)
- decide the theme or main idea in biblical text.
- recognize biblical allusions in Western literature.
- find text evidence that supports theme.
- defend a position taken in an argumentative essay.
- correct errors in standard English usage.

- share ideas with others via a discussion board.

Duration: 3-4 hours

Materials:

- Video: *Paradise Lost* Introduction
  (https://www.youtube.com/watch?v=Jbfiu-
  ss29s&list=TLPQMzAwMzIwMjK1xGHF9og3nQ&index=3)
- Book 1 of Milton's *Paradise Lost* in Modern English
  (https://www.paradiselostinmodernenglish.com/)
- Lecture: "Analysis of John Milton's *Paradise Lost*" BY NASRULLAH MAMBROL
  (https://literariness.org/2020/07/12/analysis-of-john-miltons-paradise-
  lost/)

- A computer with internet access and editing capabilities
- Paper, pen, and paper/dictionary

Procedure:

- Read Book 1 of *Milton's Paradise Lost in Modern English*
  (https://www.paradiselostinmodernenglish.com/2014/03/BOOK1.html)
- Watch the video *Paradise Lost Introduction*
  (https://www.youtube.com/watch?v=Jbfiu-
  ss29s&list=TLPQMzAwMzIwMjK1xGHF9og3nQ&index=3)

- Answer the study questions.
- Listen to the lecture: "Analysis of John Milton's *Paradise Lost*" BY NASRULLAH MAMBROL.
- Note key details.
- Respond to the study questions.
- Note key points in your notebook.
- Respond to the reflection(s)
- Edit your writing to correct errors.
- Use an online dictionary to define and pronounce unfamiliar terms.
- If you have questions or need further clarification on any assignment, e-mail me at wilmaforeman@yahoo.com or visit my website: AIBL.INFO to sign up for the online course.

Study Questions:

Video: *Paradise Lost Introduction*

(https://www.youtube.com/watch?v=Jbfiu-ss29s&list=TLPQMzAwMzIwMjK1xGHF9og3nQ&index=3)

Directions:

Based on the video, write down whether the following statements are (A) CORRECT or (B) INCORRECT.

1. The blind poet, John Milton was born in London in 1608. (A) CORRECT
2. He lived during the time of a civil war which involved political religious controversies. (A) CORRECT
3. He married Mary Powell who left him months later and did not return for three years. (A) CORRECT
4. Days after his third daughter was born, Milton's wife died. (A) CORRECT
5. A month later, his son died, and he also lost his sight. (A) CORRECT
6. Two years later, he married Catherine Woodcock. (A) CORRECT
7. The death of his first wife and losing his sight heavily influenced Milton's writing. (A) CORRECT
8. Milton took part in highly political controversies. (A) CORRECT
9. Once, he was under house arrest for six months. (A) CORRECT
10. After he married Elizabeth Mitchell, he retired from public life. (A) CORRECT
11. Parts of Milton's *Paradise Lost* are missing. (A) CORRECT
12. Milton's *Paradise Lost* is not meant to replace Hebrew Scriptures. (A) CORRECT
13. In *Paradise Lost*, the main concern of the poet was to justify the ways of God to man. (A) CORRECT
14. Milton aimed to achieve in his writing what Homer, Virgil, and Dante did for Greek, Latin and Italian cultures. (A) CORRECT
15. Homer wrote *The Iliad* and *The Odyssey*. (A) CORRECT
16. Virgil wrote *The Aeneid*, and Dante wrote *The Inferno*.
17. Mary Shelley, C.S. Lewis, and William Blake highly influenced Milton's writings. (A) CORRECT
18. As a writer, Milton pondered question: "If the world was created by a good, just, and loving God, why is there little evidence of goodness and justice in the world?" (A) CORRECT
19. He also asked the questions:" What does it mean for humankind to be created in the image of God, and how does humanity endure in a fallen world?" (A) CORRECT
20. The title of Milton's epic poem, *Paradise Lost,* alludes to the Garden of Eden. (A) CORRECT
21. Milton penned the epic poem *Paradise Lost* in blank verse. (A) CORRECT
22. A poem written in blank verse is unrhymed. (A) CORRECT

23. The people of Milton's time were familiar with poems that rhymed. (A) CORRECT
24. Milton followed the epic writing style set up by Homer. (A) CORRECT
25. He employed the practice of saying his theme and invoking the muse or a higher power to help him throughout the story. (A) CORRECT
26. In *Paradise Lost*, the *muse* alludes to the Holy Spirit. (A) CORRECT
27. Milton drew the concept of *Paradise Lost* from the Book of Genesis and the war in heaven from the Book of Revelation. (A) CORRECT
28. Genesis is the first Book in the Christian and Jewish Bibles. (A) CORRECT
29. Revelation is the last Book in the Christian Bibles. (A) CORRECT
30. Milton incorporated *iambic pentameter* and *iambic hexameter* in this epic. (A) CORRECT
31. He patterned his verses for the poem after Shakespeare's unrhymed iambic pentameter. (A) CORRECT
32. Milton's *Paradise Lost* has a logical literary pattern to it. (A) CORRECT
33. In Milton's writing, God is the omniscient or all-knowing Creator of heaven and earth. (A) CORRECT
34. In *Paradise Lost*, Jesus Christ is God's Son who has not come to earth. (A) CORRECT
35. In the poem, Jesus volunteers to give His life as a ransom for man's sin. (A) CORRECT
36. Milton poem personifies Satan and the fallen angels. (A) CORRECT
37. Satan's capital is hell in the epic poem. (A) CORRECT
38. One of the fallen angels, Beelzebub, is second in command. (A) CORRECT
39. Beelzebub is the last to speak at the devilish council that takes place in Book 1. (A) CORRECT
40. Beelzebub convinces the fallen angels to accept Satan's scheme of revenge toward God by plotting the destruction of humankind. (A) CORRECT

Study Questions

(From Literary Criticism: ANALYSIS OF JOHN MILTON'S *PARADISE LOST*)

(https://literariness.org/2020/07/12/analysis-of-john-miltons-paradise-lost/)

Directions:

Based on the article, write down whether the following statements are (A) CORRECT or (B) INCORRECT?

1. The first twenty-six lines of Book in Milton's *Paradise Lost* introduce the poem's theme-man's first disobedience. (A) CORRECT
2. According to the article, the "fruit" is consequences of eating from the Tree of Knowledge of Good and Evil. (A) CORRECT
3. The expression, "man's disobedience" relates only to male humans. (B) INCORRECT

4. The mention of "Tree" and "fruit" in Milton's poem is an allusion to Genesis, Chapter 3. (A) CORRECT

5. This article proposes that "Death" is the consequence of disobedience. (A) CORRECT

6. Milton personifies "Death" in the poem. (A) CORRECT

7. In the poem's *preface*, Milton calls upon "the heavenly *muse*" to help him narrate the story of man's Fall in the Garden of Eden. (A) CORRECT

8. A *muse* is a term related to Greek and Roman *mythology*. (A) CORRECT

9. In Greek and Roman Literature, the nine goddesses, or *muses*, are the daughters of Zeus and Mnemosyne. (A) CORRECT

10. In ancient Greek and Roman mythology, the *muses* preside over the arts and sciences. (A) CORRECT

11. A *myth* is a traditional story, especially one concerning the early history of a people. (A) CORRECT

12. *Myths* explain natural or social phenomenon (events; happenings). (A) CORRECT

13. Milton uses *apostrophe* in this line: Sing, heavenly Muse, that on the secret top of Oreb, or of Sinai, didst inspire That shepherd, who first taught the chosen seed...." (A) CORRECT

14. The reference, "that Shepherd," is an *allusion* to the biblical Moses. (A) CORRECT

15. An *allusion* is an expression designed to call something to mind without mentioning it explicitly or directly. (A) CORRECT

16. In biblical text, the expression "*the Chosen Seed*" refers to the Hebrews. (A) CORRECT

17. Milton opens the poem by asserting that he will offer a new perspective upon the undeniable truths in the Bible. (A) CORRECT

18. One should expect a writer or speaker to argue effectively against *indisputable truths*. (B) INCORRECT

19. An *epic poem* is an elaborate narrative about an important national event.

20. Based on the article, epic poetry has a "character of incredible stature and courage." (A) CORRECT

21. Usually, the main character in an *epic poem* has fought valorously in a significant battle. (A) CORRECT

22. An *epic poem* is a lengthy narrative that deals with gods or other superhuman forces. (A) CORRECT

23. The epic poem has *elevated language* and style. (A) CORRECT

24. One of the greatest attractions of classical literature is its display of creative and *elevated language.* (A) CORRECT

25. In the first section of Milton's *epic poem*, Satan and his angels have failed in a rebellion against God. (A) CORRECT

26. Milton wrote the first part of the poem in the first person. (A) CORRECT

27. In the first section, Satan tries to lift the mood of Beelzebub, his second in command. (A) CORRECT

28. In lines 27–83 of Book 1 of *Paradise Lost*, Milton introduces the reader to Satan and his 'horrid crew." (A) CORRECT

29. In this *epic poem*, Satan finds himself cast down into a recently constructed hell. (A) CORRECT

30. Based on the article, when Satan says, 'What though the field be lost? /All is not lost' (lines 105–6), he displays a degree of heroic brokenness. (A) CORRECT

31. Satan displays remorse for his rebellion in lines 105-6. (B) INCORRECT

32. The term *"stoicism"* refers to the endurance of pain or hardship without the display of feelings and without complaint. (A) CORRECT

33. The expression "stoicism in defeat" suggests that Satan accepts his present plight without any resistance. (A) CORRECT

34. In line 105-6, Milton uses military images to portray Satan. (A) CORRECT

35. While speaking to his troops, Satan refuses to show any notion of final submission to God. (A) CORRECT

For Reflection (1):

Explain the expression: "heroic brokenness" in relation to Milton's depiction of Satan in *Paradise Lost*. Write five-eight sentences. Edit your writing to correct errors. Post your work on the discussion board. Label the post: A Reflection of the "Heroic Brokenness" of Milton's Satan."

For Reflection (2):

Elaborate on the following question: If a loving, just, and caring God created a good world, why is there little evidence of goodness and justice in the world? Find evidence of the goodness that is still clear in the world. How can you contribute to the world's goodness? (Write five-eight sentences. Employ terminology from this lesson in your response. Edit your writing to correct errors. Post your work on the discussion board. Label the post: A Reflection on the Goodness in God's World?)

A Closing Thought:

"Do not forsake wisdom, and she will protect you; love her, and she will watch over you. The beginning of wisdom is this: Get wisdom, though it cost all you have, get understanding."

(Proverbs 4:6-7)

LESSON EIGHTEEN
A PHILOSOPHICAL CHARACTERIZATION OF GOD
BY THOMAS AQUINAS

Lesson Overview

The question of God's existence is one of the world's great questions The Book of Genesis introduces the concept of God's *aseity*. The expression "aseity" refers to the condition in which a Being exists in and from itself. The 13th century Catholic Dominican priest and a canonized saint, Thomas Aquinas, stood on the assumption that God is self-existent. In this lesson, students will examine the concept of God's aseity, or self-existence, as proposed in Aquinas' *Five Ways*.

Key Concepts: aseity, *Summa Theologica,* Aquinas' *Five Ways,* autonomy, philosophical, premise

Objectives:

Students will:

- show how writers in diverse cultures and ages drew from the Hebrew Bible to present their own ideas and literary works.
- discuss distinct attributes of biblical characters.
- find a theme or central idea of a text and analyze in detail its development over the course of the text.
- find the meaning of words and phrases in the text, including figurative and connotative meanings.
- analyze the cumulative impact of specific word choices on meaning and tone.
- edit writing to correct errors in spelling, punctuation, grammar, and sentence structure.

Learning Outcomes:

By the end of the lesson, students will be able to:

- decide the main idea in written passages of literature accurately and with depth of thought.
- use context clues to find the meanings of words.
- show how writers in diverse cultures and ages drew from the Hebrew Bible to present their own ideas and literary works.
- discuss distinct attributes of biblical characters.
- edit writing to correct errors in spelling, punctuation, grammar, and sentence structure.

Duration: 2-3 hours

Materials

- Article: Aquinas' "Five Proofs for the Existence of God"
(https://open.library.okstate.edu/introphilosophy/chapter/aquinass-five-proofs-for-the-existence-of-god/)

- Video: *Thomas Aquinas asks, 'Is God Self-Evident?' Or Why Bother Proving God's Existence? (Part 1 of 3)*
(*https://video.search.yahoo.com/yhs/search?fr=yhs-pty-pty_forms&ei=UTF-8&hsimp=yhs-pty_forms&hspart=pty&param1=20210503&param2=9766caf4-c28a-44ca-9b60-4d4f19b54a71&param3=forms_%7EUS%7Eappfocus1%7E&param4=d-ccc4-lp0-dsf_forms-cp_12887637018-tst1--bb9%7EChrome%7EChapter+5+%E2%80%93+The+Self-existence+of+God%7EB85D33B8065844214F83D8BF914F5AEC%7EWin10&p=a+vi+deo+by+aquinas+om+God%27s+self+evidence&type=fm_appfocus1_cr-win-%7E2021-19%7E#id=1&vid=2e34e1fa4e0687fa1a37c8f4aa783881&action=click*)

- A computer with internet access and editing capability
- Paper, pen, pencil/dictionary

Procedure:

- View the video: Thomas Aquinas asks, 'Is God Self-Evident?' Or Why Bother Proving God's Existence? (Part 1 of 3).
- Respond to the study questions.
- Note the key points in the lesson for future discussions and assessments.
- Respond to the reflections.
- Edit writing to correct errors.
- Post the reflections on the discussion board.
- Use an online dictionary to define and pronounce unfamiliar terms.
- If you have questions or need further clarification on any assignment, e-mail me at wilmaforeman@yahoo.com or visit my website: AIBL.INFO to sign up for the online course.

Study Questions (Video: *Thomas Aquinas asks, 'Is God Self-Evident?' Or Why Bother Proving God's Existence?*) *(Part 1 of 3)*

Directions:

Based on the video, are the following statements (A) CORRECT or (B) INCORRECT? (Use an online dictionary to define and pronounce unfamiliar terms.)

1. According to the video presentation, the question of God's existence is one of the world's great questions. (A) CORRECT
2. Thomas Aquinas was a 13th century Catholic Dominican priest and a *canonized* saint. (A) CORRECT
3. During his lifetime, Aquinas tried to prove the existence of God as the Creator of the universe. (A) CORRECT

4. Aquinas' argument for God's existence has withstood the criticism of the most ardent atheists. (A) CORRECT
5. His argument did not rely on faith or belief in the Bible, but it rested upon reason alone. (A) CORRECT
6. The work that Aquinas wrote about the existence of God is simply known as *Summa Theologica*. (A) CORRECT
7. The *Summa Theologica* has five proofs for God's existence, also known as Aquinas' *Five Ways*. (A) CORRECT
8. Aquinas believed in God because his reason demanded it, not simply because he wanted God's existence to be true. (A) CORRECT
9. He used both logic and scientific observation to make his deductions. (A) CORRECT
10. An argument that Aquinas had to refute is that religious people tend to believe in something in the absence of evidence. (A) CORRECT
11. One of the characters in this video presentation is Dr. Neil DeGrasse, a scientist. (A) CORRECT
12. Based on the video, scientists do not usually accept repeated observations as true. (B) INCORRECT
13. The presentation supposes that scientists believe in a strong consistency of results. (A) CORRECT
14. For over four hundred years, science has depended upon objective truths. (A) CORRECT
15. Since philosophy is an organized way of learning, it is a science. (A) CORRECT
16. The video proposes that modern science is the only way to discover the truth. (B) INCORRECT
17. Philosophy, based on logical reasoning, has successfully proven different truths about things that science cannot prove. (A) CORRECT
18. Aquinas' proofs of God's existence are *philosophical*-not scientific truths. (A) CORRECT
19. Each of Aquinas' *Five Ways* is a demonstration, or a valid argument, with true *premises*. (A) CORRECT
20. The conclusion of each of the *Five Ways* results from a universally accepted *metaphysical* principle. (A) CORRECT
21. Words associated with the term include *self-originated*, *self-sufficiency*, *independence*, and *autonomy*. (A) CORRECT
22. *Aseity* refers to the belief that God does not depend on any cause other than Himself for His existence or realization. (A) CORRECT
23. Aquinas proposes that God has His own reason for existence. (A) CORRECT
24. Thomas Aquinas, in his *Five Ways*, offers no proof of the *self-existent* God of the Hebrew Bible. (B) INCORRECT
25. Aquinas, in his *Five Ways*, offers scientific proof of the *self-existent* God of the Hebrew Bible. (B) INCORRECT

For Reflection:

Write a paragraph (5-8 sentences) about Aquinas' philosophical ideas in his *Five Ways* concerning God's self-existence. Tell why you support or refute his statements. Employ terminology from this lesson in your response. Use credible sources to complete the assignment. Document sources. Use the MLA or APA formats for documentation. Post your reflection on the discussion board. Label the post: A Reflection on Aquinas' *Five Ways*.

A Closing Thought:

For the LORD gives wisdom; from his mouth come knowledge and understanding. -Proverbs 2:6

LESSON NINETEEN

A PHILOSOPHICAL CHARACTERIZATION OF GOD

BY A.W. TOZER

Overview

Genesis 1:1 opens with four words "*In the beginning, God.*" The biblical text gives no detailed descriptions of God in the Hebrew Bible, nor does it make an argument for God's existence. The assumption is that God is self-existent. In its entirety, the Hebrew Bible portrays God (*Elohim*) as the main character. Genesis, Chapters 1 and 2 portray God as the *omnipotent* (all-powerful), *omniscient* (all-knowing), and *omnipresent* (everywhere at the same time) Creator, speaking into existence the heavens, the earth, and all the earth's creatures out of nothing. In this lesson, students will examine the concept of the self-existence of God from a passage from A.W. Tozer's *The Knowledge of the Holy, Chapter 5*.

Objectives:

Students will:

- show how writers in diverse cultures and ages drew from the Hebrew Bible to present their own ideas and literary works.
- discuss distinct attributes of biblical characters
- decide a theme or central idea of a text and analyze in detail its development over the course of the text.
- decide the meaning of key words and phrases in the text, including figurative and connotative meanings; analyze the cumulative impact of specific word choices on meaning and tone.
- edit writing to correct errors in spelling, punctuation, grammar, and sentence structure.

Learning Outcomes:

By the end of the lesson, students will be able to:

- find the main idea in written passages of literature accurately and with depth of thought.
- use context clues to find the meanings of words.
- show how writers in diverse cultures and ages drew from the Hebrew Bible to present their own ideas and literary works.
- discuss distinct attributes of biblical characters.
- edit writing to correct errors.

Duration: 2-3 hours

Materials:

- A computer with internet access
- A dictionary/paper/pen/notebook
- Video: *The Knowledge of the Holy- A.W Tozer (Ch. 5) Pt 1The Self Existence of God*
https://video.search.yahoo.com/yhs/search;_ylt=AwrDQ3LWmfRh3gQAmjE0nIlQ;_ylu=c2VjA3
NlYXJjaAR2dGlkAw--
;_ylc=X1MDMTM1MTE5NTcwMARfcgMyBGFjdG4DY2xrBGNzcmNwdmlkA1hSQ0dBREV3TG
pHcWVKMHVZSDc0U3dEbE1qWXdNUUFBQUFDUVddqRGQEZnIDeWhzLXB0eS1wdHlfZm9y
bXMEZnIyA3NhLWdwBGdwcmlkA0RMZEgyQm54U0ppaW1FQlAuLlNFcUEEbl9yc2x0AzYwB
G5fc3VnZwMwBG9yaWdpbgN2aWRlby5zZWFyY2gueWFob28uY29tBHBvcwMwBHBxc3RyAw
RwcXN0cmwDBHFzdHJsAzM2BHF1ZXJ5A2Eudy4lMjB0b3plciUyMEdvZCdzJTIwc2VsZi1ldml
kZW5jZQR0X3N0bXADMTY0MzQyMDE4OA--?p=a.w.+tozer+God%27s+self-
evidence&ei=UTF-8&fr2=p%3As%2Cv%3Av%2Cm%3Asa&fr=yhs-pty-
pty_forms&hsimp=yhs-pty_forms&hspart=pty&type=fm_appfocus1_cr-win-%7E2021-
19%7E&param1=20210503&param2=9766caf4-c28a-44ca-9b60-
4d4f19b54a71&param3=forms_%7EUS%7Eappfocus1%7E&param4=d-ccc4-lp0-dsf_forms-
cp_12887637018-tst1--bb9%7EChrome%7EChapter+5+%E2%80%93+The+Self-
existence+of+God%7EB85D33B8065844214F83D8BF914F5AEC%7EWin10#id=1&vid=d22a
4890a44fbee63cff060cf6b46b62&action=view

Procedure:

- View the video: *The Knowledge of the Holy- A.W Tozer* (Ch. 5) Pt 1The Self Existence of God.
- Read the passage below taken from A.W. Tozer's *The Knowledge of the Holy, Chapter 5*.
- Respond to the study questions.
- For future assessments, note the key points in the lesson.
- Use an online dictionary to define and pronounce unfamiliar terms.
- Write a paragraph (5-8 sentences) about Tozer's philosophical ideas about God's self-existence. Tell why you support or refute his statements. Use credible sources to complete the assignment. Edit writing to correct errors. Post the reflection on the discussion board.
- If you have questions or need further clarification on any assignment, e-mail me at wilmaforeman@yahoo.com or visit my website: AIBL.INFO to sign up for the online course.

Reading Comprehension Passage

Directions: Read the passage and respond to the study questions.

(In the fifth chapter of The Knowledge of the Holy, A.W. Tozer discusses the "Self-existence of God.")

> *"The child, by his question," Where did God come from?" is unwittingly acknowledging his creature hood. Already the concept of cause and source and origin is fixed (planted) in his mind. He knows that everything around him came from something other than itself, and he simply extends that concept upward to God. The little philosopher is thinking in true creature-idiom and, allowing for his lack of basic information, he is reasoning correctly. He must be told that God has no origin, and he will find this hard to grasp since it introduces a category with which he is unfamiliar and contradicts the bent toward origin-seeking so deeply ingrained in all intelligent beings, a bent that impels them to probe ever back and back toward undiscovered beginnings.*

> *To think steadily of that to which the idea of origin cannot apply is not easy, if indeed it is possible at all. Just as under certain conditions, a tiny point of light can be seen, not by looking directly at it but by focusing the eyes slightly to one side, so it is with the idea of the Uncreated. When we try to focus our thoughts upon One who is a pure, uncreated being, we may see nothing at all, for He dwelleth in light that no man can approach unto...since all corporeal and sensible images are immeasurably remote from God."*

> *The human mind, being created, has an understandable uneasiness about the Uncreated. We do not find it comfortable to allow for the presence of One who is outside of the circle of our familiar knowledge. We tend to be disquieted by the thought of One who does not account to us for His being, who is responsible to no one, who is self-existent, self-dependent and self-sufficient."*

Study Questions:

Directions: State whether the following statements are (A) CORRECT or (B) INCORRECT about the preceding passage?

1. Tozer implies that children are interested in what causes something to exist. (A) CORRECT
2. The writer seems to object to children asking questions about God. (B) INCORRECT
3. A "bent" is a "tendency" to do something. (A) CORRECT
4. Tozer keeps a harsh tone in discussing the child's questions about the origin of God. (B) INCORRECT
5. Tozer portrays a youngster's questions about God as a natural part of childhood. (A) CORRECT

6. "*The little philosopher*" refers to the youngster who asks the questions about God. (A) CORRECT

7. The expression "thinking in true creature-idiom" allows the boy to speak like a normal child. (A) CORRECT

8. The statement "*...it introduces a category with which he is wholly unfamiliar and contradicts the bent toward origin-seeking so deeply ingrained in all intelligent beings...*" implies that people readily ask questions about God's origin. (B) INCORRECT

9. Tozer indirectly proposes that people avoid the subject of God's origin because the unfamiliarity of the topic makes them uncomfortable. (A) CORRECT

10. The expression, "*...for He dwelleth in light...*," refers to God. (A) CORRECT

11. The writer portrays God as too pure to describe. (A) CORRECT

12. Tozer's statement: "...corporeal and sensible images are immeasurably remote from God" means that material things are far away from God. (A) CORRECT

13. According to Tozer, God is not accountable to humans. (A) CORRECT

14. "One who is pure" refers to the child mentioned in the passage. (B) INCORRECT

15. Tozer implies that God is easy to understand. (B) INCORRECT

16. In the passage, Tozer proposes that the term, *origin,* is a word that can only apply to things created. (A) CORRECT

17. Based on Tozer's premise, when one thinks of anything that has an origin, he or she is not thinking of God. (A) CORRECT

18. Tozer said that God is self-existent, while everything else "was created by *Someone* who was made of none." (A) CORRECT

19. Tozer supposed that whatever exists in the world has a cause for being in existence. (A) CORRECT

20. He proposed that anything of lesser significance cannot produce something greater than itself. (A) CORRECT

For Reflection

Explain the expression: "*…was created by someone who was made of none.*" (5-8 sentences) Justify or refute Tozer's position on the self-existence of God. Use credible sources to support your argument. Use the MLA or APA formats to document sources. Edit writing to correct errors. Post your reflection on the discussion board. Label the post: A Reflection on Tozer's View of the Self-Existence of God.

A Closing Thought:

"*We can never know who or what we are till we know at least something of what God is.*"

-A. W. Tozer

LESSON TWENTY

"THE CREATION" POEM

BY JAMES WELDON JOHNSON

Lesson Overview

James Weldon Johnson, one of the best known African American poets, wrote "The *Creation."* The poem was published in Johnson's poetry collection *The Book of American Negro Poetry* in 1922. In his poem, "*The Creation: A Negro Sermon,"* the poetic style and diction used by Johnson reflect his awareness of African American culture. This Westernized version of the story of Genesis is an indigenous expression of a black sermon. The overall poem is an allusion to the biblical episode of Genesis. An allusion is an expression designed to call something to mind without mentioning it explicitly; an indirect or passing reference. This lesson will explore the literary techniques in Johnson's poem and connect the biblical allusions to the Creation narratives in Genesis, Chapters 1 and 2.

Key Concepts: allusion, stanza, pulpit oratory, alliteration, free verse-, hyperbole, stanza, refrain, repetition, personification, anaphora, rhyming, epistrophe, consonance, synecdoche, simile, situational irony, metonymy, theme, parallelism, figurative versus literal language

Lesson Objectives:

Students will:

- analyze how an author draws on and transforms source material in a specific work (literary works in Western literature with Creation themes/allusions.
- find a theme or central idea of a text and analyze in detail its development over the course of the text.
- decide the meaning of key words and phrases used in the text, including figurative and connotative meanings; analyze the cumulative impact of specific word choices on meaning and tone.
- analyze how an author's choices concerning how to structure a text, order events within it (e.g., parallel plots), and manipulate time (e.g., pacing, flashbacks) create such effects as mystery, tension, or surprise.
- edit writing to correct errors in spelling, grammar, punctuation, and sentence structure.

Learning Objectives

Upon completion of this lesson, students will be able to:

- summarize and analyze the literary details of James Weldon Johnson's poem "The Creation" and compare Johnson's poem to the biblical text (Genesis, Chapters 1 & 2).
- examine how the author of the poem draws from the Bible to create a unique work.
- recognize literary techniques used in writings, including biblical texts.
- edit writing to correct errors in spelling, grammar, punctuation, and sentence structure.

Duration: 2-3 hours

Materials:

- A computer with editing capability
- Internet access
- A notebook/pen/pencil/dictionary
- Different translations of the Hebrew Bible (Biblehub.com) (Assigned readings: Genesis, Chapters 1 & 2)
- A pronunciation dictionary (https://howjsay.com)
- Video: *Genesis 1 - Creation Story - RARE KJV Audio Bible Videos:* *https://www.youtube.com/watch?v=ynbtg6OuZo0*
- An audio version of "The Creation" poem by *Johnson (https://video.search.yahoo.com/yhs/search?fr=yhs-pty-pty_forms&ei=UTF-8&hsimp=yhs-pty_forms&hspart=pty&param1=20210503&param2=9766caf4-c28a-44ca-9b60-4d4f19b54a71&param3=forms_%7EUS%7Eappfocus1%7E&param4=d-ccc4-lp0-dsf_forms-cp_12887637018-tst1--bb9%7EChrome%7Eaudio+version+of+the+creation+by+Johnson%7EB85D33B8065844214F83D8BF914F5AEC%7EWin10&p=audio+version+of+the+creation+by+Johnson&type=fm_appfocus1_cr-win-%7E2021-19%7E#id=1&vid=8cf05f65b8c5d4fa51d321bcfc5fe5cb&action=click)*
- Publication*: Poetry Analysis* (https://poemanalysis.com/james-weldon-johnson/the-creation/#Summary)

Procedure:

- Use a dictionary to pronounce and define the vocabulary terms below.
- Write the definitions in your notebook.
- Practice repeating the words aloud.
- Listen to the audio versions of the selections of Genesis, Chapters 1 & 2 from the Bible, then listen to the audio version of "The Creation" poem by James Weldon Johnson.
- Respond to the study questions.
- Write the key points in your notebook for future assessments.
- Write a reflection on the lesson (5-7 sentences) by sharing at least five of the similarities and differences noted in the poem and the first two chapters of Genesis.
- Label the post: A Reflection on James Weldon Johnson's "The Creation" and the Creation Narratives in Genesis 1 and 2.
- Post your response on the discussion board.

- If you have questions or need further clarification on any assignment, e-mail me at wilmaforeman@yahoo.com or visit my website: AIBL.INFO to sign up for the online course.

Understanding Common Literary Terms

Directions: Use a dictionary to pronounce and define the literary terms below. Write the words and definitions in your notebook to study for future assessments. Find examples of each term. Post your findings to the discussion board.

1. Stanza-
2. Repetition-
3. Personification-
4. Anaphora-
5. Rhyming-
6. Epistrophe-
7. Consonance-
8. Synecdoche-
9. Simile-
10. Situational Irony-
11. Chiasm-
12. Metaphor-
13. Onomatopoeia-

Study Questions

Directions:

View the video poem analysis of Johnson's "The Creation" at https://poemanalysis.com/james-weldon-johnson/the-creation/).

Based on the video presentation, state whether the following statements are (A) CORRECT or (B) INCORRECT.

1. Johnson uses multiple literary devices in this poem to make the story of the creation more appealing to the readers. (A) CORRECT
2. In the first *stanza*, the poet uses *alliteration* in the phrase, "make me." (A) CORRECT
3. A *stanza* is a group of lines forming the basic recurring metrical unit in a poem, a verse. (A) CORRECT
4. *Hyperbole* is the use of exaggeration for the effect. (A) CORRECT
5. *Hyperbole* is an overstatement of something. (A) CORRECT
6. The literary device *hyperbole* amplifies or embellishes facts.
7. The second stanza of Johnson's "The Creation" contains a *hyperbole* in the expression "blacker than a hundred midnights." (A) CORRECT
8. "Darkness covered everything" is an example of *personification.* (A) CORRECT

9. In the third *stanza*, the poet uses the literary device *anaphora*, a *rhetorical device* that features the repetition of a word or phrase at the beginning of *successive* sentences, phrases, or clauses. (A) CORRECT

10. Johnson uses *anaphora* to depict the Creation as a continuing process. (A) CORRECT

11. The poet uses a *metaphor* in the expression "a shining ball" to describe the moon. (A) CORRECT

12. *Epistrophe* is the repetition of a word at the end of *successive clauses* or sentences. (A) CORRECT

13. Johnson uses *epistrophe* in the following lines: "And the waters above the earth came down, / The cooling waters came down." (A) CORRECT

14. *Consonance* is a figure of speech in which the same consonant sound repeats within a group of words. (A) CORRECT

15. Johnson uses *consonance* in the phrase, "green grass sprouted." (A) CORRECT

16. In the ninth *stanza*, the poem is *replete* with *repetition*s. (A) CORRECT

17. *Irony* is a literary device or event in which the way things seem to be is in fact quite different from how they are. (A) CORRECT

18. In the last line, "And God said: I'm lonely still," the poet uses *situational irony*. (A) CORRECT

19. *Simile* involves the comparison of one thing with another thing of a different kind, used to (A) CORRECT make a description more emphatic or vivid.

20. The line, "Like a mammy bending over her baby" is an example of *simile*. (A) CORRECT

21. The literary expressions, *simile* and *metaphor,* involve comparisons. (A) CORRECT

22. *Metaphor* is an indirect comparison without using the words "like" or "as." (A) CORRECT

23. *Simile* is a direct comparison using the words "like" or "as." (A) CORRECT

24. A *synecdoche* is a figure of speech in which a term for a part of something refers to the whole of something or vice versa. (A) CORRECT

25. The use of a *synecdoche* is in the phrase, "lump of clay." (A) CORRECT

26. The use of is a *simile* is in the line, "Like a mammy bending over her baby." (A) CORRECT

27. Johnson's poem is an allusion to the biblical episode of the Genesis Creation narratives. (A) CORRECT

28. Since this poem is an oratory sermon, the poet utters "amen" twice at the end. (A) CORRECT

29. The expression "*amen*" means "*so be it*" and can express agreement or assent. (A) CORRECT

30. The use of "*amen*" in Johnson's poem is like the use of the expression "*it was good*" in the biblical Creation narratives. (A) CORRECT

Extended Learning

Directions: Complete the assignment as follows:

- Read the article: "The Breath of Life" by David Demick (*https://answersingenesis.org/human-body/the-breath-of-life/*).
- Read *Ellicott's Commentary for English Readers*, Genesis, Chapter 2 (*https://bibleapps.com/ellicott/genesis/2.htm*)
- Consider the last stanza of Johnson's poem. The poet focuses on how God blows the "breath of life" into the "lump of clay," and man becomes "a living soul." Compare this stanza to Genesis 2:7 (KJV) *"And the LORD God formed man of the dust of the ground and breathed into his nostrils the breath of life; and man became a living soul."* What imagery comes into your mind from the words spoken in this verse? Share your thoughts on the discussion board.

For Reflection:

Directions:

- Read the article, "The Breath of Life" by David Demick.
- Point out three facts that the writer makes about the significance of breathing.
- Compare the article to Genesis, Chapter 3 in any other Bible commentary. (Write 3-5 paragraphs.)
- Document sources by using the MLA or APA formats.
- Edit your writing to correct errors.
- Post the reflection to the discussion board or send it to the instructor by email.
- Label the paper: A Reflection on "The Breath of Life."
- Follow writing guidelines at: *Learn to Write a First Class Essay* (*https://www.researchprospect.com/essay-writing-guidelines/*).

A Closing Thought:

"If we don't have a proper fundamental moral background, we will finally end up with a totalitarian government which does not believe in rights for anybody except the State!"

– Harry Truman, Thirty third President

LESSON TWENTY-ONE

BIBLICAL CHARACTERIZATION
IN MILTON'S PARADISE LOST

Lesson Overview:

One of the most engaging ways to study the Hebrew Scriptures is through biblical characterization. For centuries, the Hebrew Bible has inspired great writers, such as the English John Milton who used the Bible to compose and publish his masterpiece, *Paradise Lost* (1667). The main ideas of the epic poem focus on the sovereignty of God, the struggle between good and evil, and humans' proclivity to sin with the later need for redemption. Using literary devices and colorful characterization, Milton recreates the biblical narratives of the Creation, the fall of Adam and Eve, and their subsequent expulsion from the Garden of Eden. One of the most interesting features of the poem is Milton's portrayal of Satan, the arch enemy of God. Different from the biblical depiction of the serpent in the Garden of Eden, however, Satan in *Paradise Lost* has extraordinary power and intellect. Despite his defeat after rebelling against God, he is still self-assertive, hateful, and revengeful. From the speeches of Satan in Milton's *Paradise Lost*, Book 1, the reader sees the epitome of evil, or the *antithesis* of all that is good. Students will analyze Milton's portrayal of Satan based on what the character says, by what he does, and how he relates to other characters in the poem.

Key Concepts: muse, chosen seed, personification, the Serpent, antithesis, characterization, apostrophe, oratory, rhetoric, synecdoche, fall from grace, themes, motifs, a universal idea, allusion, epic poem, preface, ethos, logos, justification, blank verse, elevated language, irony, iambic pentameter, and iambic hexameter

Learning Objectives:

- Decide a theme or central idea of a text and analyze in detail its development over the course of the text.
- Apply knowledge of language to understand how language functions in different contexts, to make effective choices for meaning or style, and to understand more fully when reading or listening.

Expected Outcomes:

After this lesson, students will be able to:

- Define literary terms related to the assigned readings (e.g., apostrophe, simile, personification, synecdoche, oratory skills, and antithesis).
- Find the theme or main idea in biblical text.
- Find text evidence that supports theme.
- Defend a position taken in an argumentative essay.

- Correct errors in standard English usage.
- Share ideas with others via a discussion board.

Duration: 4-5 hours

Materials:

- Book: *Paradise Lost in Modern English (https://www.paradiselostinmodernenglish.com/)*
- Book: "Satan's Speeches in *Paradise Lost* Book-I" *(https://wandofknowledge.com/speeches-of-satan-in-book-i-of-paradise-lost/)*.
- Video: *Paradise Lost Introduction (https://www.youtube.com/watch?v=Jbfiu-ss29s&list=TLPQMzAwMzIwMjK1xGHF9og3nQ&index=3)*
- Lecture: "Analysis of John Milton's Paradise Lost" BY NASRULLAH MAMBROL *(https://literariness.org/2020/07/12/analysis-of-john-miltons-paradise-lost/)*
- *Literary Criticism: ANALYSIS OF JOHN MILTON'S PARADISE LOST) (https://literariness.org/2020/07/12/analysis-of-john-miltons-paradise-lost/)*
- A computer with internet access and editing capabilities
- Paper, pen, and paper/dictionary

Procedure:

- Use an online dictionary to define and pronounce unfamiliar terms.
- Read Book 1, lines 1-90 of *Paradise Lost* in Modern English (https:/k /www.paradiselostinmodernenglish.com/)
- Respond to the study questions.
- Read Satan's speeches *in Paradise Lost* Book-I" (https://wandofknowledge.com/speeches-of-satan-in-book-i-of-paradise-lost/).
- Respond to the study questions.
- Respond to the reflection.
- If you have questions or need further clarification on any assignment, e-mail me at wilmaforeman@yahoo.com or visit my website: AIBL.INFO to sign up for the online course.

Study Questions

(from *Paradise Lost in Modern English*) (https://www.paradiselostinmodernenglish.com/)

Directions: Respond to the questions that follow.

Book 1   Lines 1-5
1. Does Milton mention the type of fruit that was eaten in the Garden of Eden? (Yes, or No?)   2. What is the "forbidden tree" to which Milton alludes?   3. Define "woe."   4. What were the consequences of eating the "forbidden fruit"?   5. Explain the expression, "…till one Greater Man Restore us…"

Book 1   Lines 6-10
6. What does Milton want from the *muse*?   7. Why does Milton mention Moses?   8. Why does Milton mention *Sinai*?   9. What is the meaning of the "*chosen seed*"?   10. How is *synecdoche* used in the expression "*chosen seed*"?

Book 1   Lines 6-20
11. What is an "oracle"?   12. Which word means "from here; from there"?   13. Which word means "ask for help or support"?   14. How is the literary device, *apostrophe* used in these words?   15. True or False? Milton wants to write like Greek philosophers,

Book 1   Lines 20-25
16. How is simile used in Milton's mention of the dove?   17. Why does Milton say, "…Thou from the first Wast present…"?   18. What did the Spirit do to darkness?   19. Explain "…what in me is dark Illumine…"   20. How is the literary technique *antithesis* used in these lines?

Book 1   Lines 26-34
21. Why does Milton want to write this epic?   22. Who were "Favoured of Heaven"?   23. Explain the expression: "…transgress His will…"   24. What was the "foul revolt":   25. Who was the "infernal Serpent"?

Book 1   Lines 35-45
26. Why did the Serpent deceive Eve?   27. What happened to the Serpent and his angels because of his pride?

28. What is an "entourage"?	
29. What was Satan's "blind ambition"?	
30. Explain the expression, "with vain expression."	
Book 1	**Lines 35-65**
31. Explain the expression, "*fall from grace.*"	
32. What does the "Almighty Power" do to the Serpent?	
33. What is the Serpent's condition in Hell?	
34. How is God "omnipotent"?	
35. Explain the expression "confounded though immortal."	
Book 1	**Lines 61-90**
36. Explain "darkness visible."	
37. Contrast heaven and hell.	
38. To whom does Satan speak first?	
39. Explain the expression, "…but Oh how fallen!"	
40. Why does Satan say, "…now misery hath joined in equal ruin…"?	

Study Questions

Directions (Assignment 2):

Read "Satan's Speeches in *Paradise Lost* Book-I" *(https://wandofknowledge.com/speeches-of-satan-in-book-i-of-paradise-lost/).*

Indicate whether the following statements are (A) TRUE or (B) FALSE?

1. Based on this analysis of Satan in Book-I in Milton's *Paradise Lost*, Satan is a type of political leader.
2. The character has political *oratory* skills.
3. Satan's speeches are the key to his character.
4. According to the article, his speaking skills surpass the best of the speeches of the ancient Romans.
5. *Rhetoric* is the art of effective or persuasive speaking or writing.
6. The use of figurative language is found in rhetoric.
7. In Milton's epic, *Paradise Lost*, Satan is the leader of the rebel-angels in Heaven.
8. According to the writer, Milton's Satan is the *uncrowned monarch* of Hell.
9. The statement that the f*allen* angels no longer have access to the "happy fields, where joy forever dwells" means that the fallen angels can never visit earth again.
10. Satan does not have to worry about keeping the loyalty of the fallen angels.
11. In the poem, Satan uses his high-pitched oratory skills to win the loyalty of the other fallen angels.
12. The expression, "*pathetic grandeur*" implies that one may receive admiration even when he is in a *pitiful* state.

13. The character, Satan, has a *lofty* position although he is in a state of sufferance and ruined splendor.
14. All the rebel angels find themselves in a fallen *stupor*.
15. A stupor is a state of near-unconsciousness or insensibility.
16. Beelzebub is Satan's first lieutenant.
17. Satan must find out if his compeer has changed his feelings.
18. Satan's first oration reveals him to be both a defiant rebel and a great leader.
19. With a fearless attitude, he encourages and sympathizes with his followers.
20. Throughout the speech, he refuses to admit the might of God.
21. Satan has nothing but scorn for God whom he believes has dismantled his merits in the eyes of his followers.
22. He defiantly refers to himself as the "tyrant of Heaven."
23. Satan's "high disdain" and "sense of injured merit" have overtones of the ridiculous.
24. His argument against God seems weak and childish.
25. He argues that a single victory does not permanently ensure God's victory.
26. Satan suggests that for the present, he and his angels may have lost the field, but that does not mean that they have lost the entire war.
27. He asserts that the "will" is unconquerable.
28. In the context of this writing, willpower is firmness of purpose.
29. He intends to study ways to gain the favor of God.
30. Satan's intention is to fight God outright or to use guile.
31. *Guile* is a type of deceit.
32. In the second speech, Satan proposes that if God tries to turn evil into good, the fallen angels must foil His attempts and turn all good to evil.
33. He proposes that all the fallen angels should reassemble and consult about the future overthrow of their enemy, God.
34. Satan plans to recover from their loss in heaven.
35. In his speech, Satan shows a high degree of self-confidence and boldness.
36. In the third speech, Satan wins over Beelzebub and puts new courage in him.
37. To avoid the presence of God, Satan welcomes the dismal horrors of the infernal world.
38. For him, hell is as good a place as heaven.
39. Satan shuns the brightness of God's goodness.
40. His mind stays unchanged by place or time.
41. When he says that it is "better to reign in Hell than serve in Heaven," he is submissive to the will of God.
42. "Farthest from Him is best" is a statement of open resistance and of moral detachment from God.
43. "Receive thy new Possessor" is characteristic of the Satanic mind to replace God's lordship.
44. The speeches of Satan are ironic in that he himself is guilty of the accusations that he voices against God.
45. The *melodramatic* line "Better to reign in Hell than serve in Heaven" shows a mixture of pride and spite.
46. In the fourth speech, Satan directly touches the fallen angels' ego by calling them, "Princes, Potentates, Warriors, the Flower of Heaven."
47. "*Potentates*" are rulers, especially those in *autocratic* positions.

48. He urges them to "wake, arise or be forever fallen."
49. In his portrayal of Satan, Milton uses sarcasm to display Satan's hatred and defiance toward God.
50. Satan's oratory skills are so strong that he arouses the fallen angels from their stupor.

For Reflection:

Explain the expression "heroic brokenness" in relation to Milton's depiction of Satan in *Paradise Lost*. (Write five-eight sentences.) Edit your writing to correct errors. Post your work on the discussion board. Label the post: A Reflection of the "Heroic Brokenness" of Milton's Satan."

A Closing Thought:

"Do not forsake wisdom, and she will protect you; love her, and she will watch over you. The beginning of wisdom is this: Get wisdom, though it cost all you have, get understanding."

(Proverbs 4:6-7)

LESSON TWENTY-TWO
DIDACTIC ETHICAL VIEWS OF GENESIS 1:27
(IN JEWISH TRADITION)

Lesson Overview:

Indirectly and directly, literature teaches ethics. This lesson allows students to read and analyze excerpts of Jewish classical and modern ethical literature related to Genesis 1:27. The original writings are in book form and instruct the Jews in religious and moral behavior. Methodically structured, the components of each chapter or section explain the ideal ways of living and show how to achieve moral virtue based on the author's systematic categories. Exposure to didactic ethics writings allows students to understand their own values and beliefs while considering the experiences, desires, and values of others in a global society. Students will examine ethical principles found in classical and modern Jewish literature related to Genesis 1:27.

Key Concepts: Torah, sages, ethics, decalogue, prohibitions, justice, compassion, free will, repentance, atonement

Learning Objectives:

The goals of the lesson are to:

- increase ethical sensitivity through the study of biblical literature.
- raise ethical issues and allow students to explore answers/solutions that reflect higher order thinking and sound reasoning.
- give students opportunities to defend her own recommendations/ positions.

Expected Learning Outcomes:

At the end of the lesson, students will be able to:

- share a dialogue with people of varying views or with those who see the world differently.
- allow room for multiple truths and take part in discussions that can help them learn and grow.

Duration: 2-4 hours

Materials:

- paper/pen/dictionary
- a computer with editing capability
- Excerpts: _Torah Book & Portion_, _Book of Genesis_, _Bereishit (Genesis 1:1-6:8)_, _Source Book Keys_, _TELVOL1_

(https://mussaria.org/Excerpt-Browser/genesis-chapter-1-verse-27-image-gen125-jewish-tradition-places-strong-emphasis-on)

- **Booklet:** THE ETHICAL TORAH: THE SAGES SPEAK No. 2 in series "LET US MAKE MAN IN OUR IMAGE" Genesis 1:26-28

(https://mussaria.org/Portals/0/adam/Content/__np4hAFsk6Uot7SlMebbQ/Link/eBooklet.hash2.pdf)

Procedure:

- Read the following passages and respond to the study questions.
- Use an online dictionary to define and pronounce unfamiliar terms.
- Write a response to the reflection questions, edit writing to correct errors, and post the reflections on the discussion board.
- If you have questions or need further clarification on any assignment, e-mail me at wilmaforeman@yahoo.com or visit my website: AIBL.INFO to sign up for the online course.

Study Questions:

Passage One

Jewish ethicists searching for universal norms within Jewish tradition will be drawn first to that body of norms specifically designated as binding upon all people… Among these laws one stands out as pertinent to issues of medical ethics, namely the prohibition against bloodshed. The rationale for this prohibition is twofold. First, it represents a fundamental requirement for a stable society. Natural tendencies toward hostility and violence must be curbed to permit the flourishing of human relationships and social institutions. Second, the prohibition against murder follows from the view that all human beings are created in God's image. As [Genesis Rabbah 34:14] put[s] it, "whoever sheds blood it is as if he diminished the Divine likeness because…"in the image of God he made man.'
PASTIMP 210-11

Based on the passage above, are the following statements (A) CORRECT or (B) INCORRECT?

1. An *ethicist* is one who specializes in moral principles. (A) CORRECT
2. *Social norms* play a key role in motivating human cooperation. (A) CORRECT
3. What members of a society judge as correct can predict positive social behavior of people. (A) CORRECT
4. Positive social behavior depends on normative information across cultures. (A) CORRECT

5. Saving human lives is an essential part of medical ethics. (A) CORRECT

6. Protecting the lives of people adds stability to the world. (A) CORRECT

7. Based on the passage, by nature, humans are hostile and violent. (A) CORRECT

8. Healthy relationships among humans strengthen a society. (A) CORRECT

9. Shedding human blood lessens the significance of the divinity assigned to humans. (A) CORRECT

10. According to the passage, humans have God-like qualities, and likening humankind to God is not irrelevant. (A) CORRECT

Passage Two

Tradition teaches that God's original intention was to create the world solely with the attribute of judgment. We can still see the results of this intention because the fundamental laws of nature are themselves immutable. If you put your hand in fire, it will be burned, no matter what you might say or think. A world created according to the quality of judgment requires that everything be a specific way, with no deviation whatever. But we are told that God realized that the world (and especially people) could not survive if the world were set up so that strict justice was exacted instantly for every error or wrongdoing. A world run only according to the principle of stern justice would leave no room for free will, learning, change, or growth, because mechanical rules would meet out the results instantly and without variation. To forestall such an insufferable rigidity, God included the attributes of compassion as an essential feature of creation, right alongside judgment. ... God reflected, "If I create the world with only the attribute of compassion, no one will be concerned for the consequences of their actions, and people will feel impunity to act badly. But if I create the world with strict judgment alone, how could the world endure? It would shatter from the harshness of justice. So, I will create it with both justice and compassion, and it will endure." Rashi. (*Genesis Rabbah 12:15*. MORINIS 77-78)

Study Questions:

1. The writer proposes that God created the world to exercise His judgment. (B) INCORRECT

2. According to the passage, the nature of God's laws is unchangeable. (A) CORRECT

3. God exacts judgment so that no one will ever break His laws. (B) INCORRECT

4. Based on the passage, humanity cannot survive strictly by God's judgment. (A) CORRECT

5. The writer proposed that extremely stern discipline will erase man's free will, learning, change, and growth. (A) CORRECT

6. God completely exchanged unbearable judgment for compassion toward humanity. (A) CORRECT

7. God's judgment and compassion are essential parts of His Creation. (A) CORRECT

8. Humans will feel exempted or free from punishment, harm, or loss if God withdraws all judgment. (A) CORRECT
9. Based on the passage, God chooses strict judgment over mercy. (B) INCORRECT
10. Justice tempered with mercy improves the hardness of the punishment. (A) CORRECT

Passage Three

The Rabbis teach that God created repentance even before He created the world. God knew that He would endow human beings with free will, which they would sometimes misuse. Thus, God needed to provide humankind with a way to atone for and correct wrongful behavior. Without a process such as teshuva (repentance), even good people would be overwhelmed by guilt, both toward God, Whose laws they had broken, and toward those whom they had hurt. TELVOL 1:151

Study Questions

Are the following statements (A) CORRECT or (B) INCORRECT?

1. The action of repenting is showing sincere regret or remorse for a wrongdoing. (A) CORRECT
2. Based on the passage, from the beginning, God knew that He would provide humans with a free will that they would misuse. (A) CORRECT
3. The passage suggests that God knew that when humans misuse their free will, He would have to make amends or reparation for their actions. (A) CORRECT
4. When one makes amends, he or she compensates for a misdeed. (A) CORRECT
5. According to the passage, God supported humans' atonement by allowing repentance. (A) CORRECT

Extended Learning Study Questions:

(THE *ETHICAL TORAH: THE SAGES SPEAK No. 2 in series "LET US MAKE MAN IN OUR IMAGE" Genesis 1:26-28.*
(https://mussaria.org/Portals/0/adam/Content/__np4hAFsk6Uot7SlMebbQ/Link/eBooklet .hash2.pdf)

Based on the assigned reading, are the following statements (A) TRUE or (B) FALSE?

1. The foundational ethical tradition of Judaism rests on the sacredness of each individual human being. (A) TRUE
2. In Judaism, humans, formed in the image of God, have a divine spirit. (A) TRUE
3. Jews believe that humanity is the crown of God's creation. (A) TRUE
4. In the Jewish culture, the person who refrains from wrongdoing and tries to do what is right is righteous. (A) TRUE
5. To Jews, man is "in the image of G-d" not in his outward form, but by how he behaves. (A) TRUE

6. Jews believe that human beings should be creative like the God of Creation. (A) TRUE
7. To Jews, humanity should complete God's unfinished artistic masterpiece-the human person. (A) TRUE
8. In Jewish culture, ethics is a way in which one creates life as a work of art. (A) TRUE
9. Jews believe that there is a single standard of ethics to measure the correctness of human conduct. (B) FALSE
10. Human values derive from religion, social customs, and conventions. (A) TRUE
11. Both economic and geographic needs shape the values of humans. (A) TRUE
12. To Jews, perfection is an abstract term subject to development and change. (A) TRUE
13. The Jewish culture has a uniform standard of ethics. (A) TRUE
14. Major religions have accepted the Jewish Decalogue, or the Ten Commandments, as the foundation of morality. (A) TRUE
15. Because of the Decalogue, Jewish, Christian, and Islamic ethics are the same. (B) FALSE
16. Jewish ethics are primarily based on the Hebrew Scriptures. (A) TRUE
17. Genesis 1:27 predetermines the structure and evolvement of Jewish culture. (A) TRUE
18. In Jewish tradition, Genesis 1:27 heightens the degree of concern and respect that humans must show in relation to his fellowman. (A) TRUE
19. Genesis 1:27 imposes on man the duty to express his godliness by imitating the divine qualities attributed to God in the Scriptures. (A) TRUE
20. In Jewish tradition, Genesis 1:27 marks a radical departure from pagan theology. (A) TRUE
21. In literature, pagan gods behave like humans in that they engage in warfare, pursue their lusts, and commit murder. (A) TRUE
22. In Jewish thought, the expression, "in God's image" means that human beings are like God in that they know good from evil. (A) TRUE
23. The Torah teaches that humanity's ability to make moral judgments enables a person to judge one's own actions and those of others. (A) TRUE
24. Based on Genesis 1:27, the Torah's acknowledges that humans can love, just as God does. (A) TRUE
25. Jews believe that to insult another person is to affront God. (A) TRUE
26. In Jewish tradition, people must treat others with respect by recognizing everyone's uniqueness and divine worth. (A) TRUE
27. Jewish ethics teach humans not to recoil from a deformed or incapacitated person, but to embrace the divine image within the person. (A) TRUE
28. The Torah demands that the executed body of a person for a capital crime be removed from the place of hanging by morning out of respect for the divine image. (A) TRUE
29. To Jews, the ability to think and speak is a divine attribution. (A) TRUE
30. In Jewish thought, humans resemble God, as well as the animals below them. (A) TRUE
31. Jews believe in the biblical account that God created humanity in His divine image and in the image of Adam. (A) TRUE
32. In Jewish tradition, killing one person is also killing all his or her potential descendants. (A) TRUE

33. To Jews, someone who saves an individual "saves an entire world." (A) TRUE
34. Jews believe that the fact that every person is unique imparts to all humans immense value. (A) TRUE
35. Thinking that the world exists for one's own sake can produce arrogance. (A) TRUE

For Reflection:

Explain the statement "Killing one person is also killing all his potential descendants." (Write five-eight sentences. Edit your writing to correct errors. Post the reflection on the discussion board. Label the post: The Value of Human Life.)

A Closing Thought:

"Ethics, too, are nothing but reverence for life. That is what gives me the fundamental principle of morality, namely, that good consists in maintaining, promoting, and enhancing life, and that destroying, injuring, and limiting life are evil. "

–Albert Schweitzer

LESSON TWENTY-THREE
THE GENESIS METANARRATIVE
(CHAPTERS ONE THROUGH ELEVEN)

Beginning with the Creation narratives, the Book of Genesis gives an account of how the universe came into existence. The early chapters also focus on humanity's proliferation of rebellion against God, their Creator. After gaining the knowledge of good and evil, humans live in disharmony with God and among themselves. The humans' proclivity to turn toward evil soon leads humans to a steady decline from their original state of goodness. Human disobedience eventually leads to widespread conflict, violence, and death throughout the earth. The themes of human rebellion against a faithful God, consequential judgment, human remorse, and God's grace unify the narratives in Genesis, Chapters 1-11. This lesson gives students more insight into the underlying plots and messages conveyed in part one of the Genesis stories that come together to form an overarching, well-unified metanarrative.

Key Concepts: historical narratives, primeval, human proclivities, plots, theme, rebellion, disharmony, divine judgment, grace, repentance, metanarrative

Lesson Objectives:

Students will:

- use online Bible study tools to access, read, interpret, and explain information.
- recognize and define literary terms (themes/plots) common in biblical text.
- use information in biblical resources to support analysis, reflection(s), and research.
- make inferences and draw conclusions based on explicit and implied information using evidence from the text as support.
- state the writer's intended purpose for writing the text.
- synthesize information from various sources.
- draw conclusions and make inferences from primary and secondary sources.
- share information about assigned biblical themes logically and accurately.

Expected Learning Objectives

At the end of this lesson, students will:

- recognize and understand common themes in biblical literature.
- discuss literary elements found in biblical text, including common unifying themes (metanarratives).
- edit writing to correct errors.

Duration: 3-4 hours

Materials:

- paper/pen/dictionary
- a computer with editing capability
- article: *"The Four Chapter Gospel: The Grand Metanarrative Told by the Bible"* by Hugh Whelchel (https://tifwe.org/the-four-chapter-gospel-the-grand-metanarrative-told-by-the-bible/)
- e-book: *Understanding the Hebrew Bible as a Metanarrative* by Wilma J. Brown-Foreman, Ed.S. (https://anyflip.com/jnqfx/zbff/basic)

Procedure:

- Read the passages that follow and respond to the study questions.
- Use an online dictionary to pronounce and define unfamiliar terms.
- Respond to the reflection, correct writing errors, and post the reflection(s) on the discussion board.
- If you have questions or need further clarification on any assignment, e-mail me at wilmaforeman@yahoo.com or visit my website: AIBL.INFO to sign up for the online course.

Passage One

Directions:

Read the excerpt from the *Four Chapter Gospel: The Grand Metanarrative Told by the* Bible by Hugh Whelchel. Respond to the study questions.

The Book of Genesis opens with the account of creation, the start of the most encompassing story that will ever be told. One of the reasons many Christians do not fully comprehend the biblical concepts of work, calling, and vocation is because we have lost the vision of the grand metanarrative told by the Bible. This metanarrative includes Creation, Fall, Redemption, and Restoration. It is called the Four-Chapter Gospel…

The story of the Bible clearly presents one over-arching narrative in the story that starts in the garden and ends in a City of God, the New Jerusalem. The New Testament tells us this story reaches its climax in the life, death, and resurrection of Jesus…The Bible begins with the creation of all things and ends with the renewal of all things, and in between it offers an interpretation of the meaning of all history. In The New Testament and the People of God, N.T. Wright says that the divine drama told in Scripture "offers a story which is the story of the whole world. It is public truth." It is the only story that explains the way things were (Creation), the way things are (Fall), the way things could be (Redemption) and the way things will be (Restoration). The biblical metanarrative makes a comprehensive claim on all humanity, calling each one of us to find our place in his story.

Study Questions:

Are the following statements (A) TRUE or (B) FALSE about the preceding passage?

1. The writer proposes that the Hebrew Bible begins with an overarching story about creation. (A) TRUE
2. He states that many Christians do not understand the metanarrative concept of the Hebrew Scriptures. (A) TRUE
3. A *metanarrative* is a narrative about narratives of historical meaning, experience, or knowledge, which offers the anticipated completion of a primary idea. (A) TRUE
4. A metanarrative is a grand story that surrounds smaller narratives. (A) TRUE
5. The statement, "*The Bible begins with the creation of all things and ends with the renewal of all things*" implies that the beginning of the Bible is comparable to the end. (A) TRUE
6. The author mentions N.T. Wright, another writer, who compares the Bible to a drama about the entire world. (A) TRUE
7. The expression, "*It is public truth*" means that truth is the same for everyone. (A) TRUE
8. Based on this article, the biblical metanarrative has four components. (A) TRUE
9. The writer proposes that metanarrative of the Bible is the story that explains (1) the way things were, (2) the way things are, (3) the way things could be, and (4) the way things will be. (A) TRUE
10. The Creation, the Fall, Redemption, and Restoration are the main themes of the biblical metanarrative. (A) TRUE

Passage Two

Directions: To demonstrate your understanding of the Hebrew Bible as a metanarrative. of the first eleven chapters of the Book of Genesis, choose the most logical word(s) for each sentence.

The biblical metanarrative gives the entire sixty-six Books in Christian translations of the Hebrew Bible and the twenty-four Books in the Jewish Bible a *(a) unifying (b) divisive* factor-God's love for *(a) all His angels (b) humankind*. In each biblical narrative, the reader can see God's *(a) hidden (b) self-revealing* character attributes. Throughout the stories, man's *(a) loyalty (b) disobedience* brings judgment and grief. Humanity's rebellion against God begins in the Garden of Eden when the serpent tempts *(a) Eve, (b) Adam* to eat from the forbidden Tree of the Knowledge of Good and Evil. The literary *(a) theme (b) prologue* of good and evil is prevalent in the Genesis narratives beginning in Genesis, Chapter 3. Human sin, God's punishment, mankind's repentance, and God's plan for the *(a) redemption (b) annihilation* of humans drive the storyline forward in the biblical text.

In their simplest form, the twenty-four books of the Jewish Bible known as the _(a) Tanach, (b) Pentateuch_– present a history of the first 3500 years from Creation until the building of the second Temple in Jerusalem. In the Jewish and Christian cultures, the underlying unifying theme centers around the God of the _(a) Hebrews, (b) Egyptians_ and His relationship with humankind. Both cultures propose that the _(a) Jews, (b) Gentiles_ are God's first chosen people with whom He desires to relate. As the narratives progress, God _(a) unfolds (b) conceals_ Himself to His people. However, because humans continue to fail in their relationship with God by the misuse of _(a) freewill, (b) language_, God works in various stages of human history to re-establish His relationship with humankind. God plans to _(a) correct, (b) destroy_ the problems that arise from man's disobedience and rebellion. In the process of dealing with humans, God reveals His own true nature and _(a) anger (b) desires_. The big picture (metanarrative) encompasses the _(a) smaller (b) larger_ narratives so that when they are studied thoroughly, they will give a more meaningful interpretation and purpose to the entire text.

For Reflection: The first eleven chapters of Genesis hold profound insights into the divine story between God and humankind. What are the main ideas and/or lessons learned from reading these smaller narratives? Give specific details and scripture references. (Write five-eight sentences. Edit writing to correct errors. Label the post: A Reflection on Genesis 1-11. Post the response to the discussion board.

A Closing Thought:

"I cannot teach anybody anything. I can only make them think."

— Socrates

LESSON TWENTY-FOUR

INTRODUCTION TO PATRIARCHAL NARRATIVES

(GENESIS TWELVE THROUGH TWENTY-THREE)

Lesson Overview:

Chapters 12-50 of the Book of Genesis recount the birth of Israel as a nation. The sagas of Abraham, Isaac, and Jacob, along with the story of Joseph, constitutes the second division the Book of Genesis. Abraham, originally called *Abram*, is the first of the Hebrew patriarchs. These *patriarchal* narratives focus on Abraham, Sarah, and their descendants. In short, God calls Abraham, Sarah, and their family to leave their homeland to go a new "Promised Land" called Canaan. God promises to make the descendants of Abraham into a great nation. The Israelite patriarchs, Isaac (Abraham's son) and Jacob (Abraham's grandson who was renamed Israel) are also prominent figures in the three largest Abrahamic religions—Judaism, Christianity, and Islam. This lesson focuses on the literary and historical aspects of the first part of the Abraham saga.

Key Concepts: saga, Hebrew patriarchs, monotheistic religions, Semitic, covenants, Hebrew customs/traditions, "Promised Land," foreshadowing

Lesson Objectives:

Students will:

- use online Bible study tools to access, read, interpret, and explain information.
- interpret the author's intended meaning of biblical text.
- decide the meaning of words and phrases based on the context of the passages.
- interpret the Hebrew Bible while allowing for use of figurative language.
- distinguish between various biblical literary genres, including historical narratives.
- use information found in online biblical resources to support analyses, reflection(s), and research.
- make inferences and draw conclusions based on explicit and implied information using evidence from the text.
- participate in discussions of literature and cultural experiences.

Expected Learning Objectives

At the end of this lesson, students will:

- interpret the author's intended meaning of biblical text.
- decide the meaning of words and phrases based on the context of the passage.

- interpret the Bible literally while allowing for normal use of figurative language.
- distinguish between various biblical literary genres, including patriarchal narratives.
- interpret biblical text accurately and respectfully.

Duration: 3-4 hours

Materials:

- Paper/pen/dictionary/notebook
- Video: Genesis Abraham and Sarah | Full Series
  https://www.youtube.com/watch?v=4BRQUC30RdQ
- Lecture: Abraham, Sarah, and Hagar
  https://online.hillsdale.edu/landing/genesis?email=wilmaforeman%40yahoo.com
- Website: *The Story of Abraham*-https://www.israel-a-history-of.com/story-of-abraham.html

Procedure:

- Read Genesis, Chapters twelve through twenty-three in any Bible translation.
- Use an online dictionary to pronounce and define unfamiliar terms.
- Watch the video(s): (1) *Genesis 12-50* by the Bible Project (https://bibleproject.com/explore/video/genesis-12-50/) and Genesis Abraham and Sarah | Full Series (https://www.youtube.com/watch?v=4BRQUC30RdQ)
- Respond to the study questions in full sentences.
- If you have questions about the assignment(s), post them on the discussion board, and wait for the instructor's clarification.
- Write key points in your notebook and study the notes for future discussions and assessments.
- Respond to the reflection(s).
- Use your computer's editing capability to correct writing errors.
- Post your reflection on the discussion board. Label the reflection "A Reflection of the Patriarchal Hebrew Narratives (Part One).
- If you have questions or need further clarification on any assignment, e-mail me at wilmaforeman@yahoo.com or visit my website: AIBL.INFO to sign up for the online course.

Genesis, Chapters 12-23

Title of the Narrative	Literary Themes	Summary	Study Questions
"The Call of Abram" (Gen. 12:1-20)	• Obedience • Faith	Without any biblical explanations, God calls Abram to leave Haran and go to Canaan. This call	1. Where is Abram living when he first encounters God.

		connects to promise that God will make Abram into a great nation through whom all the nations of the earth would receive blessings (12:2-3). Trusting and obeying God, Abram and his family set out for the land of Canaan. Arriving in Shechem, he builds an altar to the Lord in the region of Bethel. Abram, however, does not settle in the land of Canaan. He continues his wanderings further south and west as he heads toward Egypt. The region in Canaan is experiencing a famine, but Egypt is still fertile and moist. It is in Egypt that Abram lies about his wife and claims that she is his sister because he fears the Egyptians.	2. What does God instruct him to do? 3. What does God promise Abram? 4. Why does Abram build an altar in Shechem? 5. Why does Abram settle near Egypt? 6. What are the character traits revealed in Abram's actions?
	• Covenant relation between God and man • Man's wanderings • Human Fears • Divine Intervention		
"God's Covenant with Abram" (Gen. 15:1-17:27)	• Covenants • Faith • Obedience • Divine Promises	In this narrative, God sets up a covenant with Abram and his descendants. This covenant goes beyond the promise made with Noah. Abram's descendants will be as multifold as the stars.	7. Why does God set up a covenant with Abram in this part of the narrative?
"Hagar and Ishmael" (Gen. 16:1-16)	• Human Flaws • Ancient Hebrew Customs • Human Strife • Behavior and Consequence • Oppression • Mercy • Ancient Hebrew Marriage Traditions	Sarai, Abram's wife, continues to be barren despite God's promise to Abram. Following an ancient Near Eastern custom, she suggests that Abram takes her maidservant, Hagar, and impregnates her. Abram concurs, and Hagar bears Ishmael. Afterward, a personal hostility develops between Sarai and Hagar,	8. Discuss the personality flaws in the characters in Genesis, chapters 12-16. 9. Discuss problem-solving skills in ancient Hebrew societies. 10. What were the roles of women in Ancient Hebrew culture?

		and Hagar flees Sarai's harshness. God speaks to Hagar in a vision and sends her back to Sarai with her son. He promises that her son, Ishmael, will become great.	
"The Ancient Hebrew Covenant of Circumcision" (Gen. 17:1-27)	• Covenants • Name-changing • Unbelief • Human Rituals • Divine Promises	God affirms that He will be the God of Abram and his descendants. As a token of this new relationship, God changes Abram's name to *Abraham* (17:5), and Sarai becomes *Sarah* (17:15). God promises that despite their advanced age, the two will conceive a son. God promises that Abraham's successors will be the descendants of Isaac, not Ishmael. The central requirement of the covenant is the circumcision of the Hebrew males, an act regarded as evidence of being a member of the covenant people of God.	11. What was the significance of circumcision in ancient Hebrew societies? 12. What was the significance of name-changing in biblical times? 13. How is the character of God revealed in His interactions with Abraham and his family?
"Sodom and Gomorrah" (Gen. 18:1-19:38)	• Ancient Hebrew Hospitality • Biblical Customs • Human Fallibility • Divine Promises • Consequences for Behavior • Biblical Places	Three visitors in the form of angels visit Abraham. Although he has no idea who they are, he shows traditional Near Eastern hospitality by ensuring that their feet are washed and dried, and that food and drink are prepared. The purpose of the visit is to reassure Abram's wife Sarah that she will indeed conceive, although she and her husband, Abraham, have grown incredibly old. Sarah laughs at the promise. As the visitors prepare to leave, they make it clear that the	14. How is Abraham hospitable to the visitors in this part of the narrative? 15. Why do the strangers come to the region? 16. What do they reveal to Abraham? 17. How does Sarah respond to the visitors' promise? 18. What will happen to the cities of Sodom and Gomorrah? 19. How is the theme of preservation of the righteous related to

		city of Sodom, notorious for wickedness and marked for destruction. In a dialogue with one of the angels, Abraham pleads for the city. The theme of the conversation is the preservation of the righteous (KJV). The narrative then moves to Sodom, where Lot, Abraham's nephew, is sitting in the gate of the city when the angels arrive. (This suggests that he was a prominent figure in the city because the city gate in ancient Israel was a location for dispensing justice and managing local issues.) Lot is hospitable, but the other inhabitants of the city threaten to rape the visitors when they find them in Lot's house. Lot and his family rush out of the city to avoid its destruction, and they find safety in the nearby town of Zoar (19:20-22). The story continues with Lot's wife turning back to look at the burning city and turning into a pillar of salt. At the end of the narrative, Lot's daughters, hoping to ensure the continuation of the family line, make their father drunk and seduce him (19:30-38). They each bear a son out of the incestuous incident.	the theme of good versus evil?
"Lot's Wife" (Gen. 19)			20. Who is Lot, and how does he treat the strangers?
			21. Why does Lot's wife become a pillar of salt?
			22. What are Lot's character flaws?
			23. How does this narrative show human weaknesses?
			24. What are the consequences of human misbehavior?
			25. How do humans behave in the narratives when given too much autonomy?

Genesis, Chapters 21-23

"Isaac is Born" (Gen. 21)	• Divine Favor • Covenant Relationships	This Hebrew narrative focuses on the fulfillment of God's promise to Abraham	26. How is Isaac's name significant to the storyline?

		and Sarah. Isaac is born (21:1-7). In keeping the covenant set up with God earlier, Abraham circumcises Isaac. The birth of Isaac, however, alienates Sarah and Hagar. As a result, Hagar and her son must leave, yet they receive divine favor in the wilderness.	27. How does Isaac's birth alienate Sarah and Hagar?
"Abraham's Faith is Tested." (Gen. 22)	• Sacrifices • Testing of Faith • Alienation • Family Strife • Obedience • Spousal Devotion • Death • Ancient Burial Customs	God tests Abraham's faithfulness and obedience by asking him to offer Isaac as a sacrifice. Instead of sacrificing his son, Abraham God supplies Abraham a ram caught in the thorns (22:13). Abraham offers the ram as the sacrifice, and God assures him of his future greatness. Sarah later dies in the region of Canaan, occupied by the Hittites. Abraham, a "stranger and an alien," in the land, has no rights. He finally buys a part of the land as a burial site for his wife, and Sarah. He buries her in a cave in a field in Canaan.	28. How does the writer depict the personalities of Hagar and Sarah? 29. Define "divine favor" and tell how Hagar receives it. **30.** How does the idiom "There's a ram in the bush" connect the Hebrew Bible to western culture?
"The Death and Burial of Sarah" (Gen. 23)			

Study Questions/Activities

(The Story of Abraham-https://www.israel-a-history-of.com/story-of-abraham.html)

Directions: Read the article and respond to the study questions.

1. Which of the following statements is NOT CORRECT?

   A. Abraham, originally named Abram, is the perfect example of faith and trust in God.
   B. Living a prosperous life in a place called Ur, he travels to a foreign land.
   C. Without knowing the outcome, Abram leaves his home and trusted God to lead the way to the "Promised Land" (Canaan).
   D. God promises that Abraham will become the father of nations.
   E. All the above statements are correct.

2. Which of the following statements is NOT CORRECT?

   A. Abraham's family lived in an interactive society.
   B. His tribe was a wandering clan.
   C. They usually settled near urban areas.

D. The traveling clans consisted of various levels of family, servants, slaves, livestock, animals, and all other possessions.

E. *All the above statements are correct.*

3. Which of the following statements is NOT CORRECT?

A. During Abraham's times, clans were wealthy and powerful.
B. Ancient tribes traveled near ample water supplies.
C. The ancient tribes were heavily populated.
D. They engaged in business activities from place to place.

E. *All the above statements are correct.*

4. Which of the following statements is NOT CORRECT?

A. Caravans are companies of travelers that journeyed through deserts or hostile regions.
B. In ancient the Near East, caravans traveled from East to West, moving directly through the heart of the Arabian desert.
C. The routes that the caravans traveled connected Mesopotamia directly to Canaan.
D. The travel patterns described in Genesis are consistent with the discoveries of historians and archaeologists about the history of ancient Near East.

E. *All the above statements are correct.*

5. Which of the following statements is NOT CORRECT?

A. The caravan routes were shorter than the courses that the tribes or clans followed.
B. The caravan routes were more dangerous than other routes of travel.
C. The Book of Genesis narrates the story of Abraham and his father, Terah, as they travel northward alongside the Euphrates River.
D. Another term for "Aramean" is "Hebrew."

E. *All the above statements are correct.*

6. Which of the following statements is NOT CORRECT?

A. The term *Arab* originates from the expressions *Aramu* and *Habiru.*
B. These terms describe *semi nomads.*
C. Indigenous nomads and semi nomads left an imprint on the land.
D. Abraham was a semi nomad.

E. *All the above statements are correct.*

7. Which of the following statements is NOT CORRECT?

A. *Aramu* and *Habiru* people lived outside the typical structure of settled civilization.
B. Terah, Abraham's father, was a known *idolater.*
C. An *idol* is an image or representation of a god used as an object of worship.
D. An *idolator* is a person who worships an idol or idols.

E. *All the above statements are correct.*

8. Which of the following statements is NOT CORRECT?

   A. The narrative in Genesis suggests that Terah is the first receiver of God's call to leave Mesopotamia.
   B. According to the narrative, Terah does not obey God, and stops in Haran.
   C. Haran was once the capital of the Islamic empire in the eighth century AD.
   D. Remains at the site today belong to the Islamic town, Haran, from the 12th and 13th centuries AD.
   E. *All the above statements are correct.*

9. Which of the following statements is NOT CORRECT?

   A. Based on Abrahamic legend, Terah was loyal to the polytheistic system of religion in Babylon.
   B. Terah's settlement in Haran was a sign that he lacked the strength of character that Abraham displayed.
   C. The story begins with God's call for Abram (Abraham) to leave his *"father's household"* and travel toward the land of Canaan.
   D. The exact date of Abraham's life is still unknown.
   E. *All the above statements are correct.*

10. Which of the following statements is NOT CORRECT?

   A. The Book of Genesis has names from both the Pre- and Post-Flood eras.
   B. Scholars have dated the story of Abraham as recorded in Genesis as occurring during the reigns of Ur-Nammu and Hammurabi.
   C. This period was the Middle Bronze Age, from between 2100-1550 B.C.E.
   D. Hammurabi was the sixth king of the First Babylonian dynasty of the Amorite tribe, reigning from c. 1792 BC to c. 1750 BC.
   E. *All the above statements are correct.*

11. Which of the following statements is NOT CORRECT?

   A. The story of Abraham starts in Mesopotamia.
   B. Various traditions and stories in Sumerian mythology are parallel accounts of the Hebrew Bible stories.
   C. The Mesopotamian culture affected the life of Abraham.
   D. The names mentioned in the Abrahamic narrative correspond with names found throughout northwestern Mesopotamia.
   E. *All the above statements are correct.*

12. Which of the following statements is NOT CORRECT?

   A. The story of Abraham and his arrival in Canaan have been associated with northwestern-speaking *Semitic* peoples.
   B. The term *Semitic* relates to a family of languages that includes Hebrew, Arabic, and Aramaic and certain ancient languages such as Phoenician and Akkadian.

C. These languages make up the main subgroup of the Afro-Asiatic family.

D. The expression *Afro-Asiatic* refers to languages spoken in the Middle East and North Africa.

E. ***All the above statements are correct.***

13. Which of the following statements is NOT CORRECT?

   A. In his book *Walking the Bible,* best-selling author Bruce Feiler explores the spiritual roots of Abraham through the eyes of each of the major three world faiths: Judaism, Christianity, and Islam.

   B. All three religions trace their origins to Father Abraham.

   C. Feiler compares Abraham in the Bible to Abraham in the Quran.

   D. Christianity has a Jewish beginning.

   E. ***All the above statements are correct.***

14. Which of the following statements is NOT CORRECT?

   A. Genesis 11:10-26 traces Abraham's lineage from the *ante-diluvian* Patriarch Noah.

   B. The term *antediluvian* means "belonging to the time before the biblical Flood."

   C. Abraham is a direct descendant of Shem, Noah's son.

   D. In the Abrahamic biblical narrative, God continues the literary pattern (theme) of making covenants with humans.

   E. ***All the above statements are correct.***

15. Which of the following statements is NOT CORRECT?

   A. Shem was the son of Noah through whom God's promised that the "seed of the woman" would transfer to further generations (Gen. 3:15).

   B. In Christian tradition, the "seed of the woman" *foreshadows* the virgin birth of Jesus Christ.

   C. In biblical tradition, the "seed of the woman" foretells that the Son of God will conquer death, hell, and the grave.

   D. The "seed of the woman" alludes to God's punishment of the serpent in Genesis, Chapter Four.

   E. ***All the above are true.***

16. Which of the following statements is NOT CORRECT?

   A. Chronologies place Abram's (Abraham's) birth about three hundred years after the flood.

   B. The chronologies of Abraham's birth are highly debatable.

   C. Abram and Sarai (Sarah) are childless at the beginning of the narrative.

   D. Abram (Abraham) is the one through whom God chooses to give birth to the nation of Israel.

   E. ***All the above are true.***

17. Which of the following statements is NOT CORRECT?

    A. The first mention of Abram (Abraham) in the Hebrew Bible takes place in Genesis 11:26.

    B. Abram has two brothers, Nahor and Haran.

    C. According to Genesis 11:28, Haran, Abram's brother, dies before *"his father Terah in the land of his nativity, in Ur."*

    D. Abram's family came from Ur, although the reader can infer that his brother Haran lived elsewhere.

    E. All the above are true.

18. Which of the following statements is NOT CORRECT?

    A. Haran leaves Ur and dwells in the land later named after him.

    B. The Genesis story records that Haran dies while Terah, the father, is still alive.

    C. Haran is visiting his father in Ur when he dies.

    D. Terah's extended family includes members from Haran's household who have remained in Ur after their father's death.

    E. All the above are true.

19. Which of the following statements is NOT CORRECT?

    A. Based on biblical tradition, Nahor (Abraham's other brother) marries their brother's daughter, Milcah.

    B. Sarai, the wife of Abram, is also a daughter of Terah, but she is his daughter by another wife.

    C. Sarai (later Sarah) is both a wife and half-sister to Abram (Abraham).

    D. Lot is Haran's son, Abraham's nephew.

    E. All the above are true.

20. Which of the following statements is NOT CORRECT?

    A. Abraham's brother Haran leaves behind only one son named Lot.

    B. Lot becomes closely attached to his uncle Abram and leaves the land of Ur with him to journey to the land of Canaan.

    C. One can infer that Abram becomes Lot's guardian after his father Haran dies.

    D. Ur, in this era of history, is a great city, an extremely popular and busy seaport

    E. All the above are true.

21. Which of the following statements is NOT CORRECT?

    A. The city of Ur had a magnificent library, luxurious temples and royal palaces found throughout the city.

    B. The biblical narrative about Abraham continues the pattern of God's attempt to build a relationship with humanity.

    C. God's plan for Abraham and his family is to have a relational establishment with them by resettling them into a land called Canaan.

    D. Mesopotamia produced great empires in the history of the world.

E. All the above are true.

22. Which of the following statements is NOT CORRECT?

    A. Genesis 11:31 tells of Abraham's family obedience to God's instructions.
    B. At the beginning of the journey, Terah, the father, acts on pure human volition.
    C. He heads toward Canaan under the guidance of God's Providence.
    D. The ancient city state Ur was a Babylonian, or Chaldean city.
    E. All the above are true.

23. Which of the following statements is NOT CORRECT?

    A. In Genesis 11:31, Abraham and his family settle in Haran before they arrive in Canaan.
    B. The land of Ur is modern Tall al-Muqayyar or Tell el-Muqayyar, Iraq.
    C. Ur of the Chaldees (or Chaldeans) was a place in Mesopotamia.
    D. Mesopotamia is the "cradle of civilization."
    E. All the above are true.

24. Which of the following statements is NOT CORRECT?

    A. Mesopotamia is the first place where complex urban centers grew.
    B. Mesopotamia is the area between the Tigris and Euphrates Rivers
    C. The history of Mesopotamia connects to the modern nations of Egypt, Iran, and Syria.
    D. The first cities, the first writing, and first technologies originated in Mesopotamia.
    E. All the above are true.

25. Which of the following statements is NOT CORRECT?

    A. Ur of the Chaldees, the place where Abraham lived, would have had ample water and land for pasturing.
    B. One can conclude that Abraham and his family left Ur in search of a better food supply. (NOT CORRECT)
    C. Abraham's family was active in commerce.
    D. God calls Abraham and his family to an unfamiliar place.
    E. All the above are true.

Study Questions

Directions: Use credible internet sources and Bible study tools to select the best choice for each statement.

    1. How do humans behave toward God in Genesis, Chapters 3-11?
        a) The rebel against God.
        b) They worship God wholeheartedly.
        c) They obey God.
        d) They act like God.
        e) none of the above

2. In Genesis, Chapter 12, God promises to make Abram's name_____.
   a) difficult to pronounce.
   b) great.
   c) familiar.
   d) the same as His.
   e) none of the above

3. Through Abraham, God plans to_____.
   a) replace all humans
   b) bless all humans
   c) redeem all humans
   d) reject all humans
   e) none of the above

4. Israel is called a "Nation of_____."
   a) the Wealthy
   b) Holiness
   c) Peace
   d) Rebellion
   e) none of the above

5. Abraham, _____, and Jacob are the first three patriarchs of Israel.
   a) Sarah
   b) Ishmael
   c) Isaac
   d) Hagar
   e) none of the above

6. Despite the failures in Abraham's family, God is still_____.
   a) angry
   b) silent
   c) distant
   d) faithful
   e) none of the above

7. Abraham shows a character weakness when he lies about his_____.
   a) sons, Ishmael and Isaac
   b) wife, Sarah (Sarai)
   c) age and place of birth
   d) wife's servant, Hagar
   e) none of the above

8. Abraham's first son is _____,

   a) Isaac
   b) Ishmael
   c) Jacob
   d) Esau
   e) none of the above

9. God's official commitment to Abraham is a _____.

   a) relationship
   b) union
   c) covenant
   d) marriage
   e) none of the above

10. _____ is the sign of the agreement between God and Abraham.

   a) A star
   b) A handshake
   c) Bowing
   d) Circumcision
   e) none of the above

11. Jacob's name means_____.

   a) deceiver or trickster
   b) prince
   c) Israel
   d) flight
   e) none of the above

12. Jacob and his mother scheme to take Esau's_____.

   a) life
   b) clothes
   c) birthright
   d) camels
   e) none of the above

13. Jacob loves_____.

   a) Leah
   b) Rachel
   c) Hagar
   d) Zil'-pah
   e) none of the above

14. Jacob's name is changed after he_____.

   a) blesses God
   b) wrestles with an angel

c) sleeps under an olive tree
d) tells his dream
e) none of the above

15. Jacob has _____ sons by four different women.
   a) four
   b) six
   c) twelve
   d) three
   e) none of the above

16. Ironically, Laban, Jacob's_____, deceives him.
   a) brother
   b) friend
   c) uncle
   d) cousin
   e) none of the above

17. As a(n) _____Jacob has power with GOD and men and prevails.
   a) king
   b) leader
   c) angel
   d) prince
   e) none of the above

18. Rachel and Leah are _____.
   a) cousins
   b) concubines
   c) siblings
   d) Abraham's wives
   e) none of the above

19. Esau is _____twin brother.
   a) Rachel's
   b) Jacob's
   c) Abraham's
   d) Isaac's
   e) none of the above

20. Ishmael is _____half-brother.
   a) Isaac
   b) Laban
   c) Cain
   d) Abel

e) none of the above

21. The name "_____" means "Wrestled with God."
   a) Isaac
   b) Ishmael
   c) Cain
   d) Israel
   e) none of the above

22. Another word for "wrestle" is "_____."
   a) kill
   b) listen
   c) contend
   d) overcome
   e) none of the above

23. Jacob receives a wound in his thigh or_____.
   a) foot
   b) hip
   c) knee
   d) shin
   e) none of the above

24. Laban is the brother of_____, who married Isaac and bore Jacob
   a) Isaac
   b) Rebekah
   c) Eve
   d) Abel
   e) none of the above

25. Another name for Jacob is_____.
   a. Isaac
   b. Abram
   c. Sarai
   d. Israel
   e. none of the above

For Reflection:

If God's plan for Abraham and his family is to have a relational establishment with them by resettling them into a land called Canaan, what must the family learn about healthy relationships? (Write five to eight sentences. Proof-read your response before posting it on the discussion board. Label the post: A Reflection on Healthy Relationships.)

A Closing Thought:

""Nobody ever outgrows Scripture; the book widens and deepens with our years."

Charles Spurgeon

LESSON TWENTY-FIVE
THE BIBLICAL THEME OF COVENANTS

Lesson Overview:

The backbone of the biblical storyline centers on covenants. Understanding the significance of covenants is essential to understanding the Hebrew Scriptures. The lesson gives students an extensive study about the major covenants in the Hebrew Scriptures that unite the individual narratives into one grand story. Students will learn (1) the meaning of covenants, (2) how biblical characters made covenants, (3) types of covenants, and (4) how religious scholars propose that the covenants were fulfilled in the New Testament in Christian Bibles.

Key Concepts: covenants, the Adamic covenant, the Noahic covenant, protoevangelium, foreshadow, prophesy, symbolism, metanarrative, Old/New Testament, redemption, enmity, conditional, and unconditional

Lesson Objectives:

Students will:

- use online Bible study tools to access, read, interpret, and explain information.
- decide the meaning of words and phrases based on the context of the passages.
- interpret the Hebrew Bible while allowing for use of figurative language.
- distinguish between distinct types of covenants in Hebrew Scriptures.
- draw conclusions and make inferences from primary and secondary sources.
- share information about assigned biblical themes logically and accurately.

Expected Learning Objectives

At the end of this lesson, students will be able to:

- explain the meaning of contextual words and phrases, such as covenants and enmity.
- interpret the Bible normally while allowing for normal use of figurative language.
- distinguish between various biblical literary genres, including patriarchal narratives.
- explain how the literary theme of covenants in the Book of Genesis in the Old Testament foreshadows the covenant relationship between Jesus and the church in the New Testament in Christian tradition.

Duration: 3-4 hours

Materials:

- Internet access/ a computer with editing capability

- Paper/pen/notebook
- Video: *If You Understand These 8 Bible Covenants then You Understand the ENTIRE Story of the Bible! by Allen Parr (THE BEAT by Allen Parr)*
  https://www.youtube.com/watch?v=tESRUiC3CFA
- Article: "What is Protoevangelium?" By Mark Slick
  (https://carm.org/about-theology/what-is-the-protoevangelium/)
- Video: *How Is Jesus Shown in the Book of Genesis? By Josh Moody*
  ttps://www.christianity.com/jesus/is-jesus-god/old-testament-prophecies/how-is-jesus-shown-in-the-book-of-genesis.html

Procedure:

- Read the article "What is Protoevangelium?" by Mark Slick
  (https://carm.org/about-theology/what-is-the-protoevangelium/)
- Use an online dictionary to pronounce and define unfamiliar terms.
- Respond to the study questions.
- View the video(s).
- Respond to the study questions that follow.
- Write key points in your notebook and study the notes for future discussions and assessments.
- Respond to the reflection(s).
- Use your computer's editing capability to correct writing errors.
- Post your reflection on the discussion board.
- If you have questions or need further clarification on any assignment, e-mail me at wilmaforeman@yahoo.com or visit my website: AIBL.INFO to sign up for the online course.

Note: If you have questions about the assignment(s), post them on the discussion board, and wait for clarification.

Study Questions

(Video*: If You Understand These 8 Bible Covenants then You Understand the ENTIRE Story of the Bible! by Allen Parr (THE BEAT by Allen Parr)*

(https://www.youtube.com/watch?v=tESRUiC3CFA)

Based on the video, are the following statements (A) CORRECT or (B) INCORRECT?

1. A covenant is a binding agreement between two or more parties. (A) CORRECT
2. In Genesis, Chapter 2, God makes the first covenant with Adam in the Garden of Eden. (A) CORRECT
3. This first covenant is the Edenic covenant. (A) CORRECT

4. The Edenic covenant refers to the covenant made between God and Adam in the Garden of Eden. (A) CORRECT

5. Covenants can be *conditional* or *unconditional*. (A) CORRECT

6. A bilateral covenant is conditional covenant in which both parties must uphold the stipulations in the agreement or compact. (A) CORRECT

7. A unilateral covenant requires that only one party meets the requirements of an agreement. (A) CORRECT

8. The unilateral covenants in the Bible usually originate from God. (A) CORRECT

9. In each of the biblical covenants, humans barter or negotiate with God. (B) INCORRECT

10. The biblical covenants were replaceable. (A) CORRECT

11. God makes a covenant to be faithful to human beings even when they are unfaithful. (A) CORRECT

12. The term *covenant* is associated with cutting. (A) CORRECT

13. During biblical times, a covenant involved killing animals. (A) CORRECT

14. Cutting an innocent animal was indicative of the seriousness of a covenant. (A) CORRECT

15. After cutting the animal in half, parties in the agreement would walk pass the bloody pieces to symbolize the value of the oath(s). (A) CORRECT

16. The key word in the Edenic covenant is *rulership* or *dominion*. (A) CORRECT

17. In Genesis, Chapter 2, God gives Adamic dominion or rulership over the Garden of Eden. (A) CORRECT

18. God's instruction to Adam about eating from the Tree of the Knowledge of Good and Evil has a *stipulation*. (A) CORRECT

19. A *stipulation* is a condition or requirement as part of an agreement. (A) CORRECT

20. God's covenant with Adam is that if he does not eat of the Tree of the Knowledge of Good and Evil, then he will live forever. (A) CORRECT

21. Based on the narrator, if Adam had obeyed God, he would have had eternal rulership and access to God's presence. (A) CORRECT

22. Because Adam breaks the agreement, the covenant becomes invalid. (A) CORRECT

23. If an agreement becomes null and avoid, it has no legal effect. (A) CORRECT

24. The Edenic covenant is *conditional* in that two parties meet the requirements of the contract. (A) CORRECT

25. The key word in discussing the *Adamic covenant* is *redemption*. (A) CORRECT

26. *Redemption* is the act of saving or restoring. (A) CORRECT

27. God promises to redeem humans by crushing the head of the serpent, their enemy. (A) CORRECT

28. *Enmity* means intense hostility and means the state of being an enemy. (A) CORRECT

29. *Symbolically*, in Christian tradition, the serpent is the Devil or Satan. (A) CORRECT

30. *Prophetically*, in Christian tradition, Jesus will fulfill the covenant by crushing the head of the serpent's offspring. (A) CORRECT

31. In Christian tradition, the expression "bruise his heel" refers to the crucifixion of Jesus that was excruciatingly painful. (A) CORRECT

32. In the Christian faith, "crushing the head" of the serpent symbolizes Jesus' ultimate victory over death and sin. (A) CORRECT

33. The Adamic covenant in unilateral. (A) CORRECT

34. In the Adamic covenant, God stays committed to redeeming humanity. (A) CORRECT

35. In the Noahic covenant, the key word is *restraint*. (A) CORRECT

36. God retrains Himself from destroying humankind entirely because of their wickedness. (A) CORRECT

37. God spares Noah's family of eight. (A) CORRECT

38. After the flood, God makes a *unilateral* covenant with Noah. (A) CORRECT

39. In the Noahic covenant, God promises never to flood the entire earth again. (A) CORRECT

40. God stipulates the conditions of the Noahic covenant, and He is the only one that needs to fulfill the requirements. (A) CORRECT

41. In the Abrahamic covenant, the key word is "restore." (A) CORRECT

42. The Abrahamic covenant connects to the Adamic covenant in which the key word is *redemption*. (A) CORRECT

43. Redemption involves the action of regaining or gaining possession of something in exchange for payment or clearing a debt. (A) CORRECT

44. Restoration relates to the act of returning something or someone to a former position. (A) CORRECT

45. In the Adamic covenant, God wants to redeem humans. (A) CORRECT

46. In the Abrahamic covenant, God starts the process of restoring the broken relationship between humans and Himself.

47. In Genesis 12:1-3, God promises Abram (Abraham land, descendants, and blessings. (A) CORRECT

48. God promises to bless those who exalt Abraham and to bring misfortunes upon people who curse him. (A) CORRECT

49. The Abrahamic covenant is an example of how butchered animals stand for the solemnity of biblical covenants. (A) CORRECT

50. God, in the semblance of fire and light, walks through the divided pieces of dead animals. (A) CORRECT

51. In biblical text, Abraham walks pass the dead animals in the covenant between him and God. (B) INCORRECT

52. The Abrahamic covenant involves God and Abraham, but only God has an obligation to fulfill the pact. (A) CORRECT

53. The narrator proposes that Jesus in the Christian Bibles is the ultimate fulfillment of the Abrahamic covenant. (A) CORRECT

54. In Christian Bibles, both the Old and New Testaments reflect covenants. (A) CORRECT

55. In Christian tradition, the Bible is one book, composed of two testaments. (A) CORRECT

56. Comprised of thirty-nine books, the Old Testament in Jewish and Christian traditions, is God's unfolding promise to his covenant people, Israel. (B) INCORRECT

57. With twenty-seven books in Christian Bibles, the New Testament fulfills all the promises of the Old Testament through Jesus for Jews and Gentiles alike. (A) CORRECT

58. A Gentile in biblical language usually means "someone who is not a Jew." (A) CORRECT

59. In Christian Bibles, the two testaments are a literary unity, progressively revealed. (A) CORRECT

60. To understand the Christian Bible, modern readers realize that this one book has two major divisions. (A) CORRECT

For Reflection:

Study the chart that follows. How does the act of circumcision relate to God's promises to Abraham? (Write five to eight sentences. Edit your writing to correct errors. Post your reflection on the discussion board. Label the post: God's Promises to Abraham.)

Genesis 17:1-27

Title of the Narrative	Literary Themes	Summary	Study Questions
"The Covenant of Circumcision" -Gen. 17:1-27	• Covenants • Name-changing • Unbelief • Human Rituals • Divine Promises	God affirms that he will be the God of both Abram and his descendants. As a token of this new relationship, Abram's name becomes Abraham (17:5), and Sarai becomes Sarah (17:15). God promises that despite their advanced age, the two will have a son together. God promises that Abraham's successors will be through Isaac, not Ishmael. This covenant is conditional. The central requirement is circumcision of males. According to	1. What does the expression, "a covenant people of God" mean in reference to the Jews? 2. What is the significance of name-changing in biblical text? 3. What is a conditional covenant?

		Hebrew tradition, this act is evidence of being a member of the covenant people of God.	

A Closing Thought:

"I marvel at the resilience of the Jewish people. Their best characteristic is their desire to remember. No other people has such an obsession with memory."

–Elie Wiesel

LESSON TWENTY-SIX

THE BEGINNING OF THE NATION OF ISRAEL

(GENESIS TWENTY-FOUR THROUGH THIRTY)

Lesson Overview:

A vast amount of scholarly knowledge about the history of ancient Israel comes from the Hebrew Bible. According to the biblical text, Israel's origins begin with Abraham, who is considered the father of both Judaism (through his son Isaac) and Islam (through his son Ishmael). The second section of the Book of Genesis unfolds the fulfillment of the covenant made by God with Abram in Genesis 12:1-3. *"The LORD had said to Abram, 'Leave your country, your people and your father's household and go to the land I will show you. I will make you into a great nation and I will bless you; I will make your name great, and you will be a blessing."* In this encounter, God purposes to build a special relationship with the descendants of Abraham. Known as the Abrahamic covenant, God's promise to Abraham was the key to both his immediate life and to the later history of the nation of Israel. This lesson continues to explore the patriarchal historical narratives with the focus on Abraham's descendants, Isaac and Jacob as recorded in Genesis, Chapters 24-30.

Key Concepts: Abrahamic covenant, descendants, lineage, sibling rivalry, conditional and unconditional covenants, situational irony, character flaws, matriarchal, endogamy, patrilineal, segmentary system, concubine, syncretism

Lesson Objectives:

Students will:

- use online Bible study tools to access, read, interpret, and explain information.
- interpret the author's intended meaning of biblical text.
- decide the meaning of words and phrases based on the context of the passages.
- interpret the Hebrew Bible while allowing for use of figurative language.
- distinguish between various biblical literary genres, including patriarchal Hebrew narratives.
- use information found in online biblical resources to support analyses, reflection(s), and research.
- make inferences and draw conclusions based on explicit and implied information using evidence from the text.
- draw conclusions and make inferences from primary and secondary sources.
- share information about assigned biblical themes logically and accurately.

Expected Learning Objectives

At the end of this lesson, students will:

- interpret the author's intended meaning of biblical text.
- decide the meaning of words and phrases based on the context of the passage.
- interpret the Hebrew Bible normally while allowing for use of figurative language.
- distinguish between various biblical literary genres, including patriarchal narratives.

Duration: 3-4 hours

Materials:

- Internet access/ a computer with editing capability
- Paper/pen/notebook
- "What the Bible says about the Nation of Israel-Biblical Israel?"
  (From *Forerunner Commentary*) (Genesis 32:28 (KJV) - Forerunner Commentary (bibletools.org)
- (Article: "History of Israel" (https://www.factsaboutisrael.uk/history-of-israel-timeline/)
- Article: "Ancient Israelite Marriage Customs" by Jim West, ThD (http://www.theology.edu/marriage.htm)
- Article: "Hebrew Social Organization: Marriage" (https://www.umanitoba.ca/faculties/arts/anthropology/tutor/case_studies/hebrews/marriage.html)

Procedure:

- Read Genesis, Chapters 24-36 in any translation.
- Use an online dictionary to pronounce and define unfamiliar terms.
- Read "What the Bible says about the Nation of Israel-Biblical Israel?"
  (From *Forerunner Commentary*) (Genesis 32:28 (KJV) - Forerunner Commentary (bibletools.org)
- Respond to study questions in full sentences.
- Write key points in your notebook and study the notes for future discussions and assessments.
- Respond to the reflection.
- Use your computer's editing capability to correct writing errors.
- Post your reflection on the discussion board.
- Label the reflection A Reflection of the Patriarchal Hebrew Narratives -The Beginning of Israel as a Nation.
- If you have questions or need further clarification on any assignment, e-mail me at wilmaforeman@yahoo.com or visit my website: AIBL.INFO to sign up for the online course.

Study Questions

(from "What the Bible says about the Nation of Israel-Biblical Israel?")
(From *Forerunner Commentary*) (Genesis 32:28 (KJV) - Forerunner Commentary
(bibletools.org)

Are the following statements (A) CORRECT or (B) INCORRECT?

1. The first mention of Israel is in Genesis 32:28. (A) CORRECT
2. Israel is the changed name of Jacob. (A) CORRECT
3. Jacob's name is changed because he wrestled with God and men, and he won. (A) CORRECT
4. God is the first to use the name "Israel" to identify Jacob. (A) CORRECT
5. Jacob is the progenitor of the twelve tribes of Israel. (A) CORRECT
6. A "progenitor" is a person or thing from which a person, animal, or plant is descended. (A) CORRECT
7. Jacob had twelve sons who later became the head of tribes. (A) CORRECT
8. The names "Jacob" and "Israel" are used interchangeably throughout the Bible. (A) CORRECT
9. In the sentence, "And Jacob was told, 'Look, your son Joseph is coming to you'; and Israel strengthened himself and sat up on the bed," the names *Jacob* and *Israel* refer to the same person. (A) CORRECT
10. Manasseh and Ephraim are the names of Joseph's sons. (A) CORRECT
11. Israel blesses Joseph's sons before he dies.
12. Jacob places his hands upon his two grandsons. (A) CORRECT
13. Abraham and Isaac are the fore parents of Israel. (A) CORRECT
14. The promises that God makes to Abraham are passed down to Jacob (Israel) and his descendants. (A) CORRECT
15. The land of Israel is named after Jacob. (A) CORRECT

Genesis 24-30

Title of the Narrative	Literary Themes	Summary	Study Questions
"Isaac Marries Rebekah" (Gen. 24)	• Ancient Hebrew Customs • Actions and Consequences • Mercy • Divine Promises	Aware that his own death is not far away, Abraham decides that his son, Isaac, will take a wife. He dispatches his chief servant in the household to find a suitable wife for Isaac. He does not want him to marry a Canaanite because of ancient Hebrew laws against *syncretism*. In the town of Nahor, the servant meets Rebecca who has come to a well to draw water for their family. Convinced that she is the right person to marry Isaac, he arranges a meeting with her family and explains why he has come to the town. During the conversation, the family decides that she is to marry Isaac. Rebecca obeys and leaves with the servant to marry Isaac.	**Are the following statements (a) true or (b) false about Genesis, Chapter 24?** 1. This narrative mentions Abraham's old age. 2. Abraham's servant swears to find a bride for Isaac from Abraham's homeland. 3. The servant travels to Nahor in Mesopotamia. 4. He stops by a well to water his ten camels. 5. The servant asks Yahweh for a sign. 6. A girl who arrives not only gives him water, but she gives water to his camels also. 7. Rebecca (Rebekah), the beautiful virgin daughter of Abraham's nephew, acts out the servant's sign. 8. The servant gives Rebekah golden jewelry. 9. Rebekah reveals her family lineage to the servant. 10. The servant finds lodging for the night. 11. The servant blesses Yahweh for guiding him to

			the house of Abraham's brother.
			12. Rebekah's brother is Laban.
			13. Rebekah is Abraham's great-niece.
			14. Laban brings the servant and his men into the home, washes their feet, and feeds the camels.
			15. Rebekah and her servant girls leave with Abraham's servant.
			16. Rebekah falls off her camel when she first sees Isaac.
			17. In English, the term "alighted" is usually translated as "dismounted."
			18. Isaac takes Rebekah into his mother's tent and finds comfort after his mother's death.
			19. Isaac loves Rebekah.
			20. Rebekah covers her hair to show modesty.

Title of the Narrative	Literary Themes	Summary	Study Questions
"Jacob Gets Esau's Blessing" (Gen. 26:34-27:40)	• Birthrights • Sibling rivalry • Parental preference • Deceit • Broken relations	Relations between Esau and his parents deteriorate. At the age of forty, he marries two Hittite women (26:34). The Bible mentions a third wife later (28:9). This concerns his mother and father. Nevertheless, Esau is the firstborn and has certain	1. What are the names of Isaac's sons? 2. What is Isaac's physical condition? 3. For whom does Isaac call first? 4. What does Isaac ask his son, Esau, to do?

		birthrights. Esau obviously does not value such rights, for when he is hungry one day, he sells his birthright to Jacob, who later deceives his old father into blessing him instead of his brother Esau. Rebecca aids Jacob in the scheme. After the deception, relations between the two brothers fall apart.	5. Who is listening to Isaac when he is talking to Esau?
			6. To whom does Rebekah talk about what she hears from Isaac?
			7. Whom does Rebekah want Jacob to obey?
			8. Why does Rebekah want Jacob to take food to his father, Isaac?
			9. Why does Jacob think that his mother's plan will not work?
			10. What does Jacob fear?
			11. How does Rebekah dress Jacob?
			12. Where does Jacob go after he dresses in Esau's clothes?
			13. What question does Isaac ask Jacob?
			14. How does Jacob answer his father?
			15. Where does Jacob say the meal came from that he gives to his father?
			16. Why does Isaac want to touch Jacob?
			17. What does Isaac say is different about his son, Esau?
			18. What question does Isaac ask after he blesses Jacob?
			19. How does Jacob answer the question?
			20. What does Isaac smell when he kisses Jacob?

			21. In the blessing, who will bow down to Jacob?
"Jacob Dreams" (Gen. 28: 10-22)	• Dreams • Covenants • Forgiveness • Human frailties • Human potential • Divine favor • Determination • Fear • Name-Changing	In trying to escape his brother's wrath for stealing his birthright, Jacob sets out for Haran, Abraham's hometown. During this journey, he stops at a place known as Luz (Bethel). There, Jacob dreams of a stairway on which angels are descending and ascending. During this dream, God extends to Jacob the covenant he had previously made with Abraham and Isaac. Despite all his deceptions, Jacob receives God's blessings for himself and his descendants. Thus, reassured of God's promises, Jacob continues his journey to Haran.	22. What is the name of Abraham's hometown? 23. What does the name *Bethel* mean? 24. What does Jacob see in the dream? 25. Explain the expression *divine favor*. 26. How does Jacob receive his blessing in the dream?
"Laban Deceives Jacob" (Gen. 28:1-25)	• Wanderings • Male/female relationships • Parental influence • Romantic love • Commitment • Deception • Sowing and reaping • Broken promises	On arriving in Haran, Jacob looks to find Laban. However, the first member of the family he meets is Rachel, Laban's younger daughter. She is more beautiful than her older sister, Leah, who has dulled bleared eyes. After Laban welcomes him into his house, Jacob begins to work for his living. Instead of wages, Jacob desires to marry Rachel. He is willing to work for seven years to have Rachel's hand in marriage. Although Laban consents, he obviously has other plans. On Jacob's wedding night, he gives Leah to Jacob Leah instead of Rachel. Jacob discovers the deception the morning after his wedding night. Ironically, Jacob, known for deception, is now deceived. As later events unfold, Laban	27. How is Leah different from her sister? 28. How does Jacob feel about Rachel? 29. How does Jacob prove his love for Rachel? 30. Characterize Laban. 31. What personality traits do Jacob and Laban have in common? 32. Explain the *situational irony* in this narrative.

		and Jacob will continue to deceive each other.	
"Jacob Marries Rachel" (Gen. 30:29:26-30:24)	• Dedication • Romantic love • Family strife • Female rivalry • Man's frailties • Divine favor	Laban promises Jacob that he can marry Rachel for seven more years of labor. The text makes it clear that he can be with Rachel at once (29:28-30), although he owes Laban seven more years of work. Jacob has two wives simultaneously (common during ancient biblical times). It is only when God sets up the covenant with Moses as Sinai that monogamy becomes the norm. Jacob's fathers children through Leah, and later by her handmaiden when Leah is too old to conceive. Rachel is barren, so Jacob sleeps with her handmaiden and fathers sons. (This happens before he becomes the father of children by Leah's maidservant). Finally, Rachel conceives and bears a son named Joseph.	33. How were ancient Hebrew marriage traditions different from marriages in Western culture today? 34. Define the term *monogamy*. 35. As wives, how are Sarah and Rachel in similar situations?

Study Questions (Genesis, Chapters 12-30 from any translation of the Hebrew Bible. Use online Bible study tools to enhance your learning.)

Directions:

- Read/Review Genesis, Chapters 12-30. Respond to the study questions.
- Use any of the resources listed above in this lesson or other reliable internet sources to respond to the study questions/activities that follow.

Are the following statements (A) CORRECT or (B) INCORRECT?

1. In Hebrew Scriptures, God uses to Abram's descendants to begin the nation of Israel. (A) CORRECT
2. The most well-known of the biblical patriarchs is Abraham (Abram). (A) CORRECT
3. God approaches Abram in Genesis, Chapter 12, and promises to make his descendants a great nation in the land of Canaan. (A) CORRECT
4. In biblical text, the Israelites are descendants of Abraham. (A) CORRECT
5. God again makes a covenant with Abram in Genesis 17:4, promising that he would be "the father of many nations." (A) CORRECT

6. God changes Abram's name to Abraham, which means "father of a multitude." (A) CORRECT

7. Abram takes his extended family to Canaan, and they live there as *nomad*s. (A) CORRECT

8. Abram's wife, Sarai, stays barren throughout the Abrahamic narrative. (A) CORRECT

9. In desperation, she gives Abram her handmaiden, Hagar, as a concubine. (A) CORRECT

10. In Hebrew, the name "Sarah" means "princess." (A) CORRECT

11. The name "Ishmael" means "God will hear." (A) CORRECT

12. In Hebrew, the name "Hagar" can possibly mean "flight." (A) CORRECT

13. Hagar gives birth to Ishmael who is thought to be the ancestor of Arabs. (A) CORRECT

14. Although Sarah is doubtful, she later gives birth to Isaac (Genesis 21:2). (A) CORRECT

15. In her jealousy over her son's inheritance, Sarah forces Hagar and Ishmael to flee to the wilderness. (A) CORRECT

16. When Sarah dies, Abraham marries Keturah and has six more sons. (A) CORRECT

17. The line of biblical *patriarchy* runs through Isaac. (A) CORRECT

18. God instructs Abraham to sacrifice Isaac in Genesis, Chapter 22. (A) CORRECT

19. In Genesis, Chapter 24, Abraham trusts his servant to choose Rebekah as a wife for his son Isaac. (A) CORRECT

20. When Rebekah is pregnant with twins, she learns that the older child (Esau) will serve the younger (Jacob). (A) CORRECT

21. Isaac rebels against the prophesy and favors Esau anyway. (A) CORRECT

22. God's plan is that Jacob will be next in the line of patriarchs after Isaac. (A) CORRECT

23. During the birth of the twins, Jacob is holding his brother Esau's heel. (A) CORRECT

24. In Genesis, Chapter 27, Jacob (whose name means "supplanter") tricks Isaac into giving him the blessing of the firstborn. (A) CORRECT

25. Jacob runs away to escape his brother's wrath and lives with his Uncle Laban, Rebekah's brother. (A) CORRECT

26. Jacob falls in love with Laban's younger daughter, Rachel. (A) CORRECT

27. Ironically, Laban proves to be as deceitful as his nephew Jacob. (A) CORRECT

28. Laban gives Jacob to Rachel at the end of Leah's wedding week, but Jacob must work another seven years. (A) CORRECT

29. Jacob never marries Rachel. (B) INCORRECT

30. God comforts Leah by allowing her to conceive and bear sons. (A) CORRECT

31. Both Leah's and Rachel's handmaidens give birth to the sons of Jacob. (A) CORRECT

32. Rachel finally becomes pregnant, and Jacob becomes the father to twelve sons and a daughter. (A) CORRECT

33. Before reconciling with Esau, Jacob wrestles with an angel. (A) CORRECT

34. Symbolically, in Christian tradition, the angel that struggles with Jacob is the pre-incarnate Jesus Christ. (A) CORRECT

35. The angel changes Jacob's name to Israel. (A) CORRECT

36. The name "Israel" means "he who strives with God."

37. The nation of Israel takes its name from the man who fathered the nation, Jacob. (A) CORRECT
38. Each of Jacob's sons becomes a patriarch of a tribe of Israel. (A) CORRECT
39. On his death bed, Jacob blesses his twelve sons. (A) CORRECT
40. Jacob (Israel) mirrors his own inheritance by blessing Joseph's younger son, Ephraim, over the older son, Manasseh. (A) CORRECT

Extended Learning Study Questions:

(Article: "History of Israel" (https://www.factsaboutisrael.uk/history-of-israel-timeline/)

Directions: Write down whether the statements are (A) CORRECT or (B) INCORRECT.

1. Israel is known as a "chosen" nation. (A) CORRECT
2. In the Hebrew Scriptures, God wants Israel to serve as a model nation. (A) CORRECT
3. The nation of Israel is more than 3,000 years old. (A) CORRECT
4. Israel is three hundred miles long and thirty miles wide. (A) CORRECT
5. In the Book of Genesis, the covenant between God and Abraham is unconditional. (A) CORRECT
6. In Jewish and Christian traditions, all nations will be blessed through Abraham. (A) CORRECT
7. The term, "Jew" refers to the Israelites, named after Jacob, who is the grandson of Abraham. (A) CORRECT
8. Jacob's name becomes *Israel* in Hebrew Scriptures. (A) CORRECT
9. The term "Jew" relates to Judah, one of Jacob's twelve sons. (A) CORRECT
10. Ancient Israel consisted of twelve tribes that eventually divided into two kingdoms. (A) CORRECT

Extended Learning:

Study Questions

Reference: "Ancient Israelite Marriage Customs" by Jim West, ThD (http://www.theology.edu/marriage.htm)

Are the following statements (A) CORRECT or (B) INCORRECT?

1. Israel was a matriarchal culture in the Ancient Middle East. (B) INCORRECT
2. Women dominate a *matriarchal* culture. (A) CORRECT
3. In ancient Israel, males dominated family life. (A) CORRECT
4. Genesis 3:16 records that the husband (Adam) would rule over the wife (Eve). (A) CORRECT
5. As the head of the family in biblical times, the husband had the title "lord" or "master" denoting his role as the leader. (A) CORRECT

6. In ancient Israel, to remain an unmarried man deviated from the norm. (A) CORRECT

7. Marriage was not the norm in ancient Israel during biblical times. (B) INCORRECT

8. In ancient Israel, wives came from the larger family circle. (A) CORRECT

9. Women usually became wives at the beginning of puberty. (A) CORRECT

10. In ancient Hebrew culture, the purpose of marriage among relatives was to keep the purity of the family line. (A) CORRECT

11. Ancient Hebrew marriages could not be too closely blood related. (A) CORRECT

12. The ancient Israelites could not adopt the Egyptian and Canaanite cultures. (A) CORRECT

13. Israelites could not marry their father, mother, sister, or stepsister. (A) CORRECT

14. In Leviticus 18:18, God forbids rivalry in marriages. (A) CORRECT

15. Jacob, in Genesis 29: 28, takes a second wife, Rachel. (A) CORRECT

16. His second wife, Rachel, becomes a rival to his first wife, Leah. (A) CORRECT

17. In Genesis 4:19, Lamech is a polygamist. (A) CORRECT

18. Ancient Israelites forbade the offering of children as sacrifices to false gods. (A) CORRECT

19. God forbade the ancient Jews from defiling themselves by sleeping with their close relatives' wives. (A) CORRECT

20. Ancient Hebrew cultures forbade bestiality and same-sex attraction. (A) CORRECT

Study Questions:

(Reference: Hebrew Social Organization: Marriage

https://www.umanitoba.ca/faculties/arts/anthropology/tutor/case_studies/hebrews/marriage.html)

Directions: Note whether the statements are (A) CORRECT or (B) INCORRECT.

1. *Endogamy* is the practice of marrying within a specific social group, religious denomination, caste, or ethnic group. (A) CORRECT

2. The ancient Hebrews practiced endogamy based on dynamics of the patrilineal segmentary system. (A) CORRECT

3. The term "*patrilineal*" means inheriting or deciding descent through the male line. (A) CORRECT

4. A "segmentary system" refers to each of the parts into which something is divided.

5. The expression "descent" relates to birth, lineage, transmission, or transference of an estate. (A) CORRECT

6. The Genesis narrative in Genesis 29-30 about Jacob and his wives reflects status distinction. (A) CORRECT

7. In ancient Hebrew culture, childbirth related to status distinction. (A) CORRECT

8. Israel engaged in *endogamous* marriages, as well as in extramarital relationships.

9. According to the writer, the "Leah and Rachel tribes" were dominant political and territorial tribes in ancient Israel. (A) CORRECT

10. The biblical account of Reuben's seduction of Jacob's concubine serves as a rationale for excluding him and his patrimony from first-born privileges. (A) CORRECT

11. A synonym for "*patrimony*" is "*birthright*." (A) CORRECT

12. In ancient Hebrew tradition, the tribe of Judah inherited the rights to kingship. (A) CORRECT

13. The tribe of Levi received hereditary positions in the priesthood. (A) CORRECT

14. Joseph's descendants, especially Ephraim, received special birthrights.

15. Joseph's lineage primarily inherited substantial territorial allocations.

For Reflection

What are examples of the dominance of the tribes of Levi, Judah, Joseph (Ephraim and Manasseh), and Benjamin as reflected in the literature and history of ancient Israel? Write a three-five paragraph essay. Edit writing for errors. Use reliable internet sources to format the paper in APA or MLA style. Document sources. Post your reflection (five-eight sentences) on the discussion board. Label the post: A Reflection Tribal Dominance in Ancient Israel.

A Closing Thought:

"It is impossible for one who has studied at all the services of the Hebrew people to avoid the faith that they will one day be restored to their historic national home and there enter on a new and yet greater phase of their contribution to the advance of humanity.

-President Warren Harding

LESSON TWENTY-SEVEN
THE CHIASMIC EPISODIC STRUCTURE
OF THE ABRAHAMIC STORY

Lesson Overview

A *chiasm* (also called a chiasmus) is a literary device with a sequence of ideas presented and then repeated in reverse order. The Abraham story has a "mirror" effect as the main ideas "reflect" one another within the passages. (Repeated words and events connect the main ideas.) An "episodic narrative" is a story told through a series of episodes, or segments. The events are loosely connected parts or events. The biblical account of Abraham, Genesis, Chapters 12-36, is in episodes with an overreaching, larger story called a metanarrative. The chiasmic metanarrative divides into smaller, self-contained adventures about the relationship between God and Abraham. Students will examine the episodic chiasmic structure of the Abraham narratives.

Key Concepts: episodes, chiasm (also called a chiasmus), stylistic structure, continuity of plot, doublets, chiasmic metanarrative

Lesson Objectives:

Students will:

- use online Bible study tools to access, read, interpret, and explain information.

- examine the episodic chiasmic structure of the Abraham narratives.

- interpret the author's intended meaning of biblical text.

- find the meaning of words and phrases based on the context of the passages.

- interpret the Hebrew Bible while allowing for use of figurative language.

- distinguish between various biblical literary genres, including patriarchal Hebrew narratives.

- use information found in online biblical resources to support analyses, reflection(s), and research.

- make inferences and draw conclusions based on explicit and implied information using evidence from the text.

- share information about assigned biblical themes logically and accurately.

Expected Learning Objectives

At the end of this lesson, students will:

- understand literary terms related to biblical literacy, such a *chiastic episodic narrative*.

- explain the episodic chiasmic structure of the Abraham narratives

- interpret the author's intended meaning of biblical text.
- find the meaning of words and phrases based on the context of the passage.
- interpret the Hebrew Bible while allowing for normal use of figurative language.
- distinguish between various biblical literary genres, including patriarchal narratives.

Duration: 2-3 hours

Materials:

- Paper/pen/notebook/dictionary
- Video: *On the Structure of the Abraham Narratives - Prof. George Savran (https://www.youtube.com/watch?v=uc4SwO_LIjc)*

Procedure:

- Watch the video: *On the Structure of the Abraham Narratives - Prof. George Savran (https://www.youtube.com/watch?v=uc4SwO_LIjc)*
- Use an online dictionary to pronounce and define unfamiliar terms.
- Respond to study questions in full sentences.
- Write key points in your notebook and study the notes for future discussions and assessments.
- Respond to the reflection at the end of the lesson.
- Use online Bible study tools to enhance your learning.
- Use your computer's editing capability to correct writing errors.
- Post your reflection on the discussion board.
- Label the reflection: The Chiasmic Episodic Structure of the Abrahamic Story.
- If you have questions or need further clarification on any assignment, e-mail me at wilmaforeman@yahoo.com or visit my website: AIBL.INFO to sign up for the online course.

Study Questions:

Based on the presentation *The Structure of the Abraham Narratives* by Prof. George Savran, are the following statements (A) CORRECT or (B) INCORRECT?

1. The narratives about Abraham are the pivotal point of the Book of Genesis. (A) CORRECT
2. The biblical narratives about Abraham show the growth and development of Abraham's character from youth to old age. (A) CORRECT
3. The Abrahamic narratives are a continuous story about his quest for an heir and property. (A) CORRECT
4. In the narratives, Abraham endures ten trials to assess his faith in God. (A) CORRECT
5. The stylistic structure of the narratives is simple. (A) CORRECT
6. The story begins in Chapter 12 with God instructing Abraham to leave his birthplace from his father's land. (A) CORRECT

7. In reading the Abraham narratives from beginning to end, the overall pattern of his life story is complicated. (A) CORRECT

8. The narratives do not have details about Abraham's birth nor are there heroic accounts of his childhood. (A) CORRECT

9. The Abrahamic narrative begins with his migration toward the Promised land and concludes with his death in Canaan in Genesis 25. (A) CORRECT

10. The stories do not follow a clear progression, especially when compared to the more conventional chain of events in the Jacob cycle. (A) CORRECT

11. The order that the narratives recount the adventures in Abraham's life is not a normal progression. (A) CORRECT

12. Abraham, the soldier, connects to the context of Abraham as the keeper of flocks. (A) CORRECT

13. Genesis, Chapter 15 bears no relation to the plotline of Abraham's quest for land. (A) CORRECT

14. The forecast of enslavement in Egypt loosely connects to the prophecies of Abraham's offspring. (A) CORRECT

15. As the story progresses, Sarah's later initiatives to secure an heir for Abraham in Genesis 16 is unexpected to the reader. (A) CORRECT

16. The narrative fulfillment of the promise of Abraham's descendants occurs in Genesis 21. (A) CORRECT

17. The episodes in Genesis, Chapters 20 and 21 appear suddenly, and the demand to sacrifice Isaac upon the altar is unexpected. (A) CORRECT

18. *Continuity of plot* is not the central principle of the organization of the stories. (A) CORRECT

19. In addition to the difficulties in finding a clear linear progression of the events in the stories, there are *doublets*. (A) CORRECT

20. *Doublets* are two distinct words derived from the same source but by different routes of transmission. (A) CORRECT

21. The "wife-sister" Abraham story occurs near the beginning of the Abraham cycle in Chapter 12 and once again at the end of Chapter 20. (A) CORRECT

22. The promise of Isaac's birth appears twice in Chapters 17 and 18 with different divine reactions to Abraham and Sarah, respectively. (A) CORRECT

23. Bible scholars see the doublets as indications of a chiastic arrangement of the narratives. (A) CORRECT

24. Scholars suggest that the second doublet reflects a reworking of the first. (A) CORRECT

25. Another proposed organizational principle of the Abrahamic narrative structure focuses on *parallel* behaviors or actions. (A) CORRECT

26. The birth of Isaac parallels to the birth of Ishmael, and the covenant of the pieces in Genesis, Chapter 15 parallels to the covenant of circumcision in Genesis, Chapter 17. (A) CORRECT

27. The battle of Abraham with the kings in Genesis, Chapter 14 has no parallel narrative in the Book of Genesis. (A) CORRECT

28. Abraham's childlessness first mentioned in Genesis, Chapter 11 finds expression in his complaint in Genesis, Chapter 15. (A) CORRECT

29. In the Abrahamic narratives, such as the Hagar-Sarah story, a first action of Abraham results in a later behavior taken without prior consultation with God. (A) CORRECT

30. While the first actions of Abraham lead to a measure of success, the second part of the story serves as a correction to his first choices. (A) CORRECT

31. In the narratives, the unifying force is God's divine guidance that is essential to realizing the larger aims of God plans. (A) CORRECT

32. Abraham stories have a didactic emphasis of the larger narrative that focuses on a consistent walk with God. (A) CORRECT

33. Abraham is the recipient of God's ongoing instruction and continuous correction of his attempts to assert his own authority and control. (A) CORRECT

34. The episodic narratives center on Abraham's personal destiny in his role as a founder of the Hebrews. (A) CORRECT

35. Episodes in a narrative may not always have the same characters, but each episode draws from a broader group of characters. (A) CORRECT

For Reflection:

How does the episode about Sarah's initiatives to secure an heir for Abraham in Genesis 16 reflect the ancient Hebrews' marriage traditions? How do the traditions compare to modern customs in Western society? (Write five-eight sentences. Edit your writing to correct errors. Post your reflection on the discussion board. Label the post: Marriage Customs of the Ancient Hebrews.)

For Reflection:

Outline the ten trials which measure Abraham's faith in God. Edit your writing to correct errors. Post your reflection on the discussion board. Label the post: Ten Trials that Test Abraham's Faith.

For Reflection:

Select one episode from the Abrahamic narratives and discuss the significance of the story as it pertains to the promises that God makes to Abraham. Write five-eight sentences. Edit your writing to correct errors. Post your reflection on the discussion board. Label the post: A Reflection on an Episode in the Abraham Chiasm.

A Closing Thought:

"Knowledge of the Bible never comes by intuition. It can only be obtained by diligent, regular, daily, attentive reading."

— *J.C. Ryle*

LESSON TWENTY-EIGHT

THE SIGNIFICANCE OF ABRAHAM

IN JEWISH, CHRISTIAN, AND ISLAMIC TRADITIONS

Lesson Overview:

Modern day Palestine (the Promised Canaan) is the home of Jews, Christians, and Arabs. Abraham (Abram) is the common Hebrew patriarch of these Abrahamic monotheistic religions, including Judaism, Christianity, and Islam. The Abrahamic narrative in the Book of Genesis centers on the theme of posterity, land, and blessings in the Promised Land-Canaan. In Judaism, Abraham is the founding father of the special relationship between the Jews and God; in Christianity, he is the spiritual forefather of all believers in God, whether Jewish or non-Jewish; and in Islam, he is a common link to the Islamic prophets beginning with Adam and ending with Muhammad. This lesson will supply information about the conflict in the Middle East compared to the descendants of the biblical Abraham and the possession of the Promised Land. Students will review historical and current events in the Middle East and examine the complexities in resolving the issues.

Key Concepts: The Promised Land, the Middle East, Palestine, the Arab Israeli conflict, Quran, or Koran, nationalism, Mecca, the Kaaba, Hajj, intifada, The Balfour Declaration, Nakba Day, the Temple Mount, Hamas, Salam, Zionism, the "Partition Plan, the UN and Resolution 242

Objectives:

Students will:

- connect the biblical account of the life of Abraham to his descendants in Jewish, Christian, and Islamic traditions.
- compare the points of view of citizens of Israel and Palestine about the Arab Israeli conflict.
- summarize negotiations and ongoing conflicts in the Middle East.
- give a correct summary of a source.
- cite specific textual evidence to support analysis of primary and secondary sources.

Expected Learning Outcomes:

At the end of the lesson students will:

- understand the role that the Abrahamic narratives play in the Middle East land conflicts.
- compare the points of view of Palestinian citizens about the Arab/Israeli conflict.
- summarize negotiations and ongoing conflicts in the Middle East.

Materials:

- Paper/pen/notebook
- Internet access/a computer with editing capability
- Video: Abraham, Father of Many Nations
  (https://www.youtube.com/watch?v=l5ZDoGqFfxg)
- Video: The Complete Story of Abraham: The Father of Nations
  (https://www.youtube.com/watch?v=Wv9usf6BrEY)
- Video: The 12 Tribes of Israel in the Bible (Whiteboard Bible Study)
  (https://www.youtube.com/watch?v=KP-EXMy4Xas)
- Article: "Place of Abraham in Islam, Christianity, Judaism"
  (https://hp.haccessonlineforms.com/?page=newtab&cid=iliimbpbpliabblllmgebklpjkgeag
  jp&ap=appfocus1&source=d-ccc4-lp0-dsf_forms-cp_12887637018-tst1--
  bb9&uc=20210503&uid=9766caf4-c28a-44ca-9b60-4d4f19b54a71&i_id=forms_1.3&)
- Video: Conflict in Israel and Palestine
  (https://www.khanacademy.org/humanities/whp-origins/era-7-the-great-convergence-
  and-divergence-1880-ce-to-the-future/74-end-of-empires-betaa/v/conflict-in-israel-and-
  palestine-crash-course-world-history-223-beta)

Procedure:

- Read the article: "Place of Abraham in Islam, Christianity, and Judaism."
- Use an online dictionary to pronounce and define unfamiliar terms.
- Respond to the study questions.
- Watch the video lessons and respond to the study questions.
- Use online Bible study tools to enhance your learning.
- Write a reflection on the lesson. Edit writing for errors.
- Post the reflection on the discussion board,
- Label the post: A Reflection on Abraham and the Middle East Conflicts

Study Questions:

Article: "Place of Abraham in Islam, Christianity, Judaism"

https://hp.haccessonlineforms.com/?page=newtab&cid=iliimbpbpliabblllmgebklpjkgeagjp&ap=a
ppfocus1&source=d-ccc4-lp0-dsf_forms-cp_12887637018-tst1--
bb9&uc=20210503&uid=9766caf4-c28a-44ca-9b60-4d4f19b54a71&i_id=forms_1.3&

Directions:

Indicate whether the following statements are (A) CORRECT or (B) INCORRECT.

1. In Islam tradition, the name *Abraham* is *Ibrahim*. (A) CORRECT
2. Abraham is a prophet in Islamic cultures. (A) CORRECT

3. In Islam, a prophet is a person regarded as an inspired teacher or proclaimer of the will of God. (A) CORRECT
4. The phrase "Peace be unto him" (PBUH) follows Abraham's name in Islamic cultures. (A) CORRECT
5. *Salam* is a greeting in Arabic that means "Peace be upon you." (A) CORRECT
6. *As-salamu alaykum* is an Arabic greeting that Muslims worldwide use regardless of their language background. (A) CORRECT
7. In Islam, Abraham (Ibrahim) is a "friend of God" and the father of Ishmael and Isaac. (A) CORRECT
8. In Islamic tradition, Abraham is the fore parent of Jacob (Yaqub). (A) CORRECT
9. The *Quran*, or *Koran*, is the central religious text of Islam, believed by Muslims to be a revelation from God. (A) CORRECT
10. Arabic name for Mecca is *Makkah*. (A) CORRECT
11. Mecca is an Arabic city in western Saudi Arabia, found in the Ṣirāt Mountains, inland from the Red Sea coast. (A) CORRECT
12. Mecca is the holiest city in Islam. (A) CORRECT
13. The word Hajj (Hadj) means to make a resolve to visit a holy place and refers to visiting the Ka'ba in Makka (Mecca). (A) CORRECT
14. The Muslim pilgrimage to Mecca takes place in the last month of the year. (A) CORRECT
15. Hajj involves a series of rituals that take place in and around Mecca over a period of five to six days. (A) CORRECT
16. The Kaaba (Kaba) is a sanctuary attributed to Abraham and Ishmael. (A) CORRECT
17. The Kaaba is the central structure around which the Hajj takes place. (A) CORRECT
18. The visit to the Kaaba stands for devotion to Abraham, Hagar, and Ishmael. (A) CORRECT
19. In Islamic tradition, Prophet Ibrahim settled his wife and son in the valley of Makkah (Mecca) by God's order. (A) CORRECT
20. Mecca is the holiest city in Saudi Arabia. (A) CORRECT

Study Questions

Directions: View the video: *Conflict in Israel and Palestine*

(*https://www.khanacademy.org/humanities/whp-origins/era-7-the-great-convergence-and-divergence-1880-ce-to-the-future/74-end-of-empires-betaa/v/conflict-in-israel-and-palestine-crash-course-world-history-223-beta*). Respond to the study questions.

Are the following statements (A) TRUE or (B) FALSE?

1. The conflict between Israel and Palestine over the last decades relates to theological and land differences between Islam and Judaism. (A) CORRECT
2. In both Judaism and Islam, the key prophets descended from Abraham's son by Sarah, Isaac, or his son by Hagar, Ishmael. (A) CORRECT
3. The main conflict in the Middle East results from different religious views on land inheritances. (A) CORRECT
4. In the late 19th century, the Ottoman Empire ruled over what we now know as Palestine. (A) CORRECT

5. According to 1878 Ottoman records, eighty-seven percent of the population was Muslim, ten percent was Christian, and three percent was Jewish. (A) CORRECT

6. Ancient Ottoman Palestine was a place in which people of different religious faiths lived together peacefully. (A) CORRECT

7. In the late 19th century during the Golden Age of European nationalism, at least ten different nations wanted their own state. (A) CORRECT

8. A Jewish journalist named Theodor Herzl hoped that Jews could *assimilate* into European nations. (A) CORRECT

9. He later became convinced that the Jewish people needed to leave Europe and settle in their own state. (A) CORRECT

10. The concept of Jewish nationalism came to be known as *Zionism.* (A) CORRECT

11. Zionists were *secular* Jews who imagined Israel as a state for Jews different from a religious Jewish state. (A) CORRECT

12. In 1917, the British government, hoping to gain the support of Jewish people, issued the Balfour Declaration. (A) CORRECT

13. The Balfour Declaration promised "the establishment in Palestine of a national home for the Jewish people." (A) CORRECT

14. A year before the Balfour Declaration, the British had secretly promised the French that they would divide the Arab territories and Britain would keep Palestine. (A) CORRECT

15. In 1915, British officials had promised the ruler of Mecca, Sharif Hussein, that he would rule over an Arab state including Palestine if he led an Arab revolt against Ottoman rule. (A) CORRECT

16. In all, the British leaders promised Palestine to the Meccans, to themselves, and to the Zionists. (A) CORRECT

17. After the end of the war, the British set up a colony in Palestine with the assumption that they would rule until the Palestinians could govern themselves. (A) CORRECT

18. The British established separate institutions for Christians, Jews, and Muslims. (A) CORRECT

19. Palestinian Christians and Muslims were not able to cooperate with each other in peace. (A) CORRECT

20. The British were able to "divide and rule" the inhabitants of Palestine. (A) CORRECT

21. The British did try to honor the Balfour Declaration's promise to "facilitate Jewish immigration under suitable conditions." (A) CORRECT

22. In 1938, Jews were thirty percent of the population in Palestine. (A) CORRECT

23. The growing Jewish population focused on buying land from absentee non-Palestinian Arab landowners. (A) CORRECT

24. Over time, small farmers became indebted to rich families. (A) CORRECT

25. By controlling both the land and the labor, the Jewish population hoped to set up a more secure community within Palestine. (A) CORRECT

26. The land purchasing practices heightened tensions between Jewish people and Arab Palestinians between the 1920s and the 1930s. (A) CORRECT

27. Palestinian Arabs considered themselves as the Palestinian nation. (A) CORRECT

28. The growing sense of nationalism erupted in 1936, when the Palestinians revolted against the British. (A) CORRECT

29. With the help of Jewish militias, the British brutally suppressed the Palestinian revolt. (A) CORRECT

30. The British limited Jewish immigration to Palestine and called for the establishment of a joint Arab and Jewish state in Palestine. (A) CORRECT

31. The Zionists became angry at Britain for limiting Jewish immigration. (A) CORRECT

32. The Arab Palestinians were unhappy about the prospect of waiting ten years to become a state. (A) CORRECT

33. At the beginning of World War II, Palestine experienced peace, but later, the tensions resumed, and the British handed the issue of Palestine over to the newly created United Nations. (A) CORRECT

34. In November of 1947, the United Nations voted to partition Palestine into separate Palestinian and Jewish states. (A) CORRECT

35. The "Partition Plan" called for two states in Palestine of equal in size. (A) CORRECT

36. The borders of the Palestinian states are easy to define. (B) INCORRECT

37. The 1948 Arab Israeli War broke out with Israel on one side and the Palestinians and Arab states on the other. (A) CORRECT

38. The Israelis won the war, and an armistice was signed in 1949. (A) CORRECT

39. After the war, Israel occupied a third more land than they would have had under the UN proposal. (A) CORRECT

40. Jordan, an Arab region, controlled and later annexed the West Bank and the old city of Jerusalem, while Egypt controlled the Gaza strip. (A) CORRECT

41. Over 700,000 Palestinians fled their homes and became refugees in the surrounding Arab countries. (A) CORRECT

42. To Israelis, this was the beginning of their nation, but o the Palestinians, the post-war condition was the *nakba*, or *catastrophe*, as they became stateless. (A) CORRECT

43. *Nakba Day* is the day of commemoration for the *Nakba*, also known as the *Palestinian Catastrophe,* the 1948 destruction of Palestinian society and homeland. (A) CORRECT

44. In 1967, Israel and Arab states went to war again for six days. (A) CORRECT

45. Israel won the Six-Days War. (A) CORRECT

46. Israel gained control over the West Bank, the Gaza Strip, the Sinai Peninsula, and the Golan Heights. (A) CORRECT

47. The UN passed Resolution 242 that outlined a basic framework for achieving peace in the region. (A) CORRECT

48. The Resolution included Israel withdrawing from the territory gotten in the war.

49. All participants in the Six-Days war had to recognize the rights of both the Palestinians and an Israelis to exist as a state. (A) CORRECT

50. After the Six-Days-War, the broader Israeli-Arab conflict transformed into a more specific Israeli-Palestinian conflict. (A) CORRECT

51. *Palestinian* is a word used to describe the ethnic identity of those who have historically lived in Palestine, including Jews, Christians, and Muslims. (A) CORRECT

52. The Israeli government began to set up Jewish settlements in what had been Palestinian territory, including East Jerusalem, the West Bank, and the Gaza Strip. (A) CORRECT

53. By the late 1980s, Palestinians launched the first *intifada*, which means "shaking off." (A) CORRECT

54. The *intifada* began as a boycott of Israeli products and services and by refusing to pay Israeli taxes. (A) CORRECT

55. When the Israeli armed forces confronted the protesters, violence ensued. (A) CORRECT

56. In 1993, the first *intifada* resulted in the founding of *Hamas*, which launched the first suicide bombing against Israel. (A) CORRECT

57. *Hamas* gained support because of its militancy and social welfare projects in Gaza. (A) CORRECT

58. President Bill Clinton's administration came closer than any other time in recent history to forming a peace deal between the Israelis and the Palestinians. (A) CORRECT

59. Peace between the Israelis and Palestinians did not take place. (A) CORRECT

60. Ehud Barak's government was undermined, and in September of 2000, Prime Minister candidate Ariel Sharon led a group of 1,000 armed guards to the Temple Mount in the Old City of Jerusalem. (A) CORRECT

61. To Muslims, the Temple Mount is known as the Al-Aqsa Mosque, the third-holiest site in Islam. (A) CORRECT

62. The Kaaba in Mecca and the Prophet's Mosque in Medina are the holiest sites of the Muslims. (A) CORRECT

63. The Temple Mount is the holiest site in Judaism. (A) CORRECT

64. The march on the Temple Mount sparked a massive protest and led to the much more violent *Second Intifada*. (A) CORRECT

65. During the protest, more than three thousand Palestinians and one thousand Israelis died. (A) CORRECT

66. In 2002, the Israelis began construction of a wall around the West Bank to include Israeli settlements on the Israeli side. (A) CORRECT

67. In 2005, Yasser Arafat died, and in an election shortly thereafter, Hamas won a majority of the parliamentary seats. (A) CORRECT

68. Since 2005, Palestine has been poorly governed. (A) CORRECT

69. In the past ten years, Hamas has often launched rocket attacks into Israel. (A) CORRECT

70. Israel has retaliated against Hamas with violence. (A) CORRECT

71. Both parties claim that they are responding to the provocations of the other. (A) CORRECT

72. The conflict reflects the consistent failure on all sides to understand the legitimacy of the others' rights to land ownership. (A) CORRECT

73. The right to land ownership can be traced to both Ishmael and Isaac, descendants of Abraham. (A) CORRECT

74. God first gave the pledge of land ownership to Abraham and then to Abraham's descendants. (A) CORRECT

75. Ishmael's descendants are the Arabs. (A) CORRECT

For Reflection:

Genesis, Chapter 12 God makes a unilateral contract that only He must fulfill. What are the terms of the contract? What are the symbolic actions of God and Abraham in Genesis, Chapter 15 to seal the contract? Explain why the covenant is official according to the ancient Israelites' traditions of covenant making. Discuss the importance of blood in the covenants. How does the ancient covenant between God and Abraham impact the tensions in the Middle East? (Write 3-5 paragraphs.) Record your source(s). Edit your writing to correct errors. Post the reflection on the discussion board. Label the post: The Abrahamic Covenant and Tensions in the Middle East.

(Suggested reference: *"Covenant Making in Anatolia and Mesopotamia" by Moshe Weinfield - Hebrew University of Jerusalem)*
(file:///C:/Users/user/Downloads/Moshe_Weinfeld_Covenant_Making_in_Anatol.pdf).

A Closing Thought:

"The Promised Land is not a place to be conquered by armies and solidified by displacing other people. The Promised Land is a corner in the heart."

— Joseph Campbell

LESSON TWENTY-NINE
THE JOSEPH SAGA
(GENESIS THIRTY-SEVEN THROUGH FIFTY)

Lesson Overview:

The Joseph narrative is a lauded treasure of world literature. This *saga* extends thirteen chapters in the Hebrew Scriptures. A saga is a narrative telling the adventures of a hero or a family. The *literary motifs* (patterns) that appear in the Joseph saga concern family breakdown, God's promise to Abraham, divine providence, blessings, and possession of land. Each of these motifs is dominant in the Joseph story, but the overreaching theme is God's providential work in the life of Joseph to save Jacob's (Israel's) flawed family. Through divine intervention, Joseph not only preserves the descendants of Abraham, but he becomes a blessing to others outside the family. The biblical author enhances the story by using dreams, Egyptian words, proper names, and customs, inner monologue, a chiasmic structure, and an array of *doublets* (repetition with variation). Students will analyze the literary artistry in the Joseph saga and the role that God plays in keeping His covenants with humanity.

Key Concepts: saga, episodes, literary motifs, sibling rivalry, character flaws, chiasmic structure, antithetical parallelism, inner monologue, repetition with variation, divine providence, doublets

Lesson Objectives:

Students will:

- cite specific textual evidence to support analysis of primary and secondary sources.
- connect the biblical account of the life of Joseph and his descendants in Jewish, Christian, and Islamic traditions.
- summarize a source accurately and concisely.
- understand the themes of divine providence and solidarity in the saga of Joseph.
- understand the chiastic structure of a literary saga.

Expected Learning Outcomes:

At the end of the lesson students will be able to:

- use specific textual evidence to support analysis of primary and secondary sources.
- understand the themes of divine providence and solidarity in the saga of Joseph.
- understand the chiastic structure of a literary saga.
- find the presence of gaps and repetition in a story.
- explain how a story's use of repetition and gaps affects the meaning.
- analyze and evaluate the characters' roles in a story.

Duration: 4-5 hours

Materials:

- Paper/pen/notebook/dictionary
- Video: *THE STORY OF JOSEPH*
  (*https://www.youtube.com/watch?v=UI8X6ytNh7o*)
- Booklet: *The Literary Genius of the Joseph Narrative* (Pages1-3).
  (http://www.inthebeginning.org/chiasmus/xfiles/xjosephnarrative.PDF)
- Use an online dictionary to pronounce and define unfamiliar terms.
- Blog: The Joseph Saga: Turnabouts, Trade-Offs, and Transience
  (https://blog.apaonline.org/2021/02/01/the-joseph-saga-turnabouts-trade-offs-and-transience/)
- Article: Finding Meaning in Incoherence: The Joseph Story Beyond Source Criticism
  (https://www.thetorah.com/article/finding-meaning-in-incoherence-the-joseph-story-beyond-source-criticism)
- Blog: The Joseph's Saga (1): The Beloved Son by Julia Blum April 22, 2021
  (https://blog.israelbiblicalstudies.com/jewish-studies/josephs-saga-1-the-beloved-son/)

Procedure:

- Read Genesis, Chapters thirty-seven through fifty.
- Study the overview chart below.
- Watch the video: *THE STORY OF JOSEPH*
  (*https://www.youtube.com/watch?v=UI8X6ytNh7o*).
- Respond to the study questions.
- Respond to the reflection(s).
- Use online Bible study tools to enhance your learning.
- Edit your writing to correct errors.
- Post the reflection(s) on the discussion board.
- If you have questions or need further clarification on any assignment, e-mail me at wilmaforeman@yahoo.com or visit my website: AIBL.INFO to sign up for the online course.

Genesis 37-50

"Joseph Sold into Slavery"	Gen. 37:38-30	Joseph, Jacob's son by Rachel, receives special favor over his other brothers. Jacob is especially fond of this son since he gives him a coat of assorted colors. Joseph, also a dreamer, shares his dreams that suggest that he will rule over his family. Joseph's older brothers are so infuriated that they sell him	• Dreams • Sibling rivalry • Parental favoritism • Jealousy • Pride (Joseph's) • Deceit

		to a group of passing Midianite's traders. They deceive their father Jacob by dipping Joseph's rich coat in goat's blood and by pretending that a wild animal killed Joseph. In truth, they have sold Joseph into slavery in Egypt.	• Family strife • Hatred • Bondage/oppression • Parental Grief
"Joseph and Potiphar's Wife"	Gen. 39:1-23	In Egypt, Joseph is a slave in the household of Potiphar, one of Pharaoh's senior officials. Joseph is successful in all his responsibilities, and advances in position in the household. His attractive features, however, cause him trouble when the wife of Potiphar tries to seduce him. After she fails in her attempts, she accuses him of rape. Potiphar sends Joseph to prison. In this dire condition, Joseph still finds divine favor.	• Divine favor • False accusations • Man/Woman relations • A wife's influence. • Purity in character • Facing adversity
"Joseph's Dreams" "Joseph's Brothers Travel to Egypt"	Gen. 41:1-57; 41:1-57 Gen. 42:1-38	In prison, Joseph soon joins two men from Pharaoh's household. One is a cupbearer, and the other is a baker. Each of these men has dreams that Joseph can interpret. The cupbearer's dream is a prophecy of restoration to his former post. After interpreting the dream, Joseph asks the cupbearer to remember him when he assumes his freedom, but the cupbearer does not remember Joseph. Later, Pharaoh begins to dream, but he finds that there is no one to interpret his dreams for him. Finally, the cupbearer remembers the dreamer, Joseph. Summoned from prison to interpret the dreams of Pharaoh, Joseph predicts seven	• Dreams • Gratitude • Forgiveness • Divine favor • Irony of situation • Divine providence • Brotherly love

		years of rich harvest in Egypt, followed by seven years of famine. Pharaoh decides to place Joseph in charge of preparations for the forthcoming famine. Because of this decision, Egypt survives during the years of famine, just as Joseph predicted. As the famine persists, Jacob and his household are dangerously short of food. As a result, he sends his sons to Egypt for more food. Benjamin, their youngest brother, travels with them. After they arrive in Egypt, Joseph sees his brother Benjamin, and becomes emotional. He decides not to reveal himself right away, however. Instead, he plants his own cup inside Benjamin's sack of food and accuses his brother of stealing it. He then demands that the sacks someone searches the bags. When someone finds the cup in Benjamin's bag, his brothers return to Joseph and offer themselves as slaves if Joseph will spare Benjamin.	

"Jacob Travels to Egypt"	Gen. 45:47-27	After Joseph reveals his identity to his brothers, Pharaoh orders transportation so that Jacob and his household can move to Egypt. Jacob's family can settle in the land of Goshen as honored guests. This happens to be one of the richest parts of Egypt (46:25-28). Even though the famine continues in Egypt, Joseph ensures the Israelites that grain will be available to all of them.	• Brotherly love • Forgiveness • Character maturity • Divine favor

"Jacob Blesses his Sons"	Gen. 49:50-21	Before he dies, Jacob blesses each of his twelve sons individually and the tribes that will bear their names (49:50-51). He repeats his request to be buried in the family grave in the field of Machpelah in Canaan beside Abraham, Sarah, Isaac, Rebekah, and Leah. Joseph ensures him that his wishes will be honored and goes with his entire family to Canaan to bury Isaac. Afterward, the family returns to Egypt and stays there permanently (50:121). The Book of Genesis ends with the recording of the death of Joseph and his burial in Egypt.	• Fatherly love and foresight • Fore-shadowing • Inheritance • Family loyalty • Parental respect • Family history • Ancient burial customs

Study Questions (based on the video: *THE STORY OF JOSEPH*
(https://www.youtube.com/watch?v=UI8X6ytNh7o))

Are the following statements (A) CORRECT or (B) INCORRECT?

1. At the beginning of the Joseph saga, Jacob lives in the land of Canaan. (A) CORRECT

2. Genesis, Chapters 37-50 is an account of the life of Jacob's youngest son, Joseph. (A) CORRECT

3. In this narrative, Israel loves Joseph more than any of his other sons because he is born to him in his old age. (A) CORRECT

4. Israel (Jacob) makes Joseph a richly ornamented robe, called a "coat of many colors." (A) CORRECT

5. When Joseph's brothers see that their father loves him more than any of them, they hate him. (A) CORRECT

6. The brothers behave judiciously toward Joseph, as well as their father. (B) INCORRECT

7. Joseph has a dream, and when he tells it to his brothers, they are become even more malicious toward him. (A) CORRECT

8. In the dream, Joseph binds sheaves of grain in the field, and suddenly, his sheaf rises and stands upright. (A) CORRECT

9. His brothers' bundles of grain (A) CORRECT stalks gather around his and bow to his bundle. (A) CORRECT

10. According to the video, Joseph's dream in Chapter 37 symbolizes earthly matters: food, wheat, sustenance. (A) CORRECT

11. This dream also symbolizes Joseph's future elevated position in Egypt. (A) CORRECT

12. Joseph's brothers reject the idea of his reigning over them. (A) CORRECT

13. Joseph has another dream in which the sun, the moon, and eleven stars bow to him. (A) CORRECT

14. His father, as well as his brothers, rebuke him. (A) CORRECT

15. When Joseph tells his dream, his father ponders it, but his brothers despise him more than ever. (A) CORRECT

16. One day, Jacob sends Joseph to Shechem for his brothers who are grazing their father's flocks in the field. (A) CORRECT

17. Joseph finds his brothers in Dothan, about a day's journey from Shechem. (A) CORRECT

18. One of the brothers suggests that they kill Joseph and throw him into a cistern. (A) CORRECT

19. A cistern is an underground water tank, often built to store rainwater. (A) CORRECT

20. The brothers' plan is to say that an animal has killed Joseph. (A) CORRECT

21. Reuben suggests that they throw Joseph into the cistern instead of killing him. (A) CORRECT

22. When Joseph comes to his brothers, they strip him of the richly ornamented robe and throw him into the empty cistern. (A) CORRECT

23. While the brothers are eating, they see a caravan of Ishmaelites coming from Gilead with camels loaded with balm and myrrh. (A) CORRECT

24. Balm and myrrh are spices. (A) CORRECT

25. The Ishmaelites are traveling to Egypt. (A) CORRECT

26. Judah proposes that the brothers sell Joseph to the traveler. (A) CORRECT

27. The merchants buy Joseph for twenty shekels of silver. (A) CORRECT

28. Reuben becomes distraught when he returns to the cistern and sees that Joseph is not there. (A) CORRECT

29. Tearing one's clothes was an ancient sign of distress. (A) CORRECT

30. The brothers dip Joseph's robe into the blood of a slaughtered goat and take the garment back to their father. (A) CORRECT

31. They tell the father that they have found the robe and make Israel believe that a ferocious animal has killed Joseph. (A) CORRECT

32. Jacob tears his clothes, puts on sackcloth, and mourns for his son. (A) CORRECT

33. Jacob finds comfort in his wife, Leah, after a prolonged period of grieving. (B) INCORRECT

34. The Midianites sell Joseph in Egypt to Potiphar, one of Pharaoh's officials. (A) CORRECT

35. Potiphar is the captain of the guard. (A) CORRECT

36. Joseph lives in the house of his Egyptian master. (A) CORRECT

37. His master perceives that God favors Joseph. (A) CORRECT

38. God gives Joseph success in everything he does. (A) CORRECT

39. Joseph finds favor in his Egyptian master's eyes and becomes his attendant. (A) CORRECT

40. Potiphar puts Joseph in charge of his household and all that he owns. (A) CORRECT

41. One day, Potiphar's wife takes notice of Joseph and makes sexual advancements toward him. (A) CORRECT

42. Demonstrating his integrity of character, Joseph refuses her attempts to seduce him. (A) CORRECT

43. In retaliation, Potiphar's wife lies to her husband about Joseph. (A) CORRECT

44. She says that Joseph has tried to molest her. (A) CORRECT

45. She shows her husband Joseph's cloak as proof that he has behaved inappropriately toward her. (A) CORRECT

46. Infuriated, Potiphar imprisons Joseph. (A) CORRECT

47. A cloak is a loose outer garment. (A) CORRECT

48. God grants Joseph favor with the prison wardens and gives him success in all his endeavors. (A) CORRECT

49. At the end of the saga, Joseph forgives his brothers for mistreating him. (A) CORRECT

50. Joseph believes that God has intervened during his adverse circumstances and has turned evil into good. (A) CORRECT

Extended Learning Study Questions:

Directions: Read *The Literary Genius of the Joseph Narrative* (Pages 1-3). (http://www.inthebeginning.org/chiasmus/xfiles/xjosephnarrative.PDF). Respond to the study questions.

Are the following statements (A) CORRECT or (B) INCORRECT?

1. A *chiasm* (also called a chiasmus) is a literary device in which a sequence of ideas appears and then reappears *in reverse order*. (A) CORRECT
2. A chiasm produces a "mirror" effect as the ideas appear in a passage. (A) CORRECT
3. Each idea in a chiasm connects to its "reflection" by a repeated word. (A) CORRECT
4. The term *chiasm* comes from the Greek letter *chi*, which looks like our letter *X*. (A) CORRECT
5. Chiastic pattern is the same as "ring structure." (A) CORRECT
6. The structure of a chiasm, such as ABBA refers to two ideas (A and B) repeated in reverse order (B and A). (A) CORRECT
7. The common saying "When the going gets tough, the tough get going" is chiastic. (A) CORRECT

8. Benjamin Franklin's *axiom*, "By failing to prepare, you are preparing to fail" is chiastic. (A) CORRECT

9. The structure of the Joseph saga unfolds in an ad hoc or haphazard manner. (B) INCORRECT

10. The Joseph narrative is the most unified narrative in Genesis. (A) CORRECT

11. Not only is the narrative a saga, but it is a biography. (A) CORRECT

12. The life of Joseph is *paradoxical*, or contradictory. (A) CORRECT

13. The Joseph narrative is the most intricately composed, complex and lengthy unit in Hebrew Scriptures. (A) CORRECT

14. The Joseph saga divides into manageable *episodes*. (A) CORRECT

15. An episode is the simplest unit of a narrative, displaying a significant level of independence from its context. (A) CORRECT

16. The grand effect of the Joseph narrative rests upon its parts blending into one continuous whole. (A) CORRECT

17. The content, phraseology, and sequencing of events contribute to the overall literary strategy in the Joseph narrative. (A) CORRECT

18. Structural analysis of the Hebrew Scriptures has proved that ancient biblical writers relied heavily on *chiasmus* to compose their literary works. (A) CORRECT

19. *Chiasmus* produces balanced statements, in direct, *inverted*, or *antithetical parallelism*. (A) CORRECT

20. *Antithetical parallelism* is a major literary device in Hebrew Scriptures. (A) CORRECT

21. Antithetical parallelism supplies an *antithesis*, or contrast. (A) CORRECT

22. An example of antithetical parallelism is in Genesis 4:6-7: *Then the Lord said to Cain, "Why are you angry? And why has your countenance fallen? If you do well, will not your countenance be lifted up? And if you do not do*(A) CORRECT *well, sin is crouching at the door; and its desire is for you, but you must master it."*

23. The proper titles of the episodes surrounding the Joseph narrative include: "Beloved Son, Hated Brother" (Gen. 37:2-11) and "Strife and Deceit" (Gen. 37:12-36). (A) CORRECT

24. The Joseph episodes vary in length and complexity. (A) CORRECT

25. Each episode in the Joseph narrative has its own *exposition,* followed by action with a climax that leads to an end. (A) CORRECT

26. The episodes do not detract from the suspense of the Joseph narrative in its entirety. (A) CORRECT

27. An episode is a temporary resting point for the action of the narrative. (A) CORRECT

28. The *chiastic structure* rests its focus upon a central theme. (A) CORRECT

29. The Joseph narrative has *chiastic elements* that lead to a climax, then follow a second series of matching units in reverse order to bring the story to a *resolution or conclusion*.

30. The chiasmus structure in the Joseph saga depends on *inverted order*. (A) CORRECT

For Reflection:

Blog: "The Joseph Saga: Turnabouts, Trade-Offs, and Transience" **by** Steven M. Cahn (https://blog.apaonline.org/2021/02/01/the-joseph-saga-turnabouts-trade-offs-and-transience/)

Directions:

Respond to the 2021 blog by Steven M. Cahn in five -eight sentences. Focus on the thought: *"The story of Joseph suggests that turnabouts, trade-offs, and transience are features of the human condition…Such is life."* Post your reflection on the discussion board. Edit your writing to correct errors. Label the post: The Joseph Saga-Such is Life!

Documented Essay Assignment:

To become a strong leader, an individual's character needs to become fully developed in integrity, humility, patience, faithfulness, compassion, competence, and wisdom. From Joseph's own words in Genesis 50:20, one can conclude that God allows the physical, mental, and emotional sufferings of Joseph not only to fulfill His plan to save the lives of the Hebrews, but to strengthen Joseph's character as leader. In a documented 1–3-page essay, elaborate on the development of character in the Joseph saga. Discuss any of the reasons for Joseph's experiences that are listed below. You may think of more reasons for his adversities in life. Use at least three primary and secondary sources, including biblical references. Use the MLA or APA styles for formatting the paper. (See: *MLA, APA, & CMS: How To Properly Format Your Papers -Knowing the Styles and When to Use Them (http://www.collegescholarships.org/mla-apa-cms-styles.htm).* Edit the paper to remove errors. E-mail your paper to your teacher. Title the paper: Character-Building Experiences in the Life of Joseph.

Suggested Reasons for Joseph's Suffering:

- He needs to overcome his prideful attitude and to grow in humility. (Genesis 37-50)

- He must learn how to serve others. (Genesis 39:4, 22-23, 40:4)

- God wants to train him to be loyal and steadfast in his personal convictions. (Genesis 39:2-6)

- God desires to strengthen him in moral purity. (See Genesis 39:7-20)

- As a strong leader, he needs to be able to comfort others in distress. (See Genesis 50:21)

- God must prepare Joseph to become a role model for forgiveness and to know how to lead his brothers to repentance. (Genesis 50)

- He must grow in the capacity to accept delays in life. (See Genesis 40:1-14, 23)

- Joseph needs to mature in his ability to withstand life's adversities (Genesis 37-50)

- God wants Joseph to understand how He completes His purposes and fulfills His promises to humans. (Genesis 37:5-11, 41:32, 42:1-5, 45:4-7, and 50:20),

- Joseph was to become God's instrument for saving lives. (Genesis 50:20)

- God wants Joseph to experience Divine favor. (Genesis 39:2-6 and 21-23)

- God positions Joseph to show others His power. (Genesis 41:15-16, 25, 28, 32-33, and 38-44).

Additional Online Writing Resources:

A writing guide by Dr. Murray and Anna C. Rockowitz -Writing Center, Hunter College, City University of New York
(https://www.hunter.cuny.edu/rwc/repository/files/the-documented-essay/guides-to-research-and-writing-from-sources/General-guidelines.pdf)

Essay Grading rubrics: *Academic Writing Guide (https://writingguideonline.com/high-school-essay-rubric/)*

A Closing Thought:

"Nearly all men can stand adversity, but if you want to test a man's character, give him power."

-Abraham Lincoln

LESSON THIRTY

IRONY IN THE BOOK OF GENESIS

Lesson Overview

In literature, irony appears in three forms: verbal, situational, and dramatic. Irony is often used for emphasis in the affirmation of a truth. Verbal irony occurs when a character says something that is the exact opposite of what will happen or what he or she means. Situational irony takes place when the least expected happens in a scenario. Dramatic irony occurs in literary works when an incongruity takes place between the words or actions of a character and the understanding of a given situation by the audience or reader. In other words, the audience or reader has knowledge of a significant situation while the character is unaware of what is happening. Ironic literary forms can include similes, sarcasms, paradoxes, oxymorons, and litotes. Students will examine examples of irony in the Book of Genesis.

Key Concepts: verbal, situational and dramatic irony, puns, similes, sarcasms, paradoxes, oxymorons, litotes, irony of fate, irony of events, and irony of circumstance

Lesson Objectives:

Students will:

- find the diverse types of biblical irony, including situational, and verbal irony, litotes, paradoxes, and overstatements.
- decide the meaning of words and phrases as they are used in the text, including figurative and connotative meanings.
- analyze the cumulative impact of specific word choices on meaning and tone.
- demonstrate the understanding of figurative language, word relationships, and nuances in word meanings.

Expected Learning Outcomes:

At the end of the lesson, student will be able to:

- distinguish between the types of irony.
- explain how figurative and connotative words and phrases are used in biblical text.
- explain how the use of irony affects the text.

Duration: 3-4 hours

Materials:
- Paper/pen/notebook/dictionary
- Video: *Situational Irony by Christopher Warner (https://ed.ted.com/lessons/situational-irony-the-opposite-of-what-you-think-christopher-warner#review)*
- Book*: Irony in the Old Testament* by Eden M. Good (pages 80-114) (https://archive.org/details/ironyinoldtestam00good/page/98/mode/2up?view=theater)
- Article: "The Story of Joseph" (*https://www.myjewishlearning.com/article/the-story-of-joseph/*)

Procedure:

- View the video: *Situational Irony by Christopher Warner*
  (https://ed.ted.com/lessons/situational-irony-the-opposite-of-what-you-think-christopher-warner#review.)
- Respond to the study questions.
- Read the selections listed above and respond to the study questions.
- Use an online dictionary to pronounce and define unfamiliar terms.
- Refer to online Bible study tools to enhance your learning.
- Note key details for future quizzes, examinations, and class discussions.
- Respond to the reflection(s).
- Edit your writing to correct errors.
- Post the reflection(s) on the discussion board.
- If you have questions or need further clarification on any assignment, e-mail me at
  wilmaforeman@yahoo.com or visit my website: AIBL.INFO to sign up for the online
  course.

Study Questions:

(Video: *Situational Irony by Christopher Warner*)

Based on the video and expanded research, are the following statements (A) CORRECT or (B)
INCORRECT?
  1. *Situational irony* is an event or occasion in which the outcome is significantly
     different from what was expected.
  2. *Situational irony* is anything considered inappropriate.
  3. Situational irony can be called *irony of fate, irony of events*, and *irony of
     circumstance*.
  4. *Irony of fate* signifies a strange fatality which brings about something quite the reverse of
     what is *expected*.
  5. In biblical text, God reveals His purpose through *ironic* situations.

Study Questions
Book*: Irony in the Old Testament* by Eden M. Good
(https://archive.org/details/ironyinoldtestam00good/page/98/mode/2up?view=theater

Directions: In each set, look for the statement that is INCORRECT.

  1. Which statement is INCORRECT?
      a. God describes everything that He makes in the Creation narratives to be "good."
      b. The presence of sin serves as an ironic motif in God's "good" earth.
      c. The first two chapters of Genesis recount mankind's failure to live up to the
         standards of his Creator, Yahweh.
      d. Chapter 3 of Genesis begins the drama of humanity's failure to meet God's
         purpose for creating people.
      *e. **All the statements above are CORRECT.***

2. Which statement is INCORRECT?
    a. God divinely appoints humankind to rule the earth in Genesis 1:28.
    b. Ironically, humanity is ordained to serve the soil in Genesis 2:15.
    c. By partaking of the forbidden fruit in Genesis, Chapter 3, humans disregard limitations or boundaries.
    d. Ironically, man's excessive desire to be like "gods" results in his loss of divine appointments.
    e. All the statements above are CORRECT.

3. Which statement is INCORRECT?
    a. Ironically, the Tree of Knowledge of Good and Evil is indeed a source of power.
    b. The serpent speaks partial truths.
    c. Ironically, half of what the serpent says to Eve is reversed after she eats the fruit.
    d. Eating the fruit produces a sense of helplessness in the minds of the humans.
    e. All the statements above are CORRECT.

4. Which statement is INCORRECT?
    a. After sin enters the world, nakedness in biblical text is a sense of helplessness instead of innocence.
    b. In Genesis, Chapter 3, humans are introduced to shame after grasping for divine knowledge independent of God.
    c. Ironically, the divine knowledge that they gain when their eyes open causes them to hide themselves.
    d. The alteration of the relationship between God and humanity in Genesis, Chapter 3 extends to the man blaming God for what was originally meant to be a blessing.
    e. All the statements above are CORRECT.

5. Which statement is INCORRECT?
    a. Disobedience affects mankind's relationship with God.
    b. Ironically, disobedience disrupts the harmony between human and human.
    c. The relationship between earth and humanity is disrupted in the Genesis, Chapter 3 narrative.
    d. Ironically, although humans are created from the ground, they lose the earth's cooperation in yielding sustenance.
    e. All the statements above are CORRECT.

6. Which statement is INCORRECT?
    a. The sin of disobedience causes the woman to take a subordinate role in the relationship with her husband.
    b. Ironically, in grasping for more than they already have, Adam and Eve lose their home in paradise.
    c. The serpent, ironically, is reduced to a shameful position of crawling on its belly in the dirt.
    d. Ironically, instead of experiencing physical death at once, the humans in the Garden of Eden become acquainted with fear and shame.
    e. All the statements above are CORRECT.

7. Which statement is INCORRECT?
    a. God admonishes Cain about his anger before he kills his brother Abel.
    b. Ironically, Cain has time to reconsider his murderous plan.
    c. Sin lurks with the intent to ambush humankind.
    d. Ironically, Cain takes the course of sin by ambushing his brother in a field.
    e. *All the statements above are CORRECT.*

8. Which statement is INCORRECT?
    a. Cain's question, "Am I my brother's keeper?" in Genesis 4:9 has a sarcastic tone.
    b. Ironically, the obvious answer is affirmative; he is his younger brother's keeper.
    c. Because of jealousy and anger, Cain fails to perceive his true relationship to his brother as a "keeper."
    d. The Hebrew term for "keeper" is a pun that relates to Abel's vocation as a shepherd, or a keeper of sheep.
    e. *All the statements above are CORRECT.*

9. Which statement is INCORRECT?
    a. Like Adam, Cain loses his vocation as a servant of the soil.
    b. Ironically, in Genesis 4:10, the soils becomes uncooperative and accuses Cain of his crime.
    c. Cain loses his home and becomes a wanderer.
    d. Ironically, Cain cries against the possibility of being murdered after he has killed his only brother.
    e. *All the statements above are CORRECT.*

10. Which statement is INCORRECT?
    a) As the story of humanity progresses, ironically, people increase in wickedness while obeying God's command to increase in population.
    b) Cain's murderous sin nature extends to Lamech (Genesis 4:23-24).
    c) The results of one ruptured relationship between the brothers in Genesis, Chapter4 expands to a tragically ironic pattern in God's "good" world.
    d) Ironically, when humans claim divine privileges, they become "beastly" and strange.
    e) *All the statements above are CORRECT.*

11. Which statement is INCORRECT?
    a. In biblical text, God is the only giver of life.
    b. The Babel narrative shows that excessive human aspirations produce evil.
    c. In the story of the Tower of Babel, unlimited human power and fame connote an air of illegitimacy.
    d. Ironically, although they are created in the image of God, humans tend to increase in evil when they are given power and fame.

e. *All the statements above are CORRECT.*

12. Which statement is INCORRECT?
    a. The Flood narrative in Genesis, Chapter 6, depicts a "good" world that has gone astray.
    b. Chaotic waters are first introduced in the Creation narratives in Genesis 1 and 2.
    c. Ironically, the chaotic waters from the Flood serve a means of reestablishing order and "goodness" on earth.
    d. At the end of the Flood, when Noah tries to return to normalcy, he reintroduces sin when he becomes intoxicated.
    e. *All the statements above are CORRECT.*

13. Which statement is INCORRECT?
    a. In the Flood narrative, the ground has a role in man's trouble.
    b. Noah plants a vineyard and uses its produce to become intoxicated.
    c. The theme of nakedness that connects to the Creation narrative is associated with shame.
    d. Ham's sin relates to his father's nakedness.
    e. *All the statements above are CORRECT.*

14. Which statement is INCORRECT?
    a. The curse of Ham affects Canaan, Noah's grandson.
    b. For a while, God gives the descendants of Canaan the promised land.
    c. Canaan becomes "the land flowing with milk and honey."
    d. Ironically, the descendants of Ham take part in the fulfillment of God's promise made to Abraham.
    e. *All the statements above are CORRECT.*

15. Which statement is INCORRECT?
    a. Verbal irony communicates the opposite of what is said.
    b. Dramatic irony derives from the fact that the character knows less than the reader.
    c. Ironical utterances can be said in the form of questions.
    d. In verbal irony, the speaker's attitude is one of rejection or disapproval.
    e. *All the statements above are CORRECT.*

16. Which statement is INCORRECT?
    a. The writer proposes that in Genesis 11:6, God ironically mocks the attitude of the people building the tower.
    b. The first eleven chapters of Genesis use irony to emphasize how God's providential plan overrides the plans of men.
    c. The Book of Genesis uses irony in telling how God's promises override human failure and fallibility.
    d. Irony can be detected by the tone of one's voice.
    e. *All the statements above are CORRECT.*

17. Which statement is INCORRECT?

   a. An echoic utterance can be a form of irony.
   b. In literature, the use of irony can be difficult to detect.
   c. ***Dramatic irony is not present in any of the patriarchal narratives. (INCORRECT)***
   d. Dramatic irony is particularly clear in the story of Joseph (50:20).
   e. All the statements above are CORRECT.

18. Which statement is INCORRECT?

   a. Verbal irony is within the blessings that Jacob gives to his sons (Genesis 49).
   b. Jacob's repeated action of choosing the younger son over the older, reinforces the theme of God's plan to prevail over the customs and expectations of human culture.
   c. Ironically, Jacob's final blessings over his sons and grandsons reflect his own way of gaining his blessing as a younger son.
   d. A writer's use of irony in a text is usually implicit.
   e. ***All the statements above are CORRECT.***

19. Which statement is INCORRECT?

   a. An understatement (litotes) is an expression of lesser strength than what the speaker or writer means or than what is normally expected.
   b. An overstatement is an act of saying something more profoundly than it is.
   c. An overstatement is used to make a point more serious, important, or beautiful.
   d. In literature, writers use overstatement for the sake of humor, and for placing emphasis on a certain point.
   e. ***All the statements above are CORRECT.***

20. Which statement is INCORRECT?

   a. This is an example of an overstatement: "And I will make thy seed as the dust of the earth: so that if a man can number the dust of the earth, *then* shall thy seed also be numbered." (Gen. 13:16) (KJV)
   b. This is an example of an overstatement: *"That in blessing I will bless thee, and in multiplying I will multiply thy seed as the stars of the heaven, and as the sand which is upon the seashore; and thy seed shall possess the gate of his enemies…"* (Gen. 22:17) (KJV)
   c. This is an example of an overstatement: *"Your descendants will be like the dust of the earth, and you will spread out to the west and to the east, to the north and to the south. All peoples on earth will be blessed through you and your offspring."* (Gen. 28:14) (NIV)
   d. This is an example of a litotes: *"And in the morning, behold, it was Leah."* (Gen. 29:25)
   e. ***All the statements above are CORRECT.***

For Reflection:

Read each of the following scenarios and reflect on the irony in each. Write a five-eight sentence response to the events/situations below about biblical irony. Edit your writing to remove errors. Post your responses on the discussion board. Label the reflections: Irony in the Book of Genesis.

Scenario 1

God informs Abraham that his descendants will be strangers in a land that they did not own, and that their enemies will afflict them four hundred years. God also assures Abraham that He will judge the oppressive nation (Egypt) and that his descendants will come out with great possessions. How is this an example of situational irony? (Gen. 15:12)

Scenario 2

Because of Sarah's beauty, her husband Abraham who fears for his life tells Abimelech king of Gerar that Sarah is his sister. In fact, she is his half-sister. Abimelech takes Sarah into his harem, but God sends him a dream forbidding him to touch Sarah because she is Abraham's wife. What is ironic about the way that Abraham behaves after receiving such great promises from God? (Gen. 20:3–7)

Scenario 3

After Jacob deceitfully steals his brother Esau's inheritance, he flees from his brother's fury. In Genesis 28:12, Jacob dreams about a ladder reaching to heaven upon which angels ascend and descend. In the dream, God extends Abraham's blessing to Jacob. What is ironic about God's choice of people to fulfill His promise to Abraham? (Genesis 28:10-17)

Scenario 4

In a dream, God reveals to Joseph that one day his family will bow to him in deference. Instead of giving Joseph honor, however, his brothers become angry and sell him into slavery in Egypt. After countless vicissitudes in his life, and through divine providence, Joseph's dream comes to pass, and he saves his family from a severe famine. Based on the life of Joseph, how does God use irony to fulfill His plans for humans? (Genesis 37-50)

A Closing Thought:

"The patriarchal, the Jewish, and the Christian dispensations, are evidently but the unfolding of one general plan."

-Mary Hopkins

LESSON THIRTY-ONE

IDIOMS FROM THE BOOK OF GENESIS

Lesson Overview:

      An idiom is language distinct to a group of people or to a district, community, or class. All languages have idioms. In the Western tradition, idioms have become an essential element of literature and descriptions of everyday life. The phrasing of words and inflections from the King James Bible has left a profound impact on our society. In this lesson, students will examine common idioms derived from the Book of Genesis.

Key Concepts: biblical idioms, puns, metaphors, allegory

Lesson Objectives:

Students will:

- examine everyday expressions whose meanings are derived from the Book of Genesis.
- demonstrate understanding of figurative language, word relationships, and nuances in word meanings.
- engage in collaborative discussions building on others' ideas while expressing their own thoughts accurately and clearly.

Expected Learning Outcomes:

At the end of this lesson, students will:

- demonstrate an understanding of idiomatic expressions derived from the Book of Genesis.
- distinguish between figurative and literal language.
- understanding of figurative language, word relationships, and nuances in word meanings.
- exchange ideas accurately and clearly.

Duration: 1-2 hours

Materials:

- Paper/pen/notebook/dictionary
- Video: *English Idioms (https://www.youtube.com/watch?v=jdSNNy9KkEI)*
- Book: *Idioms in the Bible Explained and a Key to the Original Gospels (Chapter 5: The Book of Genesis) (https://zoboko.com/text/zo8mqm68/idioms-in-the-bible-explained-and-a-key-to-the-original-gospels/5)*
- Article: "Biblical Idioms" by Maymie Hayim
- (*http://www.mayimhayim.org/Hebrew%20Perspectives/Biblical%20Idioms.RX5.htm*)

Procedure:

- Use the resources as shown in this lesson to respond to the study questions/assignments.
- Refer to online Bible study tools to enhance your learning.
- Use an online dictionary to pronounce and define unfamiliar terms.
- Respond to the reflection(s).
- Edit your writing to correct errors.
- Post the reflection(s) on the discussion board.
- If you have questions or need further clarification on any assignment, e-mail me at wilmaforeman@yahoo.com or visit my website: AIBL.INFO to sign up for the online course.

Assignment 1

Resource: *Idioms in the Bible Explained and a Key to the Original Gospels (Chapter 5: The Book of Genesis)* (*https://zoboko.com/text/zo8mqm68/idioms-in-the-bible-explained-and-a-key-to-the-original-gospels/5*)

Directions: Select the best explanation for the idioms.

1. *"Let there be light."* (Gen.1:3)
    - **A. Let there be enlightenment/ knowledge.**
    - B. Let there be order.
    - C. Let there be peace.
    - D. Let there be an abundance.
    - E. None of the above

2. *"The Tree of the Knowledge of Good and Evil"* (Genesis 2–3)
    - **A. Moral law**
    - B. Eternity
    - C. Lack of knowledge
    - D. Ignorance
    - E. None of the above

3. *"Thorns and thistles"* (Genesis 3:17-18)
    - A. Weary and impatient
    - **B. Straits and trials**
    - C. Shame
    - D. Fear
    - E. None of the above

2. *"The serpent"* (Gen. 3:1)
    - A. A competitor
    - **B. An enemy**
    - C. A mystery
    - D. Exposure
    - E. None of the above

3. *"My spirit shall not dwell in man forever."* (Gen. 6:3)

A. "I shall not live with you."

B. "I shall not hear you."

C. "I have become weary and impatient."

D. "I have another plan."

E. None of the above

4. "Naked" (Gen. 2:25)

A. Banned

B. Afraid

C. Tempted

D. Exposed

E. None of the above

5. "I set my bow in the clouds." (Gen. 9:13)

A. "I make a promise."

B. "I establish the evening."

C. "I set the rainbow in the sky."

D. "I establish plans."

E. None of the above

6. *"I have lifted up my hands."* (Gen.14:22)

A. "I am ready to fight."

B. "I am leaving."

C. "I am ready."

D. "I am taking a solemn oath."

E. None of the above.

7. *"Thy seed"* (Gen. 17:7)

A. Your offspring; descendants

B. Your land; ground

C. Your harvest

D. Your ancestors

E. None of the above.

8. *"As the stars of heaven."* (Gen. 22:17)

A. Heavenly

B. Angelic

C. Scattered

D. Innumerable

E. None of the above.

9. Hand under thigh. (Gen. 24:2)

A. Listening to an elder

B. Forgiving an enemy

C. Swearing upon the testicles of the master

    D. Talking to a stranger
    E. None of the above

10. *Looking behind (Gen. 19:17)*
    A. Lifeless; stricken
    B. *Regretting; wasting*
    C. Having weak or gentle eyes
    D. Thought to oneself
    E. None of the above

11. *He gathered up his feet. (Gen. 49:33)*
    A. *Stretched out his feet and breathed his last breath*
    B. Restored to honor
    C. Struggled with something
    D. Captured cities
    E. None of the above

12. *Laying on of hands (Gen. 14:48)*
    A. *Blessed*
    B. Rebuked
    C. Forgot
    D. Befriended
    E. None of the above

13. *The way of women (Gen. 31:35)*
    A. Beauty
    B. Childbirth
    C. Marriage
    D. *Menstruation*
    E. None of the above

Assignment 2

Directions: Write down if the following statements are (A) CORRECT or (B) INCORRECT.

14. In biblical text, the expression "*wrestling with angels*" (Gen. 32:24) means that one is struggling with something as Jacob wrestles with an angel in Genesis. (A) CORRECT
15. A "*coat of many colors*" refers to Joseph's multicolored coat in Gen. 37:23. (A) CORRECT
16. "*He gathered up his feet into the bed*" means that he died. (A) CORRECT

17. To "*possess gates*" means to capture cities. (A) CORRECT
18. "*Said in heart*" (Gen 27.41) means that one thought to own self. (A) CORRECT
19. "*Unstable as water*" (Gen. 49:4) means that someone is undecided. (A) CORRECT

20. *"Fire and brimstone"* (Gen. 19:24) refers to the destruction the wicked cities Sodom and Gomorrah. (A) CORRECT

21. *"Am I my brother's keeper?"* (Gen. 4:9) relates to a person's responsibility to care for someone else. (A) CORRECT

22. *"By the sweat of your brow"* (Gen. 3:19) concerns hard labor. (A) CORRECT

23. *"Old as Methuselah"* refers to the oldest man in biblical text, Methuselah, age 969 years old. (A) CORRECT

24. *"To dust you shall return"* (Gen. 3:19) is a part of funeral rituals referring to the cycle of life. (A) CORRECT

25. *"Fall from grace"* (Gen. 3) means that one has lost an honorable state in life. (A) CORRECT

26. *"Forbidden fruit"* (Gen. 3) is something that is desired but not allowed. (A) CORRECT

27. An *"Adam's apple"* (Gen. 3:6) refers to the protrusion in the human neck formed by the angle of the thyroid cartilage surrounding the larynx. (A) CORRECT

28. *"Adam's apples"* are most visible in men. (A) CORRECT

29. *"Extending an olive branch"* (Gen. 8:11) is a symbol of peace. (A) CORRECT

30. *"To extend an olive branch"* alludes to the dove that carries an olive branch in the story of Noah and the Great Flood. (A) CORRECT

31. To *"offer an olive branch"* suggests that someone is tired of war, whether it be an actual war or a falling out between friends. (A) CORRECT

32. "The expression *"Adam knew his wife"* (Gen. 4:1) refers a sexual relation. (A) CORRECT

33. *"The mark of Cain"* is associated to public disgrace. (A) CORRECT

34. The *"mark of Cain"* causes Cain's death in the "Cain and Abel" narrative. (B) INCORRECT

35. The expression, *"Go to your fathers in peace"* (Gen. 15:15) refers to someone dying. (A) CORRECT

For Reflection:

Find at least five (5) more idioms from the Book of Genesis. Tell how the expressions relate to the context of the Scriptures. How relevant are the idioms today? (Write five-eight sentences. Edit your writing to correct errors. Post your response on the discussion board. Label the post: "Genesis Idioms.")

A Closing Thought:

The Hebrew Bible contains multiple provisions to ensure that no one would go hungry. The corners of the field, forgotten sheaves of grain, gleanings that drop from the hands of the gleaner, and small clusters of grapes left on the vine were to be given to the poor.

-Jonathan Sacks

LESSON THIRTY-TWO

SHAKESPEARE'S ALLUSIONS TO THE BOOK
OF GENESIS

Lesson Overview:

The renowned English bard, William Shakespeare is regarded as the greatest writer in the English language and the world's greatest dramatist. Translated in eighty languages, the words, phrases, and lines from his works have helped shape modern English. Heavily affected by the Hebrew Bible, his famous plays are known for their universal themes and insight into the human condition. At times, Shakespeare quoted the biblical text directly, but more often he included a partial quote or an allusion. The influence of the Bible on Shakespeare's plays is so deep that it is sometimes difficult to distinguish between biblical language and the writer's own word choices. In this lesson, students will examine biblical allusions in Shakespeare's writings.

Key Concepts: allusions, universal themes, direct and indirect quotations

Objectives:

Students will:

- understand the influence of the Hebrew Bible on the writings of William Shakespeare.
- apply knowledge of language to understand how language functions in different contexts to make effective choices for meaning or style, and to understand more fully when reading or listening.
- find the meaning of words and phrases as they are used in the text, including figurative and connotative meanings.
- initiate and take part in collaborative discussions.

Expected Learning Outcomes:

At the end of this lesson, students are expected to be able to:

- compare translations of the English Bible.
- understand the meaning of biblical allusions.
- recognize biblical allusions in the works of William Shakespeare.
- understand the influence of the Hebrew Bible on the works of William Shakespeare.
- explain biblical allusions in Shakespearean writings.

Duration: 2-3 hours

Materials:

- Paper/pen/dictionary/notebook
- Study Guide: *Shakespeare and the Bible* by Michael J. Cummings

(http://www.shakespearestudyguide.com/Shake2/Bible.html)

- Article: "Shakespeare and the Geneva Bible" by Leland Ryken
  (https://www.reformation21.org/articles/shakespeare-and-the-geneva-bible.php)

Procedure:

- Read the resource *Shakespeare and the Bible*
  (http://www.shakespearestudyguide.com/Shake2/Bible.html) by Michael J. Cummings.
- Use an online dictionary to pronounce and define unfamiliar terms.
- Refer to online Bible study tools to enhance your learning.
- Respond to the study questions.
- Write a reflection, edit writing, and post your reflection on the discussion board. Label the post: Shakespeare's Use of Biblical Allusions.

Study Questions:

Directions: Based on the information in the study guide, are the following statements (A) CORRECT or (B) INCORRECT?

1. The English Bibles versions available during William Shakespeare's times included: *The Tyndale Bible* (New Testament, Part of Old; first English Bible), *The Coverdale Bible, The Great Bible, The Geneva Bible, The Bishops' Bible, The Douay-Rheims Bible* (Catholic), and *The King James Bible*. (A) CORRECT
2. Scholars guess that Shakespeare read the *Geneva Bible* more often than other Bibles. (A) CORRECT
3. In general, Shakespeare did not quote a Bible passage directly, but he paraphrased or summarized it. (A) CORRECT
4. None of Shakespeare's poetry alludes to biblical characters or stories. (B) INCORRECT
5. In *The Tragedy of Macbeth*, Lady Macbeth compares to Eve (Genesis 3) in that she compels her husband to commit a forbidden act. (A) CORRECT
6. In the play *Macbeth*, Lady Macbeth suggests that her husband imitate the subtle serpent in Genesis 3, saying, *"Look like the innocent flower / But be the serpent under it"* (1.5.63-64). (A) CORRECT
7. A reader can assume that "the serpent" in Shakespeare's play alludes to the serpent in Genesis, Chapter 3 in that it appears innocent to Eve, but proves to be evil. (A) CORRECT
8. In the Bishops' Bible, Genesis, 1:1 reads: *"And the serpent was suttiller then every beast of the fielde ..."* (A) CORRECT
9. Shakespeare had a deep knowledge of both the Old and New Testaments. (A) CORRECT
10. His works have hundreds of allusions and references to Hebrew Scriptures. (A) CORRECT
11. In *Henry V*, 1.1.28-33, the lines: *"...like an angel, came And whipp'd the offending Adam out of him, Leaving his body as a paradise"* alludes to the first human, Adam,

who offends God by eating fruit from the Tree of the Knowledge of Good and Evil (Genesis 2:4-3:24). (A) CORRECT

12. The lines in the play *Richard III*, 4.3.45, *"The sons of Edward sleep in Abraham's bosom"* alludes to the Hebrew patriarch Abraham (Genesis 12) as a place of resting for the righteous after death. (A) CORRECT

13. Shakespeare alludes to the biblical Adam in *As You Like It, The Comedy of Errors, Hamlet, Henry IV Part I, Henry VI Part II, Love's Labour's Lost*, and *Much Ado About Nothing*. (A) CORRECT

14. In *Hamlet*, 5.1.34, Shakespeare alludes to the murder Abel by his brother, the biblical Cain (Genesis 4): *"That skull had a tongue in it and could sing once. How the knave jowls it to the ground, as if 'twere Cain's jawbone, that did the first murder!"* (A) CORRECT

15. In the Scriptures, Cain uses a rock instead of a jawbone to kill his brother Abel. (A) CORRECT

16. These lines from *Hamlet*, 3.42-44 allude to Cain killing his younger brother Abel: *"O, my offence is rank; it smells to heaven; It hath the primal eldest curse upon't, A brother's murder."* (A) CORRECT

17. In *The Merchant of Venice*, 1.3.52-55, the lines: *When Jacob graz'd his uncle Laban's sheep—This Jacob from our holy Abram was, As his wise mother wrought in his behalf ..."* allude to Abraham's grandson Jacob, Jacob's mother Rebekah, and Abraham's brother Laban (Genesis 24). (A) CORRECT

18. The words *"They will be kin to us, or they will fetch it from Japhet"* in *Henry IV Part II*, 2.2.44 allude to Japheth, one of Noah's three sons (Genesis 10:21). (A) CORRECT

19. The line: *"No, sir, . . .Noah's flood could not do it"* in *The Comedy of Errors*, 3, 2.91-92 refers to Noah in the Flood narrative that begins in Genesis, Chapter 3. (A) CORRECT

20. In *King Henry VI*, 2.3.15, the words, *"Thy brother's blood the thirsty earth hath drunk,"* allude to Genesis 4,10–11 when the ground cries out after Cain kills his brother. (A) CORRECT

Study Questions:

Article: "Shakespeare and the Geneva Bible" by Leland Ryken
(https://www.reformation21.org/articles/shakespeare-and-the-geneva-bible.php)

Based on the information in the study guide, are the following statements (A) CORRECT or (B) INCORRECT?

1. Mainstream scholars are indebted to studies about the influence of the Hebrew Bible on the writings of William Shakespeare. (A) CORRECT

2. Naseeb Sheheen deals with the subject of the Bible's influence on Shakespeare's works in his book *Biblical References in Shakespeare's Plays*. (A) CORRECT

3. The story of Shakespeare and the Bible partly relates to the Protestant English Bible translation in the sixteenth century. (A) CORRECT

4. Shakespeare lived during a movement in which English Reformers dedicated their energies into translating the Bible. (A) CORRECT

5. During the Protestant Reformation, children learned how to read by using the Hebrew Bible. (A) CORRECT
6. Members of Shakespeare's family were Catholics. (A) CORRECT
7. Shakespeare's drama has more references to the Bible than the plays of any other Elizabethan playwright. (A) CORRECT
8. An estimated count of biblical references in Shakespeare's works totals 1200. (A) CORRECT
9. The Bible story of Cain and Abel appears more than twenty-five times in Shakespearean writings. (A) CORRECT
10. Shakespeare's allusions are generalized, but often the biblical parallels require prior scholarly knowledge. (A) CORRECT
11. Until 1598, Shakespeare's biblical references were primarily to the Bishops' Bible. (A) CORRECT
12. As a writer, Shakespeare used the Geneva Bible in his plays during the second half of his career. (A) CORRECT
13. The Geneva Bible is commonly called the Puritan Bible. (A) CORRECT
14. The Geneva Bible was the "mass Bible" of its day because it was more portable and affordable than other English translations. (A) CORRECT
15. The writer proposes that Shakespeare's first acquaintance with the Geneva Bible took place when he was a student at the Stratford Grammar School. (A) CORRECT
16. During his studies in grammar school, Shakespeare translated passages from the Geneva Bible into Latin and English. (A) CORRECT
17. Shakespeare's writings referred to the marginal notes of the Geneva Bible. (A) CORRECT
18. In the play *Hamlet,* Shakespeare alludes to the Cain and Abel narrative when King Hamlet's brother kills him in a garden. (A) CORRECT
19. Shakespeare's contemporaries pictured him as an unlearned genius who invented his writings from his own imagination. (A) CORRECT
20. English poet and intellectual, John Milton, viewed Shakespeare as a writer who "warbled his native wood-notes wild." (A) CORRECT
21. The poem, "On Shakespeare, 1630" by John Milton describes inappropriate monuments dedicated to the life of William Shakespeare. (A) CORRECT
22. Shaheen said that "it would be strange if the most often printed book of the day was not part" of Shakespeare's library. (A) CORRECT
23. The writer, Shaheen, asserted that Shakespeare did not take story material from the Bible the way Milton did. (A) CORRECT
24. The Hebrew Bible influenced Shakespeare in choosing his subject matter. (A) CORRECT
25. During Shakespeare's times, biblical references were a part of everyday usage among the people. (A) CORRECT
26. The writer speaks of the Bible as a subtext for Shakespeare's play, showing Shakespeare how to achieve the dramatic effects that he wanted. (A) CORRECT
27. Universally, literary writers have linked fictional characters to characters in the Bible in Christian tradition. (A) CORRECT
28. Links to the Bible in works of literature can be proved through allusions. (A) CORRECT
29. According to the writer of the article, one scholar speaks of biblical phrases and images as "an echo-chamber of the imagination" for Shakespeare. (A) CORRECT
30. Shakespeare was unlearned and untutored as a young child. (B) INCORRECT

For Reflection (1)

The Renaissance historian John Strype (1737) wrote about the fervent appeal of the appearance of the vernacular Bible in England during his times. He said:

> *"It was wonderful to see with what joy the book of God was received, not only among the learned sort and all the vulgar [uneducated] and common people; with what greediness God's word was read, and what resort to places where the reading of it was. Everybody that could, bought the book and among the elderly learned to read on purpose. And even little boys flocked among the rest to hear portions of the Holy Scriptures read."*

Directions:
- Examine the list of major English Bible translations at https://carm.org/king-james-onlyism/chronological-list-of-major-english-bible-translations/.
- Find at least five additional biblical allusions in the writings of William Shakespeare.
- Explain the allusions.
- Post your findings on the discussion board. Label the post: Biblical allusions in the Writings of William Shakespeare.

Reflection (2)
Directions:
- Explain the significance of the statement: *"Everybody that could, bought the book and among the elderly learned to read on purpose."* (John Strype*)*
- Tell what made Bible-reading so special during the Renaissance period in contrast to the earlier times.
- Label the post: A Reflection on the Translation of the English Bible during the 1600s.

(An added resource: Article: "The History of Translation In The Renaissance Period" https://renaissance-translations.com/translation-in-the-renaissance/)

A Closing Thought:

"Consideration, like an angel, came
And whipp'd the offending Adam out of him,
Leaving his body as a paradise."

-William Shakespeare (*Henry V*, 1.1.28-33)

LESSON THIRTY-THREE
JOHN BUNYAN'S EXPOSITION
ON THE FIRST TEN CHAPTERS OF GENESIS

Lesson Overview:

John Bunyan (1628) was an English writer and Puritan preacher best remembered as the author of the Christian allegory *The Pilgrim's Progress*. Bunyan wrote approximately sixty works, including expanded sermons. Imprisoned for nearly thirteen years for preaching the Gospel, his only solace were his Bible and *Fox's Book of Martyrs written by* Protestant English historian John Foxe, first published in 1563. Evidence of Bunyan's earnest study of the Holy Scriptures is found in the incomplete commentary *An Exposition of the First Ten Chapters of the Book of Genesis*, published in 1691 by Charles Doe. The work was discovered in Bunyan's own handwriting after his death in 1688. This lesson will focus on Bunyan's expository comments on the first ten chapters of the Book of Genesis.

Key Concepts: exposition, commentary, allusions, universal themes, direct and indirect quotations

Objectives:

Students will:

- apply knowledge of language to understand how language functions in different contexts, to make effective choices for meaning or style, and to understand more fully when reading or listening.
- understand the influence of the Hebrew Scriptures on Western culture.
- understand expository historical expository writings.
- interpret and explain a writer's point of view.
- initiate and take part effectively in collaborative exchanges to build on others' ideas and express their own thoughts succinctly, clearly, and persuasively.

Expected Learning Outcomes:

At the end of this lesson, students are expected to be able to:

- compare translations of the English Bible.
- understand the meaning of biblical allusions and expository commentaries.
- interpret a writer's point of view.
- form and share ideas from assigned readings independently and collaboratively.
- express ideas and points of view succinctly, clearly, and accurately.
- explain how the Hebrew Bible influenced Western literature.
- paraphrase the writings of different authors.

Duration: 2-3 hours

Materials:

- Internet access/ a computer with editing capability
- Paper/pen
- Reading passages from *An Exposition of the First Ten Chapters of the Book of Genesis*, published in 1691 by Charles Doe
  (https://biblehub.com/library/bunyan/the_works_of_john_bunyan_volumes_1-3/an_exposition_on_the_first.htm)

Procedure:

- Read the following passages and respond to the study questions.
- Use an online dictionary to pronounce and define unfamiliar terms.
- Refer to online Bible study tools to enhance your learning.
- Respond to the reflection(s).
- Edit writing to correct errors.
- Post the reflection on the discussion board,
- Label the post: John Bunyan's Exposition on Genesis, Chapters 1-10.
- If you have questions or need further clarification on any assignment, e-mail me at wilmaforeman@yahoo.com or visit my website: AIBL.INFO to sign up for the online course.

Passage One (Genesis, Chapter 1) (On God)

"In his attributes of wisdom, power, justice, holiness, mercy, &c., he is also inconceivably perfect and infinite, not to be comprehended by things in earth, or things in heaven; known in the perfection of his being only to himself. The seraphim cannot behold him, but through a veil; no man can see him in his perfection and live… No act of justice is without his will, power, and wisdom; no act of mercy is against his justice, holiness, and purity…Wisdom is in his justice, holiness is in his power, justice is in his mercy, holiness is in his love, power is in his goodness …"

Study Questions

Are the following statements TRUE (A) or FALSE (B)?

1. In this passage, John Bunyan notes God's perfection in good judgment, strength, rightness, and compassion. TRUE (A)
2. Bunyan writes that God is so flawless that earthly or heavenly creatures cannot fully understand him. TRUE (A)
3. He says that angelic beings do not look upon God fully, and that humans cannot see God and continue to live. TRUE (A)
4. Based on his notes, Bunyan believed that acts of justice are derived from God. TRUE (A)

Passage Two (Genesis, Chapter 3) (On the Serpent)

> *"He tempts by means; he appeareth not in his own shape and hue, but assumeth the body of one of the creatures, the body of the serpent, and so begins the combat. And from hence it is, that in after ages he is spoken of under the name of that creature, "the dragon, that old serpent which is the devil, and Satan" (Rev. 20:2) ...He labours to make them question the simplicity of the word of God, bearing Adam's wife in hand, that there must needs be some meaning that palliates the text...Hence learn, that so long as we retain the simplicity of the word, we have Satan at the end of the staff;..."*

Are the following statements TRUE (A) or FALSE (B)?

5. Bunyan noted that Satan takes on the appearance of other creatures. TRUE (A)
6. "The combat" alludes to the struggle between the adversary, the devil, and humanity. TRUE (A)
7. He proposes that biblical text should remain simple enough to be understood. TRUE (A)

Passage Three (Genesis, Chapter 3) (On Adam and Eve)

> *"By this act of these two, the whole world became guilty of condemnation and eternal judgment (Rom 5). By this came all the blindness, atheism, ignorance of God, enmity and malice against him, pride, covetousness, adultery, idolatry, and implacableness, &c., that is found in all the world. By this, I say, came all the wars, blood, treachery, tyranny, persecution, with all manner of rapine and outrage that is found among the sons of men. Besides, all the plagues, judgments, and evils that befall us in this world, with those everlasting burnings that will swallow up millions for ever and ever; all and every whit of these came into the world as the portion of mankind, for that first transgression of our first parents."*

Are the following statements TRUE (A) or FALSE (B)?

8. The expression, "these two," refers to Adam and Eve in the Garden of Eden. TRUE (A)
9. In his writing, Bunyan proposes that all the world's ills result from the actions of the first humans in Genesis, Chapter 3. TRUE (A)
10. *Every whit of these came into the world as the portion of mankind, for that first transgression of our first parents"* means that the first sin in the Garden brought God's judgment upon people that ends in death. TRUE (A)
11. Another word for "transgression" is "infringement" or "violation." TRUE (A)
12. The writer sees sin as a violation of God's commandments. TRUE (A)

Passage Four (Chapter 3) (On Sin, Shame, and Self-Righteousness)

"And Adam and his wife hid themselves." Hence observe, That a man's own righteousness will not fortify his conscience from fear and terror, when God begins to come near to him to judgment. Why did Adam hide himself, but because, as he said, he was naked? But how could he be naked, when before he had made himself an apron? O! the approach of God consumed and burnt off his apron! Though his apron would keep him from the sight of a bird, yet it would not from the eye of the incorruptible God...Let therefore all self-righteous men beware, for however they at present please themselves with the worthiness of their glorious fig- leaves; yet when God shall come to deal with them for sin, assuredly they will find themselves naked."

Are the following statements TRUE (A) or FALSE (B)?

13. To "fortify" is to supply a place for safety. TRUE (A)
14. Bunyan suggests that Adam and Eve hid themselves to protect themselves from their own conscience. TRUE (A)
15. The writer questions Adam's motive for hiding himself. TRUE (A)
16. Bunyan implies that the coverings from fig leaves stand for self-righteousness. TRUE (A)
17. He asserts that human schemes for self-righteousness cannot withstand God's true righteousness. TRUE (A)

Passage Four (Chapter 9) (On the Sanctity of Life)

Ver. 5. "And surely your blood of your lives will I require; at the hand of every beast will I require it, and at the hand of man; at the hand of every man's brother, will I require the life of man."

Are the following statements TRUE (A) or FALSE (B)?

18. One can infer that Bunyan would have referred to this verse of Scripture to uphold the sanctity of human life. TRUE (A)
19. The verse requires the death penalty for taking human life. TRUE (A)
20. Biblical text advocates respect for life. TRUE (A)

Study Questions:

Directions: Respond to the study questions on Scott's poem.

"Man, the Enemy of Man" by Sir Walter Scott

The hunting tribes of air and earth
Respect the brethren of their birth;
Nature, who loves the claim of kind,

Less cruel chase to each assigned.
The falcon, poised on soaring wing,
Watches the wild-duck by the spring;
The slow-hound wakes the fox's lair;
The greyhound presses on the hare;
The eagle pounces on the lamb;
The wolf devours the fleecy dam;
Even tiger fell, and sullen bear,
Their likeness and their lineage spare.
Man, only, mars kind Nature's plan,
And turns the fierce pursuit on man;
Plying war's desultory trade,
Incursion, flight, and ambuscade,
Since Nimrod, Cush's mighty son,
At first the bloody game begun."

Study Questions:

Are the following statements (A) TRUE or (B) FALSE about Scott's poem?

1. The expression "hunting tribes of air and earth" refers to natural predators. (A) TRUE
2. Nature is *personified* in the poem. (A) TRUE
3. The poet asserts that nature is compassionate to all creatures, (A) TRUE
4. According to the poet, each part of creation has limited degrees of cruelty. (A) TRUE
5. The poet sees the respect that other species show toward their own kind. (A) TRUE
6. Man is the only creature that disfigures the plan of nature. (A) TRUE
7. Man engages in warlike tactics in fierce pursuits of other humans. (A) TRUE
8. The warlike plans of humans lack purpose. (A) TRUE
9. Using tactics of war, humans attack, chase, and ambush their fellowmen. (A) TRUE
10. Scott alludes to the biblical figure Nimrod of ancient Babylon mentioned in Genesis, Chapter 10. (A) TRUE

For Reflection

Internationally popular Sir Walter Scott (1771-1832) began his career writing narrative poetry, and later started his career as a novelist. His knowledge of Scottish history and legends, along with his literary skills equipped him to become a renowned historical novelist, poet, and playwright. He believed in social justice and equality. He also believed in moral living regardless of religion, social status, or ancestry. Compare notes in Bunyan's commentary to Sir Walter Scott's poem "Man, the Enemy of Man." Explain the sentiments of John Bunyan about the value of human life to Sir Walter Scott's views on the sanctity of human life and acts of violence. (Write five-eight sentences. Edit your writing to correct errors. Post your reflection on the discussion board, Label the post: A Reflection on Sir Walter Scott's Poem, "Man, the Enemy of Man" and John Bunyan's Views on Violence.)

A Closing Thought:

"Christianity and Judaism are united above all in their common affirmation and implementation of the moral teaching of the Hebrew Bible, or 'Old Testament,' and the traditions of interpretation of that teaching."

-David Novak

LESSON THIRTY-FOUR
PARALLELS OF THE "LOSS/RESTORATION" THEME
IN THE BOOKS OF GENESIS AND REVELATION

Lesson Overview:

The Book of Genesis is the first book of the Hebrew Bible, the sacred text of Judaism and Christianity. The Book of Revelation, the last Book in Christian Bibles, is a sequel to the Book of Genesis. In Christian tradition, the two books form the alpha and omega, the beginnings and the "unveilings of the end" of God's purpose and plans for His world. The Book of Genesis recounts the origins the world, God love for humanity, mankind's tragic default on a harmonious relationship with the Creator, the tragedies of sin, and God's brilliant plan to redeem and reclaim humanity and His world from the chaotic forces of darkness. In Christian tradition, the central messages in the Book of Revelation are to have hope, to endure sufferings patiently, and to remain faithful until the Son of God, Jesus Christ, returns to judge evil, to reclaim the world, and to restore the lost paradise (the Garden of Eden) and fallen humanity to perfect divine order. In this lesson, students will examine the loss/restoration motif that connects the Books of Genesis and Revelation in Christian Bibles

Key Concepts: restoration, redemption, loss/restoration motif, alpha and omega, revelation, revelation, unveilings

Objectives:

Students will:

- read biblical text to gain understanding and participate in discussions.
- recognize the literary "loss/restoration" motif.
- apply knowledge of language to understand how language functions in different contexts, to make effective choices for meaning or style, and to understand more fully when reading or listening.
- compare parallel themes in given biblical texts.
- engage in scholarly discussions of the Hebrew Scriptures from various cultural traditions.
- understand the writer's purpose in primary and secondary sources.

Expected Learning Objectives:

At the end of the lesson, students will be able to:

- explain literary motifs as they are used in the Hebrew Scriptures.
- recognize and explain parallel themes in different texts.
- engage in scholarly discussions of the Hebrew Scriptures from various cultural traditions.
- understand the writer's purpose in primary and secondary sources.

Duration: 2-3 hours

Materials:

- paper/pen/notebook/dictionary
- the Hebrew Bible in any translation
- online Bible study tools
- article: "The Restoration of the Primordial World of Genesis 1–3 in Revelation 21–22" (https://digitalcommons.andrews.edu/cgi/viewcontent.cgi?article=1373&context=jats)

Procedure:

- Read any Bible translation to respond to the study questions.
- Use an online dictionary to pronounce and define unfamiliar terms.
- Refer to online Bible study tools to enhance your learning.
- Respond to the reflection(s).
- Edit your writing to correct errors.
- Post your reflection on the discussion board,
- Label the post: A Reflection on the Parallelism in Genesis and Revelation.
- If you have questions or need further clarification on any assignment, e-mail me at wilmaforeman@yahoo.com or visit my website: AIBL.INFO to sign up for the online course.

Study Questions (Focus: The Loss/Restoration Theme in the Books of Genesis and Revelation)

Directions: Use any Bible translation or credible online resource to answer the study questions.

Are the following statements (A) TRUE or (B) FALSE?

1. In Genesis 3:1, the serpent begins a deceptive conversation with Eve by asking, "Did God really say, "You must not eat from any tree in the garden'?" (A) TRUE
2. In Christian tradition, the serpent has access to the Garden of Eden. (A) TRUE
3. In the Book of Revelation 21:27 in Christian Bibles, the serpent, called the Devil or Satan, cannot enter the holy city because of its evil nature. (A) TRUE
4. Human disobedience causes a breach in the relationship with God in Genesis 3:8. (A) TRUE
5. In Revelation 21:3, God restores the relationship with humanity. (A) TRUE
6. The serpent has free access to humans in the garden of Eden in Genesis, Chapter 3. (A) TRUE
7. In Revelation 20:10, "the devil who deceived them was thrown into the lake of fire and brimstone... and ... will be tormented day and night forever and ever." (A) TRUE
8. In the Book of Revelation, the subtle tempter, is punished forever for its deception. (A) TRUE

9. Genesis 3:15 prophesies about the seed of the woman crushing the head of the serpent. (A) TRUE
10. In Christian tradition, the "seed" of the woman is Jesus in the New Testament. (A) TRUE
11. The Book of Revelation foretells of "The Lion of Judah" buying men for God. (A) TRUE
12. In the Christian faith, humanity is redeemed (repurchased) by the blood of Jesus. (A) TRUE
13. In the Hebrew Scriptures, "the Lion of Judah" stands for one of Jacob's sons. (A) TRUE
14. Twentieth century Afro-centric cultures recognize "the Lion of Judah." (A) TRUE
15. "The Lion of Judah" and "the Root of David" are mentioned in Revelation 5:5,9. (A) TRUE
16. Both expressions symbolize victory through the blood that Jesus shed for all humanity. (A) TRUE
17. In Christian tradition, the "Lion of Judah" symbolizes Jesus' return to reclaim the earth. (A) TRUE
18. Jesus, represented as a lion in Revelation 5:5. 9, is in direct contrast to His being seen as a lamb. (A) TRUE
19. In Christian tradition, Jesus' return will end the devil's reign of sin and evil. (A) TRUE
20. Revelation 23:3 says, "No longer will there be any curse. The throne of God and of the Lamb will be within the city, and His servants will worship Him." (A) TRUE

For Reflection:

In five-eight sentences, explain how the Book of Revelation uses a lamb to symbolize Jesus and a dragon to stand for Satan. How does God use the lamb to defeat the Serpent? Find at least three additional examples of the "Loss/Restoration" theme as literary parallels in the Books of Genesis and Revelation. Use reliable internet sources to respond to the assignment. Document your sources. After editing your writing, post the reflection on the discussion board. Label the Post: The Biblical Loss/Restoration Theme in Genesis and Revelation.

A Closing Thought:

"I am the Alpha and the Omega, the first and the last, the beginning and the end"

-Revelation 22:13.

LESSON THIRTY-FIVE
THE GENESIS METANARRATIVE
("THE BIG PICTURE")

Lesson Overview:

A metanarrative is an overarching story with at least one theme that gives unity to the individual stories within a work. It is the grand story or "big picture" that brings unity to the smaller individual stories. On the surface, the Hebrew Bible may seem to be a collection of random stories, but a central theme binds the smaller stories into a greater one. The biblical metanarrative follows the concept of *creation-fall-redemption*. Students will examine the metanarrative, or grand narrative that flows throughout the Book of Genesis.

Key Concepts: metanarrative, "the fall," redemption, hermeneutics, theology, plot development, setting, resolution, epilogue, transcendental truths, theme, personification, metaphor, apostrophe, symbolism

Lesson Objectives:

Students will:

- explain the meaning of a biblical metanarrative.
- understand how the individual stories in the Book of Genesis drive the metanarrative of the entire Hebrew Bible.
- examine literary elements and techniques in the Genesis metanarrative.
- examine the themes/motifs that unify the biblical storyline.
- compare various translations of the Hebrew Scriptures.
- participate in group discussion via a discussion board.
- write an end-of course full-length essay about the literary features of the biblical metanarrative.

Expected Learning Outcomes:

At the end of the lesson, students will be able to:

- explain the meaning, literary features, and purpose of a biblical metanarrative.
- connect literary themes, elements, and symbols in Book of Genesis to the Book of Revelation (the beginning and the end of the Hebrew Bible in Christian tradition).
- elaborate on how the metanarrative gives meaning to the individual narratives in the biblical text.

Duration: 3-4 hours

Materials:

- Paper/pen/notebook/dictionary/online Bible study tools
- Video: *Lesson 1: What is the Metanarrative*
  https://www.youtube.com/watch?v=UlXBFF1Pu9E

- Video: *Metanarrative Pt. 1 || Tiny Tara Teaches Truth*
  (https://www.youtube.com/watch?v=QojAKBs40t0)

- Video: *Metanarrative Pt. 2 || Tiny Tara Teaches Truth*
  https://www.youtube.com/watch?v=DlEb6C6xrbM

- Video: *Lesson 5: The Metanarrative of Scripture*
  https://www.youtube.com/watch?v=Qy-XeRCrV40

- Article: Fulfilling the Genesis Mandate While Helping the Poor by James J.S. Johnson, J.D., Th.D.
  (https://www.icr.edu/fulfilling-genesis-mandate-while-helping-poor)

Procedure:

- Respond to the study questions assigned to each video and article.
- Use an online dictionary to pronounce and define unfamiliar terms.
- Refer to online Bible study tools to enhance your learning.
- Respond to the reflections in complete sentences.
- Edit writing to correct errors.
- Post the reflection(s) on the discussion board.
- If you have questions or need further clarification on any assignment, e-mail me at wilmaforeman@yahoo.com or visit my website: AIBL.INFO to sign up for the online course.

Study Questions/Activities

Directions:

- View the video: *Lesson 1: What is the Metanarrative*
  https://www.youtube.com/watch?v=UlXBFF1Pu9E.

- Complete the "Fill in the Blanks" exercise with the correct choice.

Fill in the blanks.

1. A metanarrative is the _____ idea of individual narratives within a book.

   a. hidden   b. short   *c. grand*   d. mysterious

2. The prefix "meta" is a Greek term that means "after" or "_____" something.

   a. round   b. grand   *c. beyond*   d. before

3. A metanarrative is the _____ idea within smaller stories.

a. comprehensive   b. weaker   c. amazing   d. disconnected

4. The metanarrative is the story about all the stories in_____.
       a. *A literary form*   b. details   c. question   **d. history**

5. A metanarrative is something within the stories that is not_____.
       a. written   **b. realized**   c. studied   d. explained

6. The reader only sees a _____ of the metanarrative.
       a. beginning   **b. part**   c. version   d. vision

7. The metanarrative in the *Wizard of Oz* centers on being content with the place that Providence gives one to call his or her_____.
       a. home   b. workplace   c. school   d. church

8. The metanarrative in the drama *Citizen Kane* that was directed, produced, and co-written by Orson Welles is that real happiness is linked to one's_____.
       a. money   b. power   **c. childhood** d. education

9. According to the lecturer, outside forces and our _____ are shaping and preparing us for what comes next.
       b. friends   b. family   **c. choices**   d. goals

10. The metanarrative concerns what comes_____
       a. At the end of one' life   **b. next**   c. sometimes   d. in one's thoughts

Study Questions

Are the following statements (A) TRUE or (B) FALSE about the passage taken from William Shakespeare's *Macbeth*?

Passage

"Out, out, brief candle! Life's but a walking shadow, a poor player that struts and frets his hour upon the stage and is heard no more. It is a tale told by an idiot, full of sound and fury, signifying nothing."

11.   The beginning of the passage "Out, out, brief candle…:" is an example of the literary device "*apostrophe.*" (A) TRUE

12.   The expression "brief candle" is *symbolic* of life. (A) TRUE

13.   "Life's but a walking shadow…" is an example of *metaphor*. (A) TRUE

14.   "…a poor player that struts and frets his hour upon the stage…" is an example of *personification*. (A) TRUE

15. Macbeth, the main character, is saying that life is worthless. (A) TRUE

16. Macbeth says that life is like a pathetic actor that performs for a short while. (A) TRUE

17. The video lecturer agrees that all stories have a metanarrative that centers on the meaning of life. (A) TRUE

18. The speaker believes that the metanarrative to all stories is: "Our meaning, value, and purpose is to improve the quality of all life, to further it into the future for the betterment of all living creatures." (A) TRUE

19. The lecturer believes that the metanarrative prepares the reader for the next event in life. (A) TRUE

20. In summary, the speaker proposes that a metanarrative ties smaller stories into one grand narrative with an expectation of a future happening. (A) TRUE

Study Questions:

Directions: View the video: *Metanarrative Pt. 1 || Tiny Tara Teaches Truth* (*https://www.youtube.com/watch?v=QojAKBs40t0*).

Are the following statements (A) TRUE or (B) FALSE about the video?

21. The teacher challenges her students to share information from torn pages of a book. (A) TRUE
22. She questions the students about the way people read the Bible in bits and pieces. (A) TRUE
23. The speaker makes the point that the Bible has a beginning, a middle, and an end. (A) TRUE
24. A reader can misinterpret the Bible's overarching narrative if the smaller stories are read incorrectly. (A) TRUE
25. The speaker's main point is that the Bible should be read in its entirety-not just in parts. (A) TRUE

Study Questions:

Directions: View the video: *Metanarrative Pt. 2 || Tiny Tara Teaches Truth* https://www.youtube.com/watch?v=DlEb6C6xrbM

Are the following statements (A) TRUE or (B) FALSE?

26. The prefix "*meta*" means "to be above" or "before." (A) TRUE
27. "*Transcendent*" means to "be above or beyond the range of normal or human experience." (A) TRUE
28. Based on the video presentation, *metanarratives* are transcendent. (A) TRUE
29. While a narrative is a story, not all narratives are fiction mythology or fairy tales. (A) TRUE
30. A story that is based on a historical record, an oral tradition, and eyewitness accounts can be a true story. (A) TRUE

31. The teacher in the video says that the Bible is a true eternal story. (A) TRUE
32. The Bible has a comprehensive message that consists of smaller individual stories. (A) TRUE
33. The smaller stories communicate an overarching storyline that supplies the meaning and purpose for all the individual stories. (A) TRUE
34. The metanarrative is a primary idea that has *transcendent truths*. (A) TRUE
35. *Transcendent realities* that are those unaffected by time or space. (A) TRUE
36. Based on the narrator, an example of a *transcendent truth* is the statement: "God is good." (A) TRUE
37. The Hebrew Bible is a sacred story about the Israelites. (A) TRUE

Study Questions:

Directions: View the video: *Lesson 5: The Metanarrative of Scripture*
(*https://www.youtube.com/watch?v=Qy-XeRCrV40*)

Are the following statements (A) TRUE or (B) FALSE?

38. Literary features common in narratives include: a *setting, prologue, initial conflict, plot development, resolution,* and *epilogue*. (A) TRUE
39. The Creation setting of Genesis is in Chapters 1 & 2. (A) TRUE
40. The first conflict in the Book of Genesis is in Chapter 3. (A) TRUE
41. Literary themes bring cohesiveness to the biblical story. (A) TRUE
42. The *Genesis mandate* is found in Chapter 1: 26-28. (A) TRUE
43. A mandate is an official order or commission to do something. (A) TRUE
44. The Creation mandate includes the following for humans: bearing the image of God, placed having authority over God's creation, living under God's blessing. (A) TRUE
45. Under the Genesis mandate, God commands humankind to populate the earth. (A) TRUE

Study Questions:

Directions: View the video:

Lesson 4: The Metanarrative of Scripture
(*https://www.youtube.com/watch?v=-4BHROxJu90)*

Are the following statements (A) TRUE or (B) FALSE?

46. Understanding the Bible as one story can affect the details of the story. (A) TRUE
47. The Christian Bible consists of sixty-six books. (A) TRUE
48. Based on the video, the Book of Genesis is a literary unit in Hebrew Scriptures. (A) TRUE
49. The Hebrew Bible has a structure of narratives. (A) TRUE
50. The speaker uses the opinions of literary, dispensation, and covenant experts to show that the Bible is a *metanarrative*. (A) TRUE
51. The frame of the Hebrew Scriptures is unfinished. (A) TRUE

52. The lecturer asserts that the Bible has an overarching story, and reading the entire Bible is necessary to see the plotline end. (A) TRUE
53. The structure of the Bible is a tightly woven storyline with no loose ends. (A) TRUE
54. Sub-themes and sub-plots appear throughout the Hebrew Scriptures. (A) TRUE
55. A narrative has a beginning called a setting. (A) TRUE
56. A setting introduces the reader to the time and place of the story. (A) TRUE
57. The setting introduces the protagonist of the story. (A) TRUE

Study Questions

Directions: Read the article: "Fulfilling the Genesis Mandate While Helping the Poor" by James J.S. Johnson, J.D., Th.D. *(https://www.icr.edu/fulfilling-genesis-mandate-while-helping-poor)*

Are the following statements (A) CORRECT or (B) INCORRECT?

58. As Noah's family leaves the ark after the worldwide Flood, God renews mankind's authority over animals. (A) CORRECT

59. God mandates that the Flood survivors resume the task to "be fruitful, multiply, and fill the earth." (A) CORRECT

60. The *multigenerational decree* proves God's love for life and biodiversity. (A) CORRECT

61. According to the article, biological diversity reflects a variety of life on earth. (A) CORRECT

62. The "Tower of Babel" narrative highlights the humans' rejection of the Genesis mandate to fill the earth and multiply. (A) CORRECT

63. In biblical text, Nimrod, whose name means "Let's rebel," is the founder of Babylon. (A) CORRECT

64. "Babel" is the same as "Babylon" in the Hebrew language. (A) CORRECT

65. The post-Flood population in Babel prided themselves in resisting God's instruction. (A) CORRECT

66. Arrogance can be detected in the words: "Let us make us a name for ourselves, lest we be scattered abroad over the face of the whole earth." (Genesis 11:4) (A) CORRECT

67. The original Genesis commandment requires humans to move outward and away from each other. (A) CORRECT

68. Scattering the people all over the earth helps to fulfill God's original mandate to humanity in Genesis 1:28. (A) CORRECT

69. Genesis 9:1 is God's post-Flood renewal to repopulate the earth. (A) CORRECT

70. In the "Tower of Babel" narrative, the will of God prevails over the humans' prideful building project. (A) CORRECT

71. God separates the people by dividing their communication into different languages and scattering humanity across the lands (Genesis 11:9). (A) CORRECT

72. The writer believes that God's plan for Noah's descendants to "fill" habitats around the world still exists. (A) CORRECT

Study Questions:

Directions: View the Video: *Lesson 7: The Metanarrative of Scripture*
(*https://www.youtube.com/watch?v=a2Jxb4Uvuxk*)

73. The speaker refers to the Garden of Eden as a sacred space where people meet God. (A) CORRECT

74. The narrator proposes that God's presence makes the Garden a sacred space. (A) CORRECT

75. The lecturer mentions Eugene Merrell's concept of a sacred space that unfolds with the progress of God's plan to make the entire world a holy ground. (A) CORRECT

76. In this presentation, the theme of the Genesis metanarrative is centered on a garden-temple. (A) CORRECT

77. In the Sacred Space theme, God creates a place on earth where man worships Him. (A) CORRECT

78. God's presence makes the place that He inhabits sacred. (A) CORRECT

79. Based on the narrator, God will fill the entire world with people who will worship Him. (A) CORRECT

80. The Sacred Space theory supports God's claim to His earth. (A) CORRECT

81. God will reestablish His kingdom on the earth and undo what exists in the modern world. (A) CORRECT

82. The last Book of the Christian Hebrew Bible, Revelation, says that there will no longer be any curse (2:23). (A) CORRECT

Study Questions:

Directions: Read the following translations of Revelation 22:3. Answer the questions that follow. (Note: Learn the names of the Bible translations for each abbreviation.)

ASV
And there shall be no curse anymore: and the throne of God and of the Lamb shall be therein: and his servants shall serve him; ...

AMP
There will no longer exist anything that is cursed [because sin and illness and death are gone]; and the throne of God and of the Lamb will be in it, and His bondservants will serve and worship Him [with great awe and joy and loving devotion]; ...

AMPC

There shall no longer exist there anything that is accursed (detestable, foul, offensive, impure, hateful, or horrible). But the throne of God and of the Lamb shall be in it, and His servants shall worship Him [pay divine honors to Him and do Him holy service] ....

CEV

God's curse will no longer be on the people of that city. He and the Lamb will be seated there on their thrones, and its people will worship God...

DARBY

And no curse shall be any more; and the throne of God and of the Lamb shall be in it; and his servants shall serve him, ...

ESV

No longer will there be anything accursed, but the throne of God and of the Lamb will be in it, and his servants will worship him.

ESVUK

No longer will there be anything accursed, but the throne of God and of the Lamb will be in it, and his servants will worship him.

EXB

Nothing that God judges guilty will be in that city [Nothing accursed will be there; or There will no longer be any curse; Gen. 3:16–19; Zech. 14:11]. The throne of God and of the Lamb will be there, and God's servants will ·worship [serve] him.

GNV

And there shall be no more curse, but the throne of God and of the Lamb shall be in it, and his servants shall serve him.

Are the following statements (A) CORRECT or (B) INCORRECT?

83. While the Book of Genesis begins the Hebrew Bible, the Book of Revelation is the last Book in Christian Bibles. (A) CORRECT

84. "The curse" mentioned in Revelation 22:3 alludes to Genesis 2:15-17 where God first promises Adam and Eve that disobedience to His command will result in their deaths. (A) CORRECT

85. "The curse" originates in Genesis, Chapter 3. (A) CORRECT

86. The Bible reader can infer that in the beginning, nothing in the world ever died before "the curse." (A) CORRECT

87. Based on the AMPC translation, the term "cursed" refers to anything that is detestable, foul, offensive, impure, hateful, or horrible." (A) CORRECT

88. The AMP translation of the Scriptures refer to sin, illness, and death as a part of "the curse." (A) CORRECT

89. The metanarrative of the Hebrew Bible peaks in Revelation, Chapter 22 when God removes "the curse." (A) CORRECT
90. When Adam and Eve sin by eating from the Tree of the Knowledge of Good and Evil, they lose access to the Tree of Life. (A)
91. All the preceding translations mention one throne of God except the *Contemporary English Version (CEV)*. (A) CORRECT
92. "The Lamb" symbolizes Jesus in the New Testament of Christian Bibles. (A) CORRECT

Study Questions:

Directions: View the video: Story of the Bible: Meta-Narrative
(https://www.youtube.com/watch?v=k5nTkpuGMVI)

93. According to the speaker, the Bible is a unified, overarching story. (A) CORRECT
94. In Christian faith, the Bible is a unified story that leads to human redemption through Jesus. (A) CORRECT
95. Genesis 1:1 and Revelation 22:5 are parallel Scriptures. (A) CORRECT
96. Based on the video, in the beginning, God created the heaven and the earth, and in the end, He will reign with His people forever. (A)
97. Humans are the crown of God's creation. (A) CORRECT
98. From the beginning to the end of the biblical narratives, God plans to have a relationship with people. (A) CORRECT
99. The speaker asserts that the Bible is not a theological weapon to prove someone's religious doctrine. (A) CORRECT
100. He proposes that the Bible is a moral resource, but not a tool to use to judge others critically. (A) CORRECT
101. The presenter says that Bible is not primarily a rule Book, but it does teach one how to live and how to lead others. (A) CORRECT
102. The speaker favors the *hermeneutical* approach in reading the Bible. (A) CORRECT
103. *Hermeneutics* is the study of biblical interpretation. (A)
104. Hermeneutics plays a role in disciplines whose subject matter demands interpretative approaches. (A) CORRECT
105. Traditionally, disciplines that rely on hermeneutics include *theology*, especially Biblical studies. (A) CORRECT
106. The disciplinary subject matter concerns the meaning of human intentions, beliefs, and actions. (A) CORRECT
107. Hermeneutics is concerned with human experience as preserved in the arts and literature, historical testimony, and other artifacts. (A) CORRECT
108. Studying biblical metanarratives relates to the hermeneutics approach. (A) CORRECT
109. The Bible story is a "God-and-human" drama that unfolds over time. (A) CORRECT

For Reflection:

As we end the lessons in this course curriculum, let us review what we have learned about biblical literacy in public education and the appreciation for the literary artistry of the Book of Genesis: (1) Teaching about the Hebrew Bible academically in public education is a First Amendment right afforded by the U.S. Constitution. (2) The Bible is "worthy of studies for its literary and historic qualities" (U. S. Supreme Court, *Abington v. Schempp*, 1963). (3) The narrative literary form is the most common type of literature found in the Bible, making up almost half of the total text. (4) The literary design of the first chapter of Genesis sets the stage for the entire Hebrew Bible. (5) The repetition of connective words, phrases, characters, themes, plots, symbols, and concepts connect the individual narratives to form a well-developed metanarrative, the "Big Picture." (6) In Christian tradition, the climax of the Bible story is Jesus' birth, death, and resurrection to redeem flawed humanity and restore humans to their first state of perfection in relationship with God. Continue to "chew on" what you have learned from this course and consider how you can use your knowledge to make this a better world!

A Closing Thought:

"Knowledge is power. Power to do evil or power to do good. Power itself is not evil. So, knowledge itself is not evil."

— Veronica Roth, Allegiant

by Wilma J. Brown-Foreman, ED. S

Note: If you have questions or need further clarification on any assignment, e-mail me at wilmaforeman@yahoo.com or visit my website: AIBL.INFO to sign up for the online course.

-Wilma J. Brown-Foreman, Author

Works Cited

"6 Common Themes of Literature You Must Know About." *Your Online Publicist*,
23 May 2022, https://youronlinepublicist.com/themes-of-literature/.

7 Best Bible Study Tools Online You Can Use for Free | Think about Such Things.
1 Apr. 2021, thinkaboutsuchthings.com/bible-study-tools-online/. Accessed
26 Aug. 2022.

"19 Websites for Reading and Searching the Bible on for All Things Bible." *For All
Things Bible*, 4 Feb. 2020, https://forallthings.bible/19-websites-for-
reading-and-searching-the-bible/.

"AAR Publishes Religious Literacy Guidelines for College Graduates." *Home*,
https://www.aarweb.org/AARMBR/Publications-and-News-/Newsroom-
/News-/AAR-Publishes-Religious-Literacy-Guidelines.aspx.

"Abraham, Father of Many Nations." *YouTube*, YouTube, 4 June 2020,
https://www.youtube.com/watch?v=l5ZDoGqFfxg.

"A Literary Study of The Book of Genesis." https://issuu.com/aibl.info/docs/ebook-
22th_of_july_2022-last_book_.

Ancient Israelite Marriage Customs, http://www.theology.edu/marriage.htm.

*An Exposition on the First Ten Chapters of Genesis, and Part of the
Eleventh*,https://biblehub.com/library/bunyan/the_works_of_john_bunyan_
volumes__1- 3/an_exposition_on_the_first.htm.

Aquinas, St. Thomas. "St. Thomas Aquinas – on the Five Ways to Prove God's
Existence." *Philosophical Thought*, Tulsa Community College, 13 Aug.
2021.https://open.library.okstate.edu/introphilosophy/chapter/aquinas-
thomas-the-five-_ways-summa-theologiae-part-1-excerpt/.

Art. "The Literary Design of Genesis 1." YouTube, 23 Apr. 2018,
www.youtube.com/watch?v=7IbeeJPpRZ0. Accessed 9 Dec. 2021.

A Teacher's Guide to Religion in the Public Schools a Teacher's Guide ...
https://religiousfreedomcenter.org/wpcontent/uploads/2014/08/teachersguid
e.pdf.

Author, No. "Aquinas's Five Proofs for the Existence of
God." *Open.library.okstate.edu*, Tulsa Community College, 18 Jan. 2021,
open.library.okstate.edu/introphilosophy/chapter/aquinass-five-proofs-for-
the-existence-of-god/.

Barmash, Pamela. "Cain (Bible Odyssey)." *Academia.edu*, 25 Sept. 2015, https://www.academia.edu/16178414/Cain_Bible_Odyssey_.

"Bereshit - Genesis Chapter 1." *Www.shalomhaverim.org*, www.shalomhaverim.org/English/torah/bereshit_english_1.htm. Accessed 26 Aug. 2022.

BiblicalIdioms.http://www.mayimhayim.org/Hebrew%20Perspectives/Biblical%0Idioms.RX5.htm.

"Bible Commentaries: What They Are and How to Use Them (4 Types, 4 Tips)." *Www.youtube.com*, www.youtube.com/watch?v=6U67Xvf-T9Y). Accessed 26 Aug. 2022.

"BLB Study Resources." *Blue Letter Bible*, (https://www.blueletterbible.org/study.cfm.)

Cahn, Steven M. "The Joseph Saga: Turnabouts, Trade-Offs, and Transience." *Blog of the APA*, Feb. 2021, https://blog.apaonline.org/2021/02/01/the-joseph-saga-turnabouts-trade- offs-and-transience/.

"Cain." *Www.bibleodyssey.org*, www.bibleodyssey.org/people/main-articles/cain.

Cain and Abel in the Bible Elie Wiese- LocalTel. http://home.nwi.net/~clark/library/Cain%20and%20Abel%20in%20the%20 Bible.pdf.

"Case Categories | the First Amendment Encyclopedia." *Mtsu.edu*, mtsu.edu/first-amendment/encyclopedia/case/98/public-schools-and-religion. Accessed 26 Aug. 2022.

Chancey, M., 2022. *How Should We Teach the Bible in Public Schools?* [online] Religion & Politics. Available at: <https://religionandpolitics.org/2014/01/07/how-should-we-teach-the-bible-in-public-schools/> [Accessed 26 August 2022].

"Chapter 5: The Book of Genesis - Idioms in the Bible Explained and a Key to the Original Gospels." *Zoboko.com*, zoboko.com/text/zo8mqm68/idioms-in-the-bible-explained-and-a-key-to-the-original-gospels/5. Accessed 26 Aug. 2022.

"Copyright and Fair Use Lesson Plans." *Copyright And Fair Use Lesson Plans |Media Education Lab*, https://mediaeducationlab.com/copyright-and-fair-use-lesson-plans-high-school-college-and-graduate-education.

"Copyright Protection: What It Is, How It Works." *Stanford Copyright and Fair Use Center*, 27 Mar. 2013, fairuse.stanford.edu/overview/faqs/copyright-protection/#when_can_i_use_a_work_without_the_author8217s_permissio n. Accessed 26 Aug. 2022.

Counselman, Rachael. "Paradise Lost Introduction Video." *YouTube*, YouTube, 23 Feb. 2015, https://www.youtube.com/watch?v=Jbfiu-ss29s.

"Creation, James Weldon Johnson (Entire Poem in Description Below)." *Www.youtube.com*,www.youtube.com/watch?v=CAuArFPmXb4. Accessed 26 Aug. 2022.

Cry of Abel's Blood - Bibleodyssey.com. http://www.bibleodyssey.com/people/related- articles/cry-of-abels-blood.aspx.

Cummings, Michael J. "Shakespeare and the Bible." *Shakespeare Allusions to the Bible*, https://shakespearestudyguide.com/Shake2/Bible.html.

David L. Hudson Jr. (updated September 2017). "Rights of Teachers." *Rights of Teachers*, https://mtsu.edu/first-amendment/article/973/rights-of-teachers.

damien. "Religion in Colonial America: Trends, Regulations, and Beliefs." *SlideServe*, 7 Aug. 2014, www.slideserve.com/damien/religion-in-colonial-america-trends-regulations-and-beliefs. Accessed 26 Aug. 2022.

Demick, David. "The Breath of Life." *Answers in Genesis*, Answers In Genesis, 29July 2015, https://answersingenesis.org/human-body/the-breath-of-life/.

"Does God Exist? - What We Can Learn from Genesis 1 and 2 - Month/Month YEAR." *Www.doesgodexist.org*, *www*.doesgodexist.org/MayJun13/WhatWeCanLearnGenesis1&2.html. Accessed 31 Aug. 2022.

"English Idioms 2." *YouTube*, YouTube, 18 Feb. 2020, https://www.youtube.com/watch?v=jdSNNy9KkEI.

ecwausa. "Genesis 3:15: The Protoevangelium or "First Gospel."" *ECWA USA*, 13 Mar. 2020, www.ecwausa.org/genesis-315-the-protoevangelium-or-first-gospel/. Accessed 26 Aug. 2022.

"Essay Writing Guidelines." *Research Prospect*, www.researchprospect.com/essay-writing-guidelines/. Accessed 26 Aug. 2022.

Ferguson, Andrea. "First Amendment and Public Schools." *Five Freedoms*, 10 Nov.2021, https://fivefreedoms.org/first-amendment-and-public-schools/.

Finding Common Ground - Religious Freedom Center
https://www.religiousfreedomcenter.org/wp-content/uploads/2014/08/rfc_publications_findingcommonground.pdf.

"Finding Meaning in Incoherence: The Joseph Story beyond Source Criticism." *TheTorah.com,*https://www.thetorah.com/article/finding-meaning-in-incoherence-the-joseph-story- beyond-source-criticism.

"First Amendment Lesson Plan: Religion in Public Schools | the Free Speech Center." *Mtsu.edu*, mtsu.edu/first-amendment/page/religion-public-schools.

"Free Online English Pronunciation Dictionary | Howjsay." *Howjsay.com*, howjsay.com. Accessed 26 Aug. 2022.

"Free Online Genesis Bible Study Course: Adam to Noah: Bibleproject™." *BibleProject*, https://bibleproject.com/course/adam-noah/.

"Fulfilling the Genesis Mandate While Helping the Poor | School of Biblical Apologetics." *Www.icr.edu*, www.icr.edu/fulfilling-genesis-mandate-while-helping-poor. Accessed 26 Aug. 2022.

"Genesis Abraham and Sarah | Full Series." *YouTube*, YouTube, 12 Mar. 2021, https://www.youtube.com/watch?v=4BRQUC30RdQ.

"Genesis - Chapter 1." *Bereshit - Genesis Chapter 1*, https://www.shalomhaverim.org/English/torah/bereshit_english_1.htm.

Genesis d1bsmz3sdihplr.Cloudfront.net. https://d1bsmz3sdihplr.cloudfront.net/media/Study%20Notes/1-Genesis-Pt.-1-Study- Guide.pdf.

Genesis 2 Ellicott's Commentary for English Readers, https://www.biblehub.com/commentaries/ellicott/genesis/2.htm.

"Genesis 3:15 the Protoevangelium or 'First Gospel.'" *GENESIS 3:15 - THE PROTOEVANGELIUM OR FIRST GOSPEL*, https://biblescripture.net/First.html.

Gerber, Jacob D. "5 Of the Best Free Bible Study Tools." *Free Daily Bible Study*, 17 Dec. 2019, https://freedailybiblestudy.com/5-of-the-best-free-bible-study-tools/.

Good, Edwin M. (Edwin Marshall), and Internet Archive. *Irony in the Old Testament. Internet Archive*, Philadelphia, Westminster Press, 1965, archive.org/details/ironyinoldtestam00good/page/98/mode/2up?view=theater). Accessed 26 Aug. 2022.

"Guidance on Constitutionally Protected Prayer and Religious Expression in Public Elementary and Secondary Schools." *Home*, US Department of Education (ED),5Apr2021https://www2.ed.gov/policy/gen/guid/religionandschools/prayer_guidance. html.

"Guidelines for Religious Activities for Students | Fairfax County Public Schools." *Www.fcps.edu,* www.fcps.edu/about-fcps/policies-regulations-and-notices/guidelines-religious-activities-students.

Gupta, Sudip Das. "The Creation by James Weldon Johnson." *Poem Analysis*, 29 May 2021, https://poemanalysis.com/james-weldon-johnson/the-creation/.

Hana M. Ryman and J. Mark Alcorn. "Establishment Clause (Separation of Church and State)." *Establishment Clause (Separation of Church and State)*, https://www.mtsu.edu/first-amendment/article/885/establishment-clause-separation-of-church-and-state.

"Hebrews: Marriage." *Umanitoba.ca,* 2021, www.umanitoba.ca/faculties/arts/anthropology/tutor/case_studies/hebrews.

"Hillsdale College Online Courses." *Online.hillsdale.edu*, online.hillsdale.edu/courses/genesis. Accessed 26 Aug. 2022.

"History of Israel Timeline: Abraham to Modern Israel: Facts about Israel." *Facts & Truth about Israel*, 9 Sept. 2019, https://www.factsaboutisrael.uk/history-of-israel-timeline/.

"How Is Jesus Shown in the Book of Genesis?" *Christianity.com*, www.christianity.com/jesus/is-jesus-god/old-testament-prophecies/how-is-jesus-shown-in-the-book-of-genesis.html. Accessed 26 Aug. 2022.

"How Should We Teach the Bible in Public Schools?" *Religion & Politics*, 4 Mar. 2017, https://religionandpolitics.org/2014/01/07/how-should-we-teach-the-bible-in-public-schools/.

"Idioms in the Bible Explained and a Key to the Original Gospels." *Chapter 5): The Book of Genesis*, https://zoboko.com/text/zo8mqm68/idioms-in-the-bible-explained-and-a-key-to-the-original-gospels/5).

"If You Understand These 8 Bible Covenants Then You Understand the Entire Story of the Bible!" *YouTube*, YouTube, 14 Sept. 2021, https://www.youtube.com/watch?v=tESRUiC3CFA.

InspiringPhilosophy. "The Tower of Babel: Biblical Archaeology." *YouTube*, 6 Nov. 2020, www.youtube.com/watch?v=ZNc-hyIRrCs. Accessed 21 Sept. 2021.

In What Else Shall He Sleep? Exodus 22:24-26; Leviticus 25:36–37 https://mussaria.org/Portals/0/adam/Content/OcsjM31-KUOA9y9Pcaqmyg/Link/eBooklet.hash28.pdf.

"Irony in The Old Testament: Good, Edwin M. (Edwin Marshall), 1928- : Free Download, Borrow, and Streaming." *Internet Archive*, Philadelphia, WestminsterPress,1Jan.1965,https://archive.org/details/ironyinoldtestam00 good.

Johnson, James J. S. "Fulfilling the Genesis Mandate While Helping the Poor." *The Institute for Creation Research*, https://www.icr.org/article/fulfilling-genesis-mandate-while-helping/.

"Joseph's Saga (1): The Beloved Son." *Biblical Hebrew and Holy Land Studies Blog - IIBS.com*, 27 Apr. 2021, https://blog.israelbiblicalstudies.com/jewish-studies/josephs-saga-1-the- beloved-son/

Jr, David L. Hudson. "Rights of Teachers." *Www.mtsu.edu*, Sept. 2017, mtsu.edu/first-amendment/article/973/rights-of-teachers.

Kneller, Sam, et al. "The Tree of Knowledge of Good and Evil. the Meaning." *The Explanation*, 26 Nov. 2020, https://theexplanation.com/the-tree-of-knowledge-of-good- and-evil-the-meaning/.

Kranz, Jeffrey. "The Book of Genesis: The Beginner's Guide and Summary." *Overview Bible*, 6 Aug. 2020, https://overviewbible.com/genesis/.

Kranz, Jeffrey, and Name *. "Genesis: The Story Begins." *Overview Bible*, https://overviewbible.com/genesis/genesis-overviewbible-com-online-bible-guide/.

Kranz, Jeffrey. "The Torah: A Quick Overview of the Pentateuch." *OverviewBible*, 17 Aug. 2019, overviewbible.com/torah. Accessed 26 Aug. 2022.

"Lesson 1: What Is a Meta-Narrative?" *YouTube*, YouTube, 11 Oct. 2013, https://www.youtube.com/watch?v=UlXBFF1Pu9E.

"Lesson 5: The Metanarrative of Scripture." *YouTube*, YouTube, 30 Sept. 2020, https://www.youtube.com/watch?v=Qy-XeRCrV40.

"Lesson 7: The Metanarrative of Scripture." *Www.youtube.com*, www.youtube.com/watch?v=a2Jxb4Uvuxk. Accessed 25 Aug. 2022.

"Literary Analysis of the Flood." *JEDP Methodology: Literary Analysis of Genesis Doublets*, http://helpmewithbiblestudy.org/5system_moses/dh11_flood.asp.

"Login." *Freeonlinesurveys.com*, freeonlinesurveys.com/app#/1413601/build.

Mambrol, Nasrullah. "Analysis of John Milton's Paradise Lost." *Literary Theory and Criticism*, 12 July 2020, https://literariness.org/2020/07/12/analysis-of-john-miltons-paradise-lost/.

"Metanarrative Pt. 1 || Tiny Tara Teaches Truth." *YouTube*, YouTube, 25 July 2018, https://www.youtube.com/watch?v=QojAKBs40t0.

"Metanarrative Pt. 2 || Tiny Tara Teaches Truth." *YouTube*, YouTube, 29 July 2018, https://www.youtube.com/watch?v=DlEb6C6xrbM.

Moody, Josh. "How Is Jesus Shown in The Book of Genesis?" *Christianity.com*, Christianity.com, 3 Oct. 2012, https://www.christianity.com/jesus/is-jesus-god/old-testament-prophecies/how-is-jesus-shown-in-the-book-of-genesis.html."Mussaria.org > Excerpt Browser." *Mussaria.org*, https://mussaria.org/Excerpt- Browser/genesis-chapter-1-verse-27-image-gen125-jewish-tradition-places-strong-emphasis-on.

"Mussaria.org > Excerpt Browser." *Mussaria.org*, mussaria.org/Excerpt-Browser/genesis-chapter-1-verse-27-image-gen125-jewish-tradition-places-strong-emphasis-on. Accessed 26 Aug. 2022.

National Coalition Against Censorship. "The First Amendment in Schools: Resource Guide: Religious Expression in the Public Schools." *Ncac.org*, 2019, ncac.org/resource/the-first amendment-in-schools-resource-guide-religious-expression-in-the-public-schools.

"Noah and Human Etymology." *Www.icr.org*, www.icr.org/article/noah-human-etymology/). Accessed 26 Aug. 2022.

Noah's Ark Discovered Documentary! Evidence for Its Location, Genesis Flood! Proof Bible Is True! (https://www.youtube.com/watch?v=9f4uF4Va9gI

Norman, Bruce. "The Restoration of the Primordial World of Genesis 1-3 in Revelation 21-22." *Journal of the Adventist Theological Society*, vol. 8, no. 2, 1997, pp. 161–169, digitalcommons.andrews.edu/cgi/viewcontent.cgi?article=1373&context=jats.

"On the Structure of the Abraham Narratives - Prof. George Savran." *YouTube*, YouTube, 3 Aug. 2014, https://www.youtube.com/watch?v=uc4SwO_LIjc.

OverviewBible. "The Torah: A Quick Overview | Whiteboard Bible Study." *YouTube*, 16 Aug. 2019, www.youtube.com/watch?v=7e-z1R62FtI. Accessed 23 Sept. 2020.

"Paradise Lost Introduction Video*." *Www.youtube.com*, www.youtube.com/watch?v=Jbfiu-ss29s&list=TLPQMzAwMzIwMjK1xGHF9og3nQ&index=3. Accessed 26 Aug. 2022.

Paradise Lost in Modern English, https://www.paradiselostinmodernenglish.com/.

Parr, Allen. "If You Understand These 8 Bible Covenants Then You Understand the ENTIRE Story of the Bible!*" Www.youtube.com* www.youtube.com/watch?v=tESRUiC3CFA.*

"Protoevangelium." *Christian Apologetics & Research Ministry, 19 Oct. 2020,* https://carm.org/dictionary/protoevangelium/.

"Religion in Colonial America: Trends, Regulations, and Beliefs." *Facing History and Ourselves*, https://www.facinghistory.org/nobigotry/religion-colonial-america- trends-regulations-and-beliefs.

Rockowitz, Anna. *THE DOCUMENTED ESSAY General Guidelines.* General-guidelines.pdf (cuny.edu).

Roth, Elana. "The Story of Joseph." *My Jewish Learning*, My Jewish Learning, 15 Jan. 2010, www.myjewishlearning.com/article/the-story-of-joseph/.

Saddleback Kids. "Creation (Genesis 1-2)." *YouTube*, 4 Jan. 2019, www.youtube.com/watch?v=teu7BCZTgDs.

Shea, William H. "Literary Structural Parallels between Genesis 1 and2." *Www.grisda.org,*www.grisda.org/origins16049www.grisda.org/origins-16049. Accessed 26 Aug. 2022.

Slick, Matt. "What Is the Protoevangelium*?" Christian Apologetics & ResearchMinistry*, 2 June 2015, carm.org/about-theology/what-is-the-protoevangelium/. Accessed 26 Aug. 2022.

Stim, Rich. "Welcome to the Public Domain." *Stanford Copyright and Fair Use Center*, 11 Apr. 2017, fairuse.stanford.edu/overview/public-domain/welcome/.

Schwimmer, Brian. "Hebrew Social Organization: Marriage." *Hebrews: Marriage*, https://www.umanitoba.ca/faculties/arts/anthropology/tutor/case_studies/hebrews/marriage e.html.

"Shakespeare Allusions to the Bible." *Www.shakespearestudyguide.com*, www.shakespearestudyguide.com/Shake2/Bible.html.

"Shakespeare and the Geneva Bible." *Reformation 21,*https://www.reformation21.org/articles/shakespeare-and-the-geneva-bible.php.

Simonds, Robert L. "Teaching the Bible in Public Schools?" *The Institute for Creation Research*, https://www.icr.org/article/teaching-bible-public-schools/.

"Sir Walter Scott." *Poems by the Famous Poet - All Poetry*, https://allpoetry.com/Sir-Walter-Scott.

"Situational Irony: The Opposite of What You Think - Christopher Warner." *TED*, TED-Ed, https://ed.ted.com/lessons/situational-irony-the-opposite-of-what-you- think-christopher-warner.

Slick, Matt. "What Is the Protoevangelium?" *Christian Apologetics & Research Ministry*, 18 Mar. 2021, https://carm.org/about-theology/what-is-the-protoevangelium/.

"Statement on the Bible in Public Schools: A First Amendment Guide." *American Civil Liberties Union,* https://www.aclu.org/other/statement-bible-public-schools-first- amendment-guide.

Stim, Richard, and Rich Stim Attorney at law. "Fair Use." *Stanford Copyright and Fair Use Center*, 25 Nov. 2021, https://fairuse.stanford.edu/overview/fair-use/.

"Story of the Bible: Meta-Narrative." *Www.youtube.com*, www.youtube.com/watch?v=k5nTkpuGMVI. Accessed 26 Aug. 2022.

"Teaching about the Bible in Public Schools: How to Do It Right." *Americans United*, www.au.org/the-latest/church-and-state/articles/teaching-about-the-bible-in-public-schools/. Accessed 26 Aug. 2022.

Team, Wand of Knowledge. "Speeches of Satan in Book I of Paradise Lost (by John Milton)."*Wandofknowledge*,15July2021,https://wandofknowledge.com/speeches-of-satan-in-book-i-of-paradise- lost/.

tech@whyislam.org. "Place of Abraham in Islam, Christianity, Judaism." *Facts about the Muslims & the Religion of Islam - Toll-Free Hotline 1-877-WHY-ISLAM*, 2017, www.whyislam.org/common-ground/place-of-abraham-in-islam-christianity-judaism/.

"The Bible and Public Schools: A First Amendment Guide." *ERIC,* Vanderbilt University, Freedom Forum First Amendment Center, 1207 18th Avenue South, Nashville, TN 37212. Tel: 800-830-3733 (Toll Free); Tel: 615-321-9588; Web Site: Www.freedomforum.org., 30 Nov. 1998, https://eric.ed.gov/?id=ED443746.

"The Complete Story of Abraham: The Father of Nations." *YouTube*, YouTube, 30 Apr. 2022, https://www.youtube.com/watch?v=Wv9usf6BrEY.

"The Constitution | the National Constitution Center." *National Constitution Center – Constitutioncenter.org*, 2022, constitutioncenter.org/interactive-constitution/interpretation/amendment-i/interps/264). Accessed 26 Aug. 2022.

"The Creation" by James Weldon Johnson. *Issuu*, 23 July 2022,https://issuu.com/aibl.info/docs/ebook-22th_of_july_2022-last_book_/s/16414581.

"The First Amendment Encyclopedia." *Case Categories | The First Amendment Encyclopedia*, https religion.

The First Amendment Lesson Plan: Religion in Public School (https://mtsu.edu/first-amendment/page/religion-public-schools)

"The Genesis Story: Reading Biblical Narratives: Hillsdale College Online Courses." *Hillsdale College*, https://online.hillsdale.edu/landing/genesis/?email=

The Hebrew Creation Narrative (Genesis 1-3), https://www2.nau.edu/~gaud/bio301/content/hebnar.htm.

"The Holy Bible - Genesis Chapter 1 (KJV)." *Www.youtube.com*, www.youtube.com/watch?v=ynbtg6OuZo0. Accessed 26 Aug. 2022.

"The Knowledge of the Holy- A.W Tozer (CH 5) PT 1The Self Existence of God." *YouTube*, 23 Oct. 2018, https://www.youtube.com/watch?v=ois-IwsYx8I.

The Literary Genius of the Joseph Narrative - Inthebeginning.org. http://www.inthebeginning.org/chiasmus/xfiles/xjosephnarrative.PDF.

The Meta-Narrative. "Lesson 1: What Is a Meta-Narrative?" *YouTube*, 11 Oct. 2013, www.youtube.com/watch?v=UlXBFF1Pu9E. Accessed 8 July 2020.

"The Story of Abraham." *Israel*, https://www.israel-a-history-of.com/story-of-abraham.html.

"The Story of Joseph." *YouTube*, YouTube, 4 Aug. 2018, https://www.youtube.com/watch?v=UI8X6ytNh7o.

"The Thirteenth Amendment: The National Constitution Center." *"The Establishment Clause" by the Constitution Center*, 9 Aug. 2022, http://alpha.bits-stl.com/charm-https- constitutioncenter.org/interactive-constitution/interpretation/amendment-xiii/interps/137.

"The Torah: A Quick Overview | Whiteboard Bible Study." *YouTube*, YouTube, 16 Aug. 2019, https://www.youtube.com/watch?v=7e-z1R62FtI.

"The Tower of Babel: Biblical Archaeology." *YouTube*, YouTube, 6 Nov. 2020, https://www.youtube.com/watch?v=ZNc-hyIRrCs.

"The 12 Tribes of Israel in the Bible [Whiteboard Bible Study]." *YouTube*, YouTube, 13 June 2020, https://www.youtube.com/watch?v=KP-EXMy4Xas.

"Thomas Aquinas Asks 'Is God Self-Evident?' or Why Bother Proving God'sExistence? (Part 1 of 3)." *YouTube*, YouTube, 12 Jan. 2022, https://www.youtube.com/watch?v=Ks6Zo8eDwm4.

"Tips for Writing an Effective Essay." *Examples*, Examples.com, 22 Aug. 2017, https://www.examples.com/education/tips-for-writing-effective-essay.html.

Tumino, Melissa. "7 Best Bible Study Tools Online You Can Use for Free." *Think About Such Things*, 1 Apr. 2021, https://thinkaboutsuchthings.com/bible-study-tools-online/.

Vollmer, Timothy. "The Public Domain and 5 Things Not Covered by Copyright." *Creative Commons*, 16 Jan. 2017, creativecommons.org/2017/01/16/public-domain-5-things-not-covered-copyright/.

"Watch: Conflict in Israel and Palestine (Video)." *Khan Academy*, Khan Academy, https://www.khanacademy.org/humanities/whp-origins/era-7-the-great-convergence-and-divergence-1880-ce-to-the-future/74-end-of-empires-betaa/v/conflict-in-israel-and-palestine-crash-course-world-history-223-beta.)

What Is Intellectual Property? 2020 - Wipo. https://www.wipo.int/edocs/pubdocs/en/wipo_pub_450_2020.pdf.

"Who Wrote the Bible? (A History of the Torah)." *YouTube*, YouTube, 4 Aug. 2019, https://www.youtube.com/watch?v=k8vYLSBCAF8.

Writingguide. *High School Essay Rubric - Evaluate the Student's Writing.* 21 Feb. 2022, writingguideonline.com/high-school. Accessed 26 Aug. 2022.

Zondervan. "Understanding the Creation Story in Genesis." *YouTube*, 12 July 2019, www.youtube.com/watch?v=Iv2mePpin6A. Accessed 3 Sept. 2020.

Made in United States
North Haven, CT
11 January 2023